ELISHA
A Prophet for Our Times

D1431273

Books by F. W. Krummacher

Elijah the Tishbite

Elisha: A Prophet for Our Times

The Suffering Saviour

ELISHA
A Prophet for Our Times

F. W. Krummacher

kregel
PUBLICATIONS

Grand Rapids, MI 49501

Elisha: A Prophet for Our Times by F. W. Krummacher.

Copyright © 1993 by Kregel Publications, a division of Kregel, Inc.,
P.O. Box 2607, Grand Rapids, MI 49501. This edition, with minor
improvements, is reprinted from The Religious Tract Society's 1838
edition published in London.

Cover and book design: Alan G. Hartman

Library of Congress Cataloging-in-Publication Data

Krummacher, F. W. (Friedrich Wilhelm), 1796-1868.
    Elisha: A Prophet for Our Times / F. W. Krummacher.
        p.   cm.
Originally published: London: Religious Tract Society, 1838.
    1. Elisha (Biblical prophet) 2. Bible. O.T.—Biography.
3. Prophets—Palestine—Biography. I. Title.
BS580.E5K74 1993   222'.54092—dc20   93-4548
                    [B]   CIP
ISBN 0-8254-3060-7 (pbk.)

        1 2 3 4 5 printing / year 97 96 95 94 93

Printed in the United States of America

Contents

1. Elisha's Appearance (2 Kings 2:19-22) 7

2. The Judgment at Bethel (2 Kings 2:23-25) 17

3. The Expedition Against Moab (2 Kings 3:9-12) 29

4. The Miraculous Relief (2 Kings 3:13-19) 39

5. The Augmentation of the Oil (2 Kings 4:1-7) 47

6. The Shunammite (2 Kings 4:8-37) 57

7. "Death in the Pot" (2 Kings 4:38-41) 69

8. The Man from Baal-shalisha (2 Kings 4:42-44) 79

9. Naaman (2 Kings 5:1, 2) 95

10. The Little Maid from a Foreign Land (2 Kings 5:3) 103

11. The Journey to Samaria (2 Kings 5:4-7) 107

12. The Beggar (2 Kings 5:8-10) 123

13. The Way of Recovery (2 Kings 5:11-14) 135

14. The Cure (2 Kings 5:14, 15) 145

15. The Decision (2 Kings 5:15, 16) 155

16. A Flower of Sincerity (2 Kings 5:17) 169

17. A Scruple of Conscience (2 Kings 5:18, 19) 185

18. Gehazi (2 Kings 5:19-27) 205

1

Elisha's Appearance

The inspired prophet Micah, foretelling a blessed period yet to come which is styled "the last days," says of it, in the fourth verse of his fourth chapter, that then men "shall sit, every one under his vine and under his fig tree; and none shall make them afraid." What a touching representation of peaceful privacy and delightful repose is given by this single sentence of prophecy! The period, indeed, which it describes was very "far off" to the prophet himself; and even at our Lord's incarnation it had only begun to dawn for the New Testament still speaks of it as "the last days." Nevertheless, from the earliest ages of the Old Testament, there were blessed periods of shorter and longer tranquillity, in which the delightful preludes of that eagerly desired "last time" were conspicuously displayed.

The patriarchal age immediately after the flood strikes us as a prophetic type of the great gospel year of jubilee. Childlike simplicity and confidence characterized the relationship which prevailed between the Almighty and the saints of that period: the thunders of Sinai were not yet heard, and the terrors of the law had not yet begun to constrain the children of the promise. But they were constrained by love, arising from the kindness and condescension of Him who now graciously rejoiced again in the habitable parts of His earth, and whose delights were with the sons of men (Prov. 9:31). In the tents of Abraham and in the grove of Mamre, a spirit reigned similar to that at Emmaus where the two disciples sat familiarly at table with the Man who was God in the highest or like that which was manifested at Bethany with Lazarus and his much favored sisters.

A similar period, transcendently peaceful and benign, smiled upon Israel when Elisha appeared. To that happy, enlightened period, we

7

propose to direct our present meditations. May the Spirit of the Lord, the only Interpreter of the sacred oracles, graciously be with us, direct our observations, and instruct us to find much profit and delight in what has thus been written aforetime for that purpose!

2 Kings 2:19-22

> And the men of the city said unto Elisha, Behold, I pray thee, the situation of this city is pleasant, as my lord seeth: but the water is naught, and the land barren. And he said, Bring me a new cruse, and put salt therein. And they brought it to him. And he went forth unto the spring of the waters, and cast the salt in there, and said, Thus saith the Lord, I have healed these waters; there shall not be from thence any more death or barren land. So the waters were healed unto this day, according to the saying of Elisha which he spake.

Here then we are again returned to those times and scenes of wonders wherein so many sources of consolation and encouragement were recently opened to us in the achievements of Elijah the Tishbite and in the occurrences of his eventful life. The very country is not unknown to us. We seem acquainted and at home in it; and the eye scarcely alights upon a district, a mountain, a valley, or a hamlet that is not associated in our minds with some important and beneficial recollection of our previous spiritual excursions. On this stage a new history will now unfold to us a variety of most important incidents— the history of Elisha, the man of God. May this glorious narrative accomplish the design of Him who caused its insertion in His Word and become to us who believe a spring of manifold refreshment, a well of deep and lasting consolation in seasons of distress!

Our considerations will be at present but preparatory, and will concern, I. The character of Elisha's mission; and II. His first prophetic appearance.

The Character of Elisha's Mission

I. Elisha entered upon his course immediately after his great predecessor had been taken up into heaven. Let us briefly recollect the state of public affairs in Israel. King Ahab, by the judgment of God, had been slain in battle at Ramoth Gilead, and Ahaziah, his son and successor, was no more among the living. Because he had sent to inquire of Baal-zebub, the god of Ekron, as if there had been no God in Israel, the prophet Elijah had been sent to him with the alarming communication, "Thou shalt not come down from that bed on which thou art gone up, but shalt surely die." And his unrepenting death had terminated a life spent in forgetfulness of God.

From the brow of this Ahaziah, the crown, stained with a thousand crimes, had now passed to Jehoram his brother, the second son of Ahab and Jezebel, and it is in his reign that Elisha begins his prophetic labors. Of Jehoram, with whom we become acquainted in the course of Elisha's history, the Scriptures relate that "he wrought evil in the sight of the Lord" but not quite to the same extent as his father and profligate mother had done. Alarmed by the divine judgments which he had seen inflicted upon Ahab and Ahaziah, he had thought proper to remove the image of Baal which his father had set up and worshiped; but he still adhered to the golden calves in Bethel and in Dan; he fully restored and supported the order of Jeroboam's idolatrous priests; and though he sometimes did homage to the God of Abraham, of Isaac, and of Jacob, it was only in acts of momentary and hypocritical constraint.

His mother, the widowed queen Jezebel, continued, with his connivance, her vile and infatuated practices and used all her influence with the unstable monarch to confirm him in his iniquities and to increase the moral depravity of the people to a frightful degree. A disgusting idolatry, mingled with every kind of vice, continued to be the religion of the state. The whole realm was filled with this darkness from the bottomless pit; and the little church of God, though it glistened above the midnight covering with sublimity and brightness, was but as a green spot in the desert or as a solitary isle in the stormy ocean.

And now, like a rainbow on the dark cloud of those troublous times, appears the beneficent and evangelical mission of Elisha. Many regard it only as a faint sequel to the career of the Tishbite, but a little deeper insight into the matter will lead to a very different conclusion. Was Elijah an original phenomenon? Elisha was equally such. Who would think, because he had seen a rose, that the apple blossom has no beauty of its own? The appointment of Elisha was no repetition of Elijah. It was essentially different from that of his illustrious predecessor; and the entire organization of the man, no less than the manner of his appearance and acting, exactly harmonized with those special duties which devolved upon him. The former prophet casts no shade upon the latter; but each in his proper station serves beautifully to set off the other.

We anticipated in our reflections upon Elijah's history something of this peculiar difference of the calling of Elisha. We anticipated it in the still small voice upon the mount of Horeb as indicative of that milder season of providential dealings with Israel which the son of Shaphat was to usher in. Elisha was a kind of evangelist and forerunner of Him whose feet are beautiful upon the mountains; whereas Elijah, like another Moses, had to restore and vindicate the dignity of the law which was then neglected and despised. Elisha was to conduct back to Jehovah any who had been aroused from their deathlike slumber by the awful ministry of Elijah. For this benign office he had been unconsciously trained by the providence of God.

The earlier circumstances of his life, as well as the disposition of his mind, had tended to prepare him for it. Habituated to a peaceful, but active, rural life, he appears to have grown up under the combined influence of cheering natural scenery and simple family piety. When his affectionate parents expressed, as they evidently did, the sanguine and pious joy of their hearts by giving the name Elisha to their newborn son, they probably little expected how significantly appropriate that name would one day become. For its meaning is "God is SALVATION" or "God is my SAVIOR," and the son of Shaphat was designated to announce Him, in this character, to Israel.

Whereas the office of Elijah, as his name imports, was rather to demonstrate to the thoughtless multitude the awesome *judicial* power and majesty of Jehovah, that of Elisha, on the contrary, was neither alarming, imposing, nor overwhelming; it inspired confidence and rendered approach easy; it indicated a messenger less awful than the man of God upon Mount Carmel. The Lord, who dwells in the high and holy place, now humbled Himself to behold with special condescension the poor and the wretched. And this great and precious truth, Elisha, by his preaching and his acts, was to make manifest to Israel. How gracious is the King of kings who thus early disclosed to sinners the freeness of His mercy and His love! Never did He forget the poor of the flock.

His First Prophetic Appearance

II. The first act of Elisha's public life sets forth at once the character of his mission. It was at Jericho, that very city upon which

Joshua had pronounced a divine curse, that Elisha's mission commenced with the removal of a curse. Thither he repaired immediately
after his illustrious predecessor had been taken up into heaven, and
there he intended to await the first commands of Jehovah. In a few
days he was called forth to action. The inhabitants of Jericho, aware
that they had still a prophet among them, were soon eager to avail
themselves of the advantage. Oh that the light of every Christian
brother beamed with the mild radiance of an Elisha! And this it
would do, if we were only contented to appear as vessels of mercy,
representative of the meek and lowly Savior. Still, however, there are
some, whose light is thus beneficially shining before men. They are
dead unto themselves, but Christ lives in them. Their "life is hid with
Christ in God"; they live above the world. There is something
unspeakably soothing and animating in the company of such humble Christians. Their faith has taken firm hold of the world to come,
and their heartfelt peace sheds a blessed influence around them. The
oppressed, the doubting, and the afflicted have recourse to them and
obtain alleviation and succor; for they follow the steps of Him who
invited the weary and heavy laden to come to Him that He might
give them rest. In their words and actions His own love seems to
smile upon us; and we seldom leave them without obtaining clear-
er views and more exalted hopes.

What the inhabitants of Jericho wished to lay before the man of
God was this. The situation of the city had been once remarkable for
its beauty. The soil, favorable to vegetation, had rivaled in fruitfulness the most productive parts of the Holy Land. But it no longer
retained its ancient beauty and fertility for the devastating effects of
the curse, pronounced upon it by Joshua, were strikingly visible. The
palms drooped dejected; the gardens no longer yielded their perfumes;
the cattle languished upon the pastures once so luxuriant; the flocks
cast their young in the fold; and the people themselves were afflicted with disease and early death. All these calamities had their origin
in the water which had been rendered pernicious by the curse. The
complicated miseries which accrued from these causes made it almost
a matter of regret that Hiel, the Bethelite, had rebuilt the city.

What could the inhabitants of Jericho more earnestly desire than
the deliverance of their district, in every other respect so well situated, from this distressing and mortifying remembrance of the past?
Doubtless many attempts had been made, and much treasure and art

uselessly expended to accomplish it; yet the evil was not removed. But as Elisha was now resident among them, the thought occurred that he might possibly befriend them. They were sensible that the chastisement which God had inflicted on them, God alone could remove. They therefore applied to the man of God. They found him among the sons of the prophets, and, having been encouraged by the kindness of his manner, they modestly intimated to him their desire: "Behold, we pray thee, the situation of this city is pleasant, as my lord seeth; but the water is naught, and the land barren."

Would to God that this description given by the men of Jericho were not, in another sense, so applicable to many places in our own country, equally beautiful and delightful, except that the water is bad—I mean the spiritual water; and, therefore, the moral field is bar-ren and unfruitful. Here the spiritual fountains are corrupted, and, from the pulpit and the professor's chair, instead of the pure truth of the gospel, multitudes imbibe the poison of modern infidelity. However tinctured with Christianity, yet, by causing a forgetfulness of Bethlehem and Golgotha, stimulating proud man to seek salvation in himself, it spreads desolation and death in every direction; there a more destructive curse prevails than that which rested on the fields of Jericho. The pastures may be clothed with flocks, and the gardens pour forth their sweets; but the moral field is uncultivated and waste. There, science may furnish its splendid but perishable garniture, and men may adorn themselves with its specious covering; but hope, peace, and joy are banished from the mind, and spiritual death reigns triumphant. Oh that the God of Elisha may heal waters like these around us! The grace of Christ crucified is the only healing virtue here; and where this is experienced, the wilderness is transformed into "a fruitful field," and the desert is made to "rejoice and blossom as the rose."

No sooner had the men of Jericho declared to the prophet their desire, than he showed the most cheerful readiness to comply with it. Perceiving that the thing was from the Lord and instructed by His Spirit how to act, he replied, "Bring me a new cruse, and put salt therein"; and the men flew with joy and expectation to execute his commands. Elisha, in the performance of this miracle, was directed to the use of means; though the means he made use of were *in them-selves* of no efficacy whatever. But the very unsuitableness of the remedy necessarily contributed to make the reality of the miracle more apparent. Thus Moses was divinely directed to lift up his rod over the Red Sea; and thus, in after times, the laying on of hands was enjoined to the apostles. Moses' rod, without which Moses himself was powerless, was intended both to remind him and to impress upon the witnesses of his miracles, that he was only an *instrument* in the hands of God and immediately dependent on His power. The same end was to be answered by the means which the Lord prescribed to His servant Elisha. Had Elisha healed the waters by a wave of the hand or by the simple expression of "Be it so," it might have seemed as though the power rested in himself; and the miracle would have failed of its object. But by the method here adopted, it appeared in a different light; and the power of God, in giving efficacy to means so insignificant, was abundantly manifested. Nor was it without design that the inhabitants of Jericho were directed *themselves* to produce the salt and the cruse. It gave prominence to the main purport of Elisha's mission which was designed to show forth the glory of the Almighty, as a God of mercy and salvation, making use of common instruments—mere household vessels—to effect his great and gracious purposes. All this was strikingly evangelical.

Elisha, receiving the cruse, went forth to the spring of the waters attended by the men of the city, and, without any preliminary parade or pompous solemnity, cast its contents into the spring, exclaiming, "Thus saith the Lord, I have healed these waters; there shall not be from thence any more death or barren land." Observe, how scrupulously Elisha guarded the interests of his Master! How studiously he ascribed all the glory to Him to whom alone it belonged! How careful was he to prevent the smallest portion of such honor from attaching to himself or to the means employed! The Lord alone was to be glorified; and, therefore, the miracle was to appear as the pure act of His own goodness and mercy.

"Thus saith the Lord." With these words did the prophet approach the spring; and with the power that authorized them, it was not difficult to perform miracles. Such a power could even have called new worlds into existence. The work of God is perfect and superior to all difficulties. "He spake and it was done; He commanded, and it stood fast." We, indeed, are not gifted with the word of healing as Elisha was; but if we are God's faithful people, we possess words of even greater and more blessed import. We can say, "Thus saith the Lord, None shall pluck my sheep out of my hand."

And we are certain that these words will confound the powers of darkness. We can say, "Thus saith the Lord, Father I will that they also whom thou hast given me, be with me where I am!" and are warranted to believe, without a doubt, that, would mountains and seas impede our course thither, even seas shall be dried up and mountains be cast down before us. We can say, "Thus saith the Lord, Behold the fowls of the air! O ye of little faith, are ye not much better than they?" We can say, "Thus saith the Lord, All things shall work together for good, to those who love God!" With divine assurances like these, we are encompassed as with a wall; and they will prove no less efficacious than the words of Elisha, "Thus saith the Lord, I have healed these waters."

The words were uttered, and at once the change was accomplished. From that hour, the water became all that could be wished for refreshment and health and imparted both wherever it flowed. The fields recovered their ancient fertility, and man and beast could rejoice in renovated life and vigor. All traces of former desolation disappeared; the inhabitants of Jericho were filled with joy; and a cheerful, stirring activity became everywhere visible in young and old. The happy shouts of the reaper resounded anew between the vine-clad hills, while the shepherd, with his lambs sporting around him, answered from the plain with the melody of his solitary pipe. The native husbandman contemplated with unmingled joy the rich promise of the coming harvest, and the traveler could commend, and celebrates to this day, the exhilarating freshness of the waters of Jericho.

How gloriously was the Almighty revealed in this miracle! What a striking instance was it of His power and goodness! What a notable seal did it affix to the divine call of the prophet! Who could now doubt in whose name and authority he appeared upon the plains of Jericho? And what a mild luster did it reflect upon the whole prophetic character of the holy man! Surely no herald of Jehovah had ever entered upon his course in a more evangelical spirit than Elisha. The removal of a curse that had afflicted the land for centuries was his first act. The restoration of a withered earthly paradise was the first seal of his high commission.

We want to see this miracle at Jericho spiritually repeated in our times. We long for it; we implore it. Alas! our streams have become stagnant, corrupted, poisoned, and send forth rivers of death, threatening with moral destruction not merely a city and neighborhood, but a world. The springs to which I allude are the modes of thinking so prevalent in this age; the immoral, anarchical, and antichristian principles, that, like a corrupting leaven, infect the mass of the people and control the judgments and actions of thousands.

Witness our pursuits of science, falsely so called, which, casting aside all restraint and giving loose to the most unbridled pretensions, seek to reduce all divine mysteries within their own narrow limits. Witness our poetry, whose wit is kindled from beneath, whose inspiration is worldly or carnal lust, and in which a bold contempt of all that is moral and decent often assumes the air of genius. Witness our philosophical theology, the object of which is to disprove the necessity of an atonement, to undeify the Savior of the world, and to annul all difference between the creation and Him whose word called it into existence.

Who can fail to perceive, while reflecting on these things, that our situation is similar to that of Jericho, that our moral springs are poisoned? Our journals and periodicals are conveying these bitter waters through every region; and who, that rightly appreciates them, can forbear taking up the lamentation of Jericho, the city of palms: "Alas! the water is naught, and the land barren!" But, oh! you of the spirit of Elisha, you faithful few to whom the good salt of the Word is entrusted, withhold not your hand. Produce it upon all occasions in your new vessels, yes, in any new form you please, but take heed that it be the unadulterated salt, for that alone, under the divine blessing, can effect the marvelous healing which is needed everywhere. In the name of the Lord cast it into our polluted streams and rivers, and you will accomplish incomparably greater things than did Elisha, for you will renovate a world.

2

The Judgment at Bethel

"They compassed me about like bees," says the psalmist; and his words may well direct our thoughts from the tried believer to Him whose sufferings are often portrayed in the Psalms.

The words have been fulfilled respecting Christ in every age; and wherever His divine image is faithfully represented, His people also find that His opposers are restless and active. But, let Christ be our refuge and strength, and the more we are opposed, the more diligently let us abide in Him.

2 Kings 2:23-25

> And he went up from thence unto Bethel: and as he was going up by the way, there came forth little children out of the city, and mocked him, and said unto him, Go up, thou bald-head; go up, thou bald-head. And he turned back, and looked on them, and cursed them in the name of the Lord. And there came forth two she-bears out of the wood, and tare forty and two children of them. And he went from thence to Mount Carmel, and from thence he returned to Samaria.

This event has, at first sight, a very repulsive aspect; and we feel as if it would have surprised us less, had we met with it in the history of Elijah. In that of Elisha it appears, at first, opposed to that peaceful character we have described. A deadly burst of vengeance upon a troop of wanton youths; a curse pronounced upon them in the name of the Lord! How characteristic of the legal dispensation! But how opposite to all we have said of the character and call of Elisha as a messenger of the kindness and love of God our Savior! Yet sum-

17

mer does not cease to be summer on account of an occasional chilling tempest, which, clearing away the vapors, opens to the earth freer
access for the genial warmth of heaven. This apparent dissonance, as
will soon appear, serves only to heighten the general harmony.

Here then is impious mockery cast at the prophet. Let us consider
I. its origin; II. its nature; and III. its consequences.

Its Origin

I. Elisha now departs from Jericho on his way to Bethel and,
doubtless, under divine direction. Carnal minds enjoy following their
own dictates; but it is infinitely more safe and blessed to know that
"the steps of a good man are ordered by the Lord, and that he
delighteth in his way." Elisha quitted Jericho alone, but followed by
the prayers and blessings of many grateful hearts. The peaceful and
happy days which the sons of the prophets had enjoyed in his society would not be forgotten by them. The whole city would bless the
man of God, the instrument of their preservation; the benefits he had
been the means of conferring being of more value than silver and
gold. It was an honorable memorial which Elisha had established for
himself in the hearts of the people and in the surrounding country;
or rather, it was a glorious memorial to the praise of Him, whose
interpreter and minister he was, and who has declared, "My glory will
I not give to another."

Bethel, toward which he now directed his steps, was, as its name
imports, a city once renowned as the house of God; but it now no
longer merited that glorious distinction. The indignant prophet
called it Beth-aven, that is, *the house of vanity or iniquity* (Hos. 10:5),
because, together with Dan, it had become the seat of that idolatrous
worship which Jeroboam's impious policy had established for the purpose of effecting an entire separation between Israel and Judah. To
annihilate all desire in his subjects after the temple worship of
Jerusalem, he caused two new stations of central worship to be erected. The golden calves, one of which was set up at Bethel and the
other in Dan, were to supply the place of the cherubim above the
mercy-seat; for the king said unto the people, "These be thy gods, O
Israel, which brought thee up out of the land of Egypt." An illiterate
priesthood, arbitrarily selected, without regard to lineage and
divine appointment, was to occupy the place of the house of Aaron;
and instead of the beautiful and figurative worship of the temple, a

variety of insignificant heathenish ceremonies was substituted which tended not only to banish all hopes concerning the Messiah, but likewise gradually to eradicate from the minds of the infatuated multitude all idea of the true worship of God. How impious thus to lower the highest interests of man into subserviency to mere worldly policy! And how lamentable that the case of Israel is not the only instance of so detestable a scheme! Similar attempts have frequently been made in the world, though nothing is more offensive and provoking to the Almighty.

That Jeroboam succeeded in his nefarious scheme is not surprising, if the natural depravity of man be considered. Many in our own days can boast of similar achievements. To divert the people from the temple of the true church, Jeroboam did not directly deny the necessity of the temple worship, but erected another to resemble and to rival it; and having done so, he cried, "Come up hither! This is the true church! This is Jerusalem! Here the pure light shines!" In like manner the modern corrupters of the church have also their Christianity; but it is a Christianity as essentially different from that of Christ as was the worship of the golden calves from the religion of Abraham and of Moses. To the Christ whom they profess to honor, they have denied the crown of Deity and the priestly garments, and have left Him but a fragment of His prophetic mantle. The devotion of their worship is but a self-complacent glow of natural feeling and sentimentality; and their prayers are of the most extraordinary character, being dictated by unmeaning sensibility and expended in exclamations without an object. And yet our modern Beth-aven teems with worshipers; our Israel has forsaken the spiritual Jerusalem and the true temple. Thus "evil men and seducers wax worse and worse, deceiving, and being deceived; but their folly shall be manifest unto all men."

Elisha could take no complacency in such a Bethel, nor could the Bethelites bestow any welcome on *him*. He was a messenger of Israel's covenant God; no wonder, therefore, that he was assailed with scoffing and derision in this abode of darkness and unbelief. It is not under the Christian dispensation alone that the children of God have had to feel the truth of the declaration, "I came not to send peace, but a sword." The saints in all ages have painfully experienced the rancor of that enmity, which, from the beginning, was suffered to arise between the seed of the woman and the seed of the serpent. If the world's enmity against the children of God appear a mystery, it is sufficiently explained by that declaration of our Lord: "If ye were of the world, the world would love his own; but because ye are not of the world, but I have chosen you out of the world, therefore the world hateth you." The world cannot tolerate our separation from themselves, or that we should rise above their standard of moral excellence. They require us courteously to follow in their track, to adopt their thoughts and sentiments, and to copy their actions, and if we only comply, we secure their favor and friendship. But the moment we show symptoms of desertion, the question of peace is at an end. The reason is obvious. Our departure from their ranks, our rejection of their maxims and customs, their vanities and enjoyments, is a more decided and emphatic condemnation of them than can possibly be expressed in words. Every converted man is too powerful a contrast to their own character: he admonishes them, too forcibly, of the necessity of a change and of the possibility of rising into a more holy and elevated sphere of action than their own. But they love darkness and cannot bear the light; they love vanity and sport themselves with their own deceivings. They wish not to be disturbed in their carnal security. What wonder, then, if they have the strongest antipathy for those who cause the light to shine around them!

Brethren, if we experience personally little or nothing of this enmity from the world, it is no very favorable sign for us, but should make us pause and consider how far we are really faithful to our Lord and Master. Has He not said, "Woe unto you, when all men shall speak well of you"? Can His true disciples easily avoid being at one time or at another reviled, persecuted, or calumniated for His name's sake? The indications of our high birth must surely be too faint, and its light can shine but little before men, if the worldly can take complacency in it and remain worldly at our side. Surely, then, we are indulging them in their self-delusion by our own conformity to the world. The courtesy we commonly receive from them may be attributed to the lifelessness of our religion; which, if it contained more of the divine unction, of the fire from off the altar of the sanctuary, would cause the whole appearance of things to be changed. The true man of God can never expect to pass unmolested through Dan or Beth-aven; for, while He is "a savor of life" to all that believe, He is to the unbeliever "a savor of death unto death."

Its Nature

II. Elisha was pursuing his solitary way to Bethel, and we may believe him to have been not without recollections and meditations of the deepest interest, if we reflect only upon his recent experiences. We here can hardly help being reminded of his forefather Jacob on his solitary journey to this very place and of his communion with God; but we can better imagine than describe the prophet's present emotions. Elevated and invigorated by his contemplations of the past, how painful must have been the contrast of the scenes of moral darkness which actually surrounded him! The holy ground where Jacob was constrained to exclaim, "How dreadful is this place! this is none other but the house of God, and this is the gate of heaven"; how entirely, how mournfully, was it changed! Bethel had become a Bethaven, a house of wickedness. The place once dedicated to the glory and praise of Jehovah was now a refuge of lies and of every idolatrous abomination.

But for what purpose, might Elisha have thought, could the Lord be sending him to this place? Perhaps many a bright ray of hope had begun to shine through the gloom of his melancholy reflections, and he might suppose that possibly God intended by his means to transform this place again into a Bethel. However, he advances toward the polluted city.

It is not unlikely that it was already known in Bethel what sort of a man was approaching its gates, and the prince of darkness was already on the alert to keep his palace and to guard his territories. In Elisha he beheld an enemy whom, probably, he dreaded more than he had dreaded the Tishbite. This may seem at first sight incredible; for how simple and unpretending was the appearance of the husbandman from Abel-meholah compared with that prophet whose spirit and power were as the lightnings of heaven; so swiftly could they inflict death and destruction. But the most zealous asserters of the law are not regarded by the adversary as his most formidable opponents. He well knows that the holy law of God, far from melting the hardened heart into a willing surrender of itself to the Lord, becomes, through human depravity, the occasion whereby sin works in us all manner of concupiscence; for the rebellious disposition of man only spurns its holy restraint the more, the nearer it is brought to him. The gospel, on the contrary, the sweet message of mercy, fills the enemy of souls with real alarm for his kingdom. He knows its secret energy, its power to allure, convince, and subdue; and he is never more active in opposition than when its sounds penetrate within his dominions.

How then could he remain neutral when he beheld Elisha approaching one of his most devoted cities? He was aware of the blessings which this man of God had conferred upon Jericho, which portended to him the loss of that city and neighborhood, and for aught he knew, the loss of Bethel also. He, therefore, hastens to take his measures and has his agents ready at hand—most probably those lying priests who were always his willing instruments. He suggests to them the danger that threatens them; he incites their jealousy and rage and points out to them the carnal weapons with which they might most readily assail the enemy of their dignity and rule. The priests, we may suppose, instigated a rabble of hardened and impudent youths to try the prophet's firmness by going out of the town to meet him and insult him. This young generation of vipers think themselves men enough to encounter the odious prophet.

Elisha arrives within the precincts of the idolatrous place, not to curse and to destroy it, no, but with the gracious design of collecting backsliders under the banner of love; when, behold, the rabble of rude clamorous youths rush wildly out of the gates of the city! Our version says, "little children," but the words in the original also signify young people. They come behind the man of God as he is going up to the town; they raise a loud and insolent laugh and are not ashamed to cast at him the lowest and most offensive mockery, making even his venerable appearance the subject of their profane raillery.

Baldness was regarded by the lower orders as a kind of disgrace as it was one of the usual consequences of the leprosy. So it was accounted a sign of personal and mental degradation. Hence, in using this opprobrious epithet, the young profligates had a most malicious intention. Their expressions are not to be viewed as a mere burst of youthful wantonness, but as poisoned arrows, pointed and directed by refined and satanic malignity. It is as if they had said, "Thou effeminate leper! Thou would-be prophet! We fear thee not! Go up! Go up!" As if they meant, "Imitate thy master! Enter thy fiery chariot, and follow him through the clouds!" It seems to have been a scoffing allusion to the ascent of Elijah—partly skeptical, and partly in derision of Elisha. "Wilt thou ape the dreaded Elijah? Then magnify thy office, and show thyself." At all events, it was more than a mere sally of childish unruliness; it was the deliberate rancor of rooted and audacious impiety. The well-known and mild demeanor of Elisha (for he was no stranger to them) seems to have unfettered their impious spirits. And the fact that their hatred could overcome the power of that love, which beamed upon them in the whole appearance of this man, renders their crime the more aggravated.

Who is not penetrated with grief while contemplating this melancholy spectacle? Alas! we cannot but believe that these youths were hastening to perdition. Better had it been for them to have been sacrificed in their infancy to the fiery idol Moloch, than to have thus survived to become the victims of sin and Satan and to die the death of the impenitent. But did such an evil generation disappear from the earth with the forty and two at Bethel? Alas! the present rising generation everywhere proves the contrary. It is one of the greatest afflictions of these evil times, that we look to many of them in vain for the hope of better times at hand. It is heart-rending to behold our youth drinking of those intoxicating fountains at which their fathers have so intemperately indulged, and to know that they are initiated in vain, theoretic, and infidel notions which alienate the heart from God and dissolve the most sacred obligations. Alas! the seed so thickly sown is already springing up around us, luxuriantly rank.

"The fathers have eaten sour grapes, and the children's teeth are set on edge." O parents, masters, and teachers, how many of you have torn down long ago the barrier of God's Word and destroyed all reverence for it! And now you have yourselves to blame that you are surrounded by a youthful band of rebels whom you despair of controlling. You have taught them to view scriptural Christianity as an ignominious chain, forged by superstition in a dark age, and to regard those who preach it as canting hypocrites or weak and gloomy fanatics; and though we now admonish them, in the name of God, to honor and obey their parents, yet with what effect we do it, you yourselves are painfully aware. You have filled them with conceits of the independence of man and of human reason, and it is but a just retribution that you have been the first bitterly to feel, in their misbehavior to yourselves, the sad consequences of your pernicious instructions.

Should any imagine this description of our youth to be overwrought, let them only inspect many families and schools, and the most superficial observation will convince them of its truth. Alas! how many of our young plants are corrupted at the core! The very roots are rottenness; undutiful, and presumptuously obstinate; initiated from infancy in every mystery of iniquity and impiety, of whom no one would say, "Theirs is the kingdom of heaven"; strangers even to the show of filial obedience, modest submission, and respect to parents and superiors; they laugh at the rebuke of love, and spurn restraint with rebellious defiance. Those of low degree are vulgar, headstrong, and licentious; those of high degree are morally enervated, filled with vanity, and trusting in a lie. May God have mercy on the future age for which this generation is ripening! My brethren, the foundations of antichrist are laid; they are laid in the hearts of our children. The man of sin will have only to shake this human tree, and his disciples will fall into his arms like ripe fruit! The budding branches of the fig tree are full of sap, and their maturity is nigh. May God, in His mercy, overrule the approaching ruin and desolation!

Its Consequences

III. Such then was the origin and character of the young but presumptuous blasphemers who insulted the prophet at the gates of Bethel. They were instigated by the agency of the father of lies and had entered upon a course the very opposite to that of goodness, righteousness, and truth. Had not this conduct been punished in the awful manner in which it was, the authority of Elisha among the people might have been greatly impaired; the insolence of his opposers would have been raised to a higher pitch and might have known no bounds. Doubtless, this was what our inveterate adversary desired to accomplish, that Elisha's spiritual influence might be put down at once, his prophetic work abolished, his mission stripped of its glory, and his person rendered ridiculous (as a false prophet) in the eyes of the people.

The same method is still pursued by our great adversary in his opposition to the witnesses of God. If he cannot make them suspected as hypocrites or fanatics, he derides them to the multitude as contemptible and weak men, and therefore as false prophets. In this manner has he sought to destroy the influence of many a faithful Christian minister, and especially of one whom you well remember among yourselves. Nevertheless, that holy man stood (like an ancient confessor) unshaken as a rock and continued joyfully to testify of

Christ. He did not, as is so frequently the case at present, aim at countervailing the offense of the cross by diluting the gospel or by dressing it up in high flown eloquence. God was with that worthy man and blessed his ministry. No wild beasts devoured his revilers, but they were visited with the thunderbolts of bankruptcy and penury—the badges of public contempt. He raised his servant from the dust wherein they had sought to trample him; he gave double energy and point to his words, and so remarkably owned and prospered his work, that even the ungodly were constrained secretly to acknowledge that "the Lord was with him!"

The transaction then before the gates of Bethel was not one that could be silently passed over. The attack on the cause of God was too serious to be met with clemency and forbearance. Of this Elisha was perfectly sensible. The indignity offered to himself he might easily have brooked, but higher considerations prescribed to him, in this case, a different course. His authority in Israel was at stake, and with it the results of his prophetic mission. His rising feelings of compassion and love must, therefore, here be sacrificed to the honor and cause of Jehovah, the true God of Bethel and of Israel. This required the exercise of painful self-denial in a man of Elisha's gentle character; but a sacred public spirit sustained him, and higher considerations for the general good prevailed over him. The man of God turned toward the reckless mob, beheld them with holy indignation, and "cursed them in the name of the Lord."

Many interpreters, wishing to soften the matter, represent the prophet as only reproving them for their impiety, and threatening them, unless they reformed, with divine judgments. But this attempt to save Elisha's honor is gratuitous and misplaced. The words here used by the inspired penman oblige us to believe that Elisha, under divine direction, positively announced to his revilers the divine displeasure of the God of Israel. The Lord confirmed the word of His servant and affixed to it a dreadful seal. Scarcely had the awful words escaped the prophet's lips, when, behold, two raging bears, the terrible executioners of heavenly vengeance, rush forth from a neighboring wood, commence the work of destruction upon the godless rabble, and do not cease until forty and two of them are torn in pieces. Those fierce avengers then returned quietly into the gloom of their forest without the least molestation offered to the man of God. But what an awful judgment!

What an astounding event to Bethel, and to the whole country! That it was a divine visitation could admit of no dispute; otherwise it had not been even a likely occurrence that so many human beings should have been destroyed, as in a moment, by such means as these. Nothing but the keenest hunger could have incited such animals to attack the human species, and not even that to attack so many at once. That two such creatures should rush upon a whole band of vigorous youths was a thing unnatural and unknown. That hunger had not impelled them was evident from their tearing one victim after another, and then deserting them all; for the history implies that they did not devour them. It is, therefore, most evident, which indeed the sacred history with equal plainness intimates, that this was a special visitation of God, who, in the exercise of His almighty power, can appoint at one time ravenous birds to carry sustenance to His servants, and at another, raging bears to become the agents of His righteous displeasure.

The event produced some salutary results. Though it did not suffice to change the minds of the idolatrous Bethelites, it put them under the restraint of bit and bridle and served to secure, at least for a time, not only to the prophet but to all the pious remnant in Israel, exemption from gross outrage and injustice. It is of the same character with the summary execution of the golden calf worshipers at the foot of Sinai; with the judgment inflicted on Ananias and Sapphira at the very commencement of the New Testament church; and was intended to produce a similar effect. It proclaimed in characters of blood, "Be not deceived; God is not mocked"; and great fear must naturally have come upon all the people. A deep and awful impression of the divine severity must have bound the spirit of blasphemy and scorn as with chains of brass; and the children of the prophets, those at least in Bethel, would enjoy some respite from persecutions and indignities to which we may well suppose they had been hitherto exposed. The horrible image of the two terrible avengers would seem to guard like sentinels the dwellings of God's servants. The shields of the mighty were now seen to cover the prophet's head, and the glittering sword of the Lord to be ready, if required, to devour the adversaries.

But greatly as the punishment inflicted on this impious band of youths contributed to establish the dignity of the prophet, and important as was the impulse given by it to his work in Israel and to the advancement of the word of truth, meekness, and righteousness, the spirit of the man of God would be far from elated at any triumph of his own. Doubtless, if any one lamented that the honor of God rendered such severity needful, it was Elisha himself. Many, had they been honored with such a triumph as his, would not have retired till they had witnessed the splendid consequences of the fearful infliction, or at least had gratified themselves with the altered position and obsequious respect of their opponents.

Elisha desired no such gratification but hastened from the place, as though he had been the vanquished party and sought retirement on Mount Carmel. Does this surprise us? It need not, if we consider that the prophet found himself in a sphere of action directly at variance with his amiable and evangelical spirit. He, who was so disposed to forbearance and pardon, had been the instrument of a dreadful punishment; he, who was so especially fitted by the peculiar structure of his mind to administer consolation and healing, found himself suddenly armed with the sword of divine vengeance, and, for a while, commissioned to scatter death and destruction around him.

We may imagine that he hardly recognized himself and that his very office seemed changed, so heavily would the horrible catastrophe depress his affectionate spirit. Not only would the mangled carcasses of his revilers be constantly present to his imagination, but the awful condition of the souls whom his curse had precipitated into the presence of their Judge would continually distress a mind like his. How should he regain that former happy serenity of which this tragical event must have greatly deprived him? How should he hush that tumult of horror, pity, and amazement which must have agitated his soul? He was, indeed, aware that the Lord had commissioned him to pronounce the judgment; but this consciousness would be insufficient of itself to restore composure. What else could he do except to seek in retired solitude fresh converse with his God? In the shadow of the Lord's hand must he hide himself and there regain his self-possession. From Him, he must obtain renewed assurances that he had done right, that he had acted in His name, by His imperative command, and as His instrument. He, therefore, flees from Bethel and hastens to Mount Carmel, to pour out, in the solitude and silence of its groves, his oppressed soul before the Lord and to calm its agitating impressions in devotional retirement.

Here we leave him and conclude our reflections with rejoicing in the strengthening conviction that God identifies the honor of His faithful servants with His own, and that all contempt of them is regarded by Him as a contempt of Himself. Supported by this consideration, we may well deem it a small thing to be judged of man's judgment or to bear with the injustice of the world. If their arrows fly upward, we may well allow them to pass harmlessly over our heads without exciting our envy at the evil-doers, for rather should we pity them and cry, "Father, forgive them." It is true, God at present endures with much long-suffering those who oppose His cause and despise His people. He seldom inflicts summary judgment as He did for Elisha at Bethel. If in this life He punish the revilers of His faithful servants, it is rather by concealing from them the true glory of real Christians than by displaying it openly. Such is the nature of that service to which we belong, that it is the service of the cross; and the inscription on its banner for our direction on the way is "Onward." But a day will come when the King shall assert the honors of Zion and present her to His enemies as His chosen bride, arrayed in His own glory. What astonishment and confusion of face will then be manifested! Till then let us bear the cross patiently and be contented to be despised and unknown. We know ourselves. We already see though darkly, yet assuredly, in the mirror of God's Word, something of what we shall be; therefore let us never faint, nor be discouraged that the world knows us not, because it knew Him not. Amen.

3

The Expedition Against Moab

"**M**y tongue is the pen of a ready writer" (Ps. 45:1). So speaks the royal psalmist, when about to utter glorious mysteries concerning the King, who is fairer than the children of men. David, like all the other prophets of God, was an instrument of the Holy Spirit, who spoke by his tongue, and pen, and song; employing these to convey to mankind enlarged ideas of His everlasting kingdom, as also to express reproofs, corrections, and instructions.

Probably those inspired writers themselves sometimes knew but little of the import of what they uttered, though they never appear to have been entire strangers to it. David not only said, "My tongue is the pen of a ready writer"; but he introduced it by saying, "My heart is inditing a good matter," so that his heart was likewise engaged. Such divine messengers were themselves feasted, while they administered to others. But, beyond a doubt, much passed through their hearts that was but half appreciated; much that was but darkly understood; and much that was quite enigmatical and veiled. No authors ever occupied a position so peculiar with reference to their own productions or ever felt so deep an interest in those very productions, as did the penmen of prophecy (1 Peter 1:10-12). Their own writings afforded them abundant matter for reflection and research. How often must they have afterward discovered depths and wonders in their inspired songs and addresses of which they were hardly conscious while penning them! How many unsuspected treasures of wisdom and consolation must they have met with in their

29

own writings as their minds became more and more enlightened for that purpose! Surely, then, the great truths which they declared should deeply interest our minds, especially as it was to us, more than to themselves, that they ministered them (1 Peter 1:12). After the Sun of Righteousness had arisen, the shadows of the Old Testament passed away, and all its wonderful mysteries and prophecies began to receive their luminous fulfillment. Christ has the key of David to open every mystery, having brought life and immortality to light.

The lives and actions, as well as the writings, of Old Testament prophets and kings were not infrequently full of sacred mystery.

2 Kings 3:9-12

> So the king of Israel went, and the king of Judah, and the king of Edom: and they fetched a compass of seven days journey: and there was no water for the host, and for the cattle that followed them. And the king of Israel said, Alas that the Lord hath called these three kings together, to deliver them into the hand of Moab. But Jehoshaphat said, Is there not here a prophet of the Lord, that we may inquire of the Lord by him? And one of the king of Israel's servants answered and said, Here is Elisha, the son of Shaphat, which poured water on the hands of Elijah. And Jehoshaphat said, The word of the Lord is with him. So the king of Israel and Jehoshaphat and the king of Edom went down to him.

The scene is here changed to war and battle; but it presents much that is interesting and instructive. The embarrassment of the kings and their application to Elisha are the two subjects to which we are to direct our attention.

The Embarrassment of the Kings

I. Jehoram is incited by a vexatious occurrence to prepare for war. The Moabites, a heathen people on the southern frontier of his kingdom, had raised the standard of revolt. This unruly people, whom God had given into the hands of the Israelites, and of whom David once triumphantly declared, "Moab is my washpot!" had again and again struggled to throw off the yoke but had invariably experienced how vain it is to fight against God. Their rebellion, however, had now assumed a more important and alarming character. They had risen in mass, with king Mesha at their head, declaring themselves independent and seemed resolved to perish rather than to continue to pay the tribute that had been imposed on them by the princes of Israel. The revolt of Moab was unquestionably an act of national guilt; but it was no less a divine chastisement upon Jehoram, who had forsaken the God of his fathers and had addicted himself to the idolatry of the golden calves. Of this wickedness he was to be made sensible; and, therefore, God let loose the lion-like men of Moab and permitted them to rebel.

Jehoram was not a little disturbed at the intelligence of this event; and, spurning negotiation which he rightly considered derogatory to his dignity, he adopted the most energetic measures and drew the sword. He had nothing to apprehend from other neighboring powers; nevertheless, he requested Jehoshaphat, the pious king of Judah, to render his important aid and to conduct into the field a part of his own numerous army. "I will come up," replied Jehoshaphat to the king of Israel; "I am as thou art, my people as thy people, and my horses as thy horses." When the two princes had united their forces, it became necessary to deliberate on their line of march. Jehoram advised proceeding through the wilderness of Edom, and this route was the one which they adopted. When they arrived in Edom, the king of that country, who was a tributary of Jehoshaphat, joined the army with his horsemen; they then advanced together through the desert to attack the enemy, who, drawn out upon the plain and confident in their numbers and enthusiasm, were exulting in the anticipation of a glorious triumph.

The three allies likewise flattered themselves with the same hopes. But they, or at least Jehoram and the king of Edom, had trusted in an arm of flesh. The admirable equipment and discipline of their troops had inspired them with a courage which left them no room to doubt that the first encounter would be decisive in their favor and open to them a way to the capital. But, as often happens in similar circumstances, Israel had miscalculated, as well as Moab. The affair takes quite a different turn from what either party had expected. Both the Israelites and the heathen were again to feel that whatever might be the issue, it was not to be brought about by an arm of flesh or by human wisdom, but only by Him who does according to His will in the army of heaven and among the inhabitants of the earth. He is the dispenser of courage and of fear. He directs the arrow to its mark or turns it aside. His alliance is victory, and His displeasure, destruction. At His command the sun can put forth its hottest beams,

and whole armies languish and pine away. He can send forth irresistible frost, and the limbs of His adversaries are fettered with
invisible chains. He can bring pestilence and famine upon a country, and what then avails the warrior's prowess, or the commander's
skill?

It was, indeed, an imposing force, at the head of which the two
kings advanced against Moab, and the general impression was that
the sight of such an army would be sufficient to annihilate insur-
rection and revolt. But another enemy unexpectedly appears,
against which none had calculated; and the combined armies of
Israel, of Judah, and of Edom were threatened with imminent
destruction before they had even reached the Moabite frontier: for
after they had advanced some days march through the wilderness, the
heat had become intolerable, the waters in every direction had dried
up, and the troops were exhausted and enervated. The increasing
thirst of the soldiers soon consumed the supply of water in the camp;
and now, weak, dejected, and languishing, they were in danger of per-
ishing by a most terrible death. Their leaders would have pushed on
to reach, if possible, a more favorable and better watered region; but
in vain. Nowhere was a spring or a supply of water to be found nor
even a shady wood where they might take shelter and repose. On
every side was only a flat and parched heath, swept by a burning and
suffocating wind. After "fetching a compass seven days" their
march is totally arrested. The fainting warrior falls gasping to the
earth; the horse, overpowered with fatigue and thirst, can no longer
proceed, and the camels sink exhausted under their burdens.

In this extreme embarrassment and peril, the idolatrous Jehoram
becomes uneasy on another account. His conscience, like a lion
invigorated by sleep, awakens within him and suggests to him something about the cause and consequences of this unforeseen
emergency. It is natural for all evil conscience to give things a dismal
tinge for it is from conscience that every condition in this life bor-
rows its coloring. Yes, and let it be only cleansed by the blood of the
Lamb, and it sheds brightness upon whatever may happen to us;
cheering interpretations are suggested by it, and it robs each affliction of its sting. On the other hand, the whole world cannot furnish
a power equal to that of a condemning conscience. It is a power that
can make the hero tremble and deprive the most valiant of their
courage; it can force its upbraidings through the plaudits of a world,

so as to convert the choicest earthly possessions into dreariness and wretchedness. "An evil conscience," says Luther, "is like a tormenting spirit, it is alarmed in the midst of outward prosperity." Scripture also declares that "the wicked flee when no man pursueth," and that "the sound of a shaken leaf shall chase them."

"Alas!" cried the king of Israel, "that the Lord hath called these three kings together, to deliver them into the hand of Moab!" "With the pure," sings David, "thou wilt show thyself pure; and with the froward thou wilt show thyself unsavory." Even when the designs of God are fraught with mercy, the surmises of an evil conscience are evil. In the divine chastisements it discerns only a rod of anger; and in circumstances which He has brought about for the display of His power to save, it sees only preparations for destruction. "These three kings," says Jehoram; he considers not only the viceroy of Edom, but also the pious Jehoshaphat, as included with himself in the same condemnation. The great difference between his own character and that of the king of Judah, he entirely overlooks. That the sentence had gone forth against himself alone, he neither will perceive nor suffer others to intimate. Sinners imagine to themselves consolation from having companions in their guilt and punishment; but the Lord, who knows those that are His, will in due time cast down every such imagination.

Their Application to Elisha

II. To Jehoram's desponding exclamation, Jehoshaphat, the noble king of Judah, quickly replied. *His* words evince more firmness and composure and appear to have proceeded from a heart accustomed to recognize in the God of heaven not only a Judge, but a Friend. But, it may be asked, if Jehoshaphat was so in favor with the Almighty, why was he involved in the same calamity with apostate Jehoram? We answer, that for this he had himself to blame. If good men make common cause with the ungodly, they must not complain if the lightning, which descends upon the house where they are met, should involve them in one common ruin. The king of Judah was justified in lending help to Jehoram; but to reply with such an excess of cordiality and friendship, "I am as thou art, and my people as thy people," and to abstain from even the most remote intimation that he had merited the revolt of the Moabites by his own apostasy from the God of his fathers, was unworthy of a son of David. Such obse-

prince of idolatry; yet anything was to be apprehended, rather than that he would "be swallowed up with overmuch sorrow." If he did but obtain help, his pusillanimous fears would be allayed which was all he cared for.

How strikingly is the same discrimination of divine providence as was here exhibited in the wilderness of Edom, still observable from time to time! The preservation or victory of an army, though ascribed by the world to its discipline or to the skill of its commander, is always far more properly attributable to God's care of His people, some of whom had probably marched unnoticed in the ranks while many more had remained otherwise defenseless at home. Thus, also, an alarming danger has passed harmlessly away from a town or village, and the preservation of the place has been attributed to some fortunate accident or to the wise measures of magistrates; while the sole occasion of deliverance might, perhaps, have been sought in a few of the humblest intermingled dwellings where prayers and intercessions were made by some "that feared the Lord, and that thought upon his name."

The Minstrel

II. Elisha having thus addressed Jehoram, a scene opens which at its commencement must have appeared strange and unaccountable. Elisha, without assigning any reason, desires a minstrel to be brought before him. A minstrel is conducted into his presence, probably from among the military. At Elisha's bidding he tunes his instrument, strikes the chords, and plays before the prophet in the solitary wilderness. Elisha and the kings listen to the sweet minstrelsy in profound silence; the latter in anxious doubt as to what was to ensue; the former, soaring with the melodious harmony into higher regions. Of the kind of music which the minstrel played we are not informed. A trifling air or a martial song, it is not likely to have been. The awful seriousness of the moment and the presence of the man of God on which the hopes of the whole army depended must have sufficiently intimated to the musician what was proper for the occasion. Probably it was one of the well-known songs of Zion, which we may suppose were sometimes played and sung in the army.

Though music is one of the gifts of God, it is not to be numbered with those of the first order, such as our daily bread, his holy Word, and many similar blessings. It must rather be classed with the flowers that shed their fragrance around us and with the various delicious fruits that ripen for our enjoyment. It is intended to redound to the glory of His name and to contribute to, to adorn, to cheer, and to soothe our existence. It is the universal dialect of feeling and constitutes the appropriate medium of a sensibility too refined for common language. As giving expression to some of the tenderest susceptibilities of the soul, it is the most wonderful of the arts and sometimes acts with very powerful influence. Hence it is a dangerous art, when employed in the service of the world, of vanity, and sin. But when applied to the uses for which it was originally intended, to the praise of the Lord and the glory of His holy name, to celebrate the works of His hands in the beautiful objects of nature and the goodness of His ways of providence and grace, and thus to give utterance and emphasis to the nobler and better feelings of the heart, how much of genuine beauty and blessing does it serve to diffuse over our personal and social existence in the life that now is! Luther, our great reformer, who is even celebrated to this day for his sublime compositions on sacred music, has feelingly expressed in some of his writings his own experience of the truth of the preceding remarks.

Music was in frequent use among the ancient prophets and was sedulously cultivated in their school. Saul met at the hill of God a company of prophets with psaltery, tabret, pipe, and harp, to the sound of which they sang their inspired songs (1 Sam. 10:5, 10). Music was here put to its legitimate use, for it was employed in the service of holiness. Its inspiration was the love of God, its breathings were raised by the Spirit of the Lord, and the glory of the Lord was its end and object. Thus consecrated from on high and allied to the harmony of heaven, it ministered to peace and serenity around, to dispelling of discontent and care, to the suggestion and exercise of thought upon the highest subjects, and to the preparation of the mind for every gracious impression. To show how music, applied to holy purposes, can be the means of direct salutary influence upon the soul, it is not necessary to adduce the example of David with his harp playing before Saul. Many of us have experienced it ourselves, and Elisha, who was a man of like passions as we are, was evidently not insensible of it. His spirit, which had been agitated with holy indignation against the son of Ahab, required immediate calming to its wonted equanimity, that it might be a fit mirror of heavenly and oracular light. And now, at the moment of recovered composure and self-possession, Jehovah approaches His prophet in the power of inspiration, as it is written, "The hand of the Lord came upon him." The Spirit of Christ, which was in him, did then signify what he was to declare, advise, and do.

The Prophet's Message

III. The minstrel ceases, and Elisha communicates agreeable intelligence. How great are the mercies of God! Israel is not only to obtain water, but to subdue the rebels. "Thus saith the Lord, Make this valley full of ditches. Ye shall not see wind, neither shall ye see rain; yet that valley shall be filled with water, that ye may drink, both ye, and your cattle, and your beasts. And this is but a light thing in the sight of the Lord: he will deliver the Moabites also into your hand. And ye shall smite every fenced city, and every choice city, and shall fell every good tree, and stop all wells of water, and mar every good piece of land with stones."

Such was the utterance of the prophet at which every dejected countenance must have brightened with joy. The command was obeyed with alacrity, and ditches were formed. And when they had drawn the deep furrows over the parched soil of the valley, at which they appear to have worked all night, lo! the thirsty country glistens everywhere the next morning with rills of water which had come by the way of Edom; and thereby was the whole fainting army not only rescued from death, but revived to new life and vigor. Now, this is but one of the many instances of that peculiar, but infinitely wise, method by which the God of providence displays His sparing mercy and preserving love.

Yet it may be asked, Why was such an indirect method as this adopted? Would not the preservation of Israel's army have been more simply and naturally secured by a prevention of the drought altogether? It would; but then Jehoram would have retained his golden calves; Jehoshaphat would have had one humbling experience less of the faithfulness of his God; and the army, attributing victory to their own prowess, would have thought, *We* are the men! *We* can command success! The pride of human nature would have been fostered, and Jehovah yet more dishonored and despised. But by the arrival of help and deliverance, after every fleshly arm had been enfeebled, the Lord alone was exalted in that day. His power and faithfulness were magnified in the sight of the nations; apostates were put to shame; the high looks of the high ones were brought down; believers were confirmed in their faith and courage; and enjoyment was enhanced by such an immediate vouchsafement of the goodness and beneficence of the Almighty. O ye children of God, take notice of all this, that you may not be too much cast down when He leads you over rugged paths and through desert places. Does the day of your earthly prosperity close in night? It is only that you may behold the Star of Bethlehem. Do the supports of human wisdom and counsel break under you? The Lord would only erect above them His throne of power and faithfulness.

The Moabites, who had received intelligence of the advance of their enemies, were now assembled in battle array upon their frontiers. When the sun was up and his rosy light first fell upon the water, the vanguard of the rebels, beholding it at a distance, supposed it to be blood. Thus the notion was rapidly spread from one to another that the kings were surely slain, having fallen out among themselves. Hence there was a universal shout, "Moab to the spoil!" and they rush forward, confident of victory. But who can describe their consternation at beholding the Israelite squadrons advancing to meet them sword in hand! In a moment they are confounded and flee in the utmost panic and disorder. The allied forces press hard upon them into their country; and, as had been predicted by the word of Jehovah, they demolished their cities, and on every good piece of land cast every man his stone and filled it; and they stopped all their wells of water and felled all the good trees; only Kir-haraseth, the capital, they did not demolish, but they encompassed it about with their slingers and threatened to level it likewise with the ground.

Into this place the king of Moab had thrown himself with the remainder of his fugitive troops; but soon perceiving that he should not be able to defend the city, he formed the desperate resolution of cutting his way through the enemy. He, therefore, sallied forth on that side of the city which was invested by the king of Edom, but being overpowered by numbers, he was again driven back within the walls. And now a horrible scene ensued. The king, frantic and desperate, suddenly appeared with his firstborn son upon the battlements of Kir-haraseth. Here he caused an altar to be erected and sacrificed upon it his own child to propitiate the gods. The Israelites, at beholding such a horrifying spectacle of rage and despair, raised the siege, and retired to their own land, leaving the unfortunate king, with the wreck of his army, to seek safety in flight. The object of the campaign had been attained; the power of Moab was broken, the rebellion suppressed, and the country again placed under the scepter of the king of Israel.

"The Lord is a man of war, great and mighty in battle." It is well for us, if we are on His side and He on ours. Then we advance from victory to victory; we break in pieces the mighty, like earthen vessels.

Man's extremity is God's opportunity. He takes from us our cisterns, to supply us from his own fountains. He strikes away our supports from under us, not that we may fall, but that He may be Himself our stay and staff; and He makes use of our perplexities to give us experience of His power, mercy, and truth.

A heathen sage is said to have exclaimed, "Never complain of misfortune while Cæsar is your friend!" But what shall we exclaim to those whom the King of kings and Lord of lords is not ashamed to call His friends and His brethren! He has said to every one of them, "I will never leave thee, nor forsake thee." Should not this gracious declaration forever banish all their fears and anxieties? He who has Christ dwelling in his heart by faith, though he seem as having nothing, is truly possessing all things.

Privations, difficulties, and trials are God's providential means of hiding pride from man; and it is only when pride will not be thus subdued that men in their afflictions yield to despair. Pride, as in the case of Jehoram, is ever the cause of despair and no wonder, for it is the cause of unbelief and of all the bitter fruits of unbelief. And why, but because it will not deign to offer unto God one word of heartfelt supplication. What an insane and contemptible thing then is pride in the fallen children of Adam! Even "the *fear of man*," which "bringeth a snare," proceeds from pride. Do we not therefore see what a righteous thing it is in God to rebuke and punish this sin? Can we wonder that the fearful and the unbelieving, those who live and die under the influence of pride, must have their portion in the lake which burns with fire and brimstone? But God gives grace to the humble. He is to the true Israel a Father of mercies and a God of all comfort; and with the Lord for our Shepherd, we can lack nothing. Therefore never can we be too dependent on Him; never too humble and poor in spirit. Herein is that saying true, "When I am weak, then am I strong."

5

The Augmentation of the Oil

The spiritual Zion is no abode of famine, drought, or desolation. Its fields are always green with abundance both in summer and winter because "THE LORD IS THERE." Of this we are furnished with a pleasing instance in the history before us.

2 Kings 4:1-7

> Now there cried a certain woman of the wives of the sons of the prophets unto Elisha, saying, Thy servant my husband is dead; and thou knowest that thy servant did fear the Lord: and the creditor is come to take unto him my two sons to be bondmen. And Elisha said unto her, What shall I do for thee? tell me, what hast thou in the house? And she said, Thine handmaid hath not any thing in the house, save a pot of oil. Then he said, Go borrow thee vessels abroad of all thy neighbors, even empty vessels; borrow not a few. And when thou art come in, thou shalt shut the door upon thee and upon thy sons, and shalt pour out into all those vessels, and thou shalt set aside that which is full. So she went from him, and shut the door upon her and upon her sons, who brought the vessels to her; and she poured out. And it came to pass, when the vessels were full, that she said unto her son, Bring me yet a vessel. And he said unto her, There is not a vessel more. And the oil stayed. Then she came and told the man of God. And he said, Go, sell the oil, and pay thy debt, and live thou and thy children of the rest.

The Moabite war having terminated in the signal defeat and reduction of the revolters, Elisha, who had returned home, is again employed in ministering blessings among the lowly and quiet in the land. Thus we have now to contemplate another instance of the peculiar character of his mission as a messenger and instrument of grace. The account is beautifully affecting and well adapted to the strengthening of our faith. It relates, I. A poor widow's distress; II. Her application to the prophet; and III. Her miraculous relief.

A Poor Widow's Distress

I. The place of this remarkable occurrence is not mentioned. It may have been at Gilgal, where there was also a prophet's seminary like those in Jericho and Bethel (1 Sam. 10:8-10). These institutions, of which Samuel appears to have been the originator and founder, were voluntary associations of men and youths, residing together under the same roof or occupying cottages in the immediate vicinity of each other, supporting themselves by the labor of their hands, either at the plow or in the vine and olive gardens. Their chief business was spiritual; and they devoted their time principally to the study of sacred history and the divine revelations, as also to sacred music and other arts and sciences dedicated to the service of God. A prophet always governed these institutions as their teacher and paternal guide, who, when not commissioned to other service by the word of the Lord, resided as a welcome guest, sometimes at one and sometimes at another of them, imparting wisdom by his conversation, quietly assembling them for instruction in the things of God, and uniting them in prayer and cheerful praise.

These enlightened societies, to which can best be compared the missionary seminaries of modern days, contained the flower of Israel and constituted those living temples wherein the fire of Jehovah shone purest and brightest. They were to Israel what Israel was to the world—the repositories of divine truth. Often was the little remaining vigor of that nation's spiritual life concentrated here where it issued forth afresh to revive the whole languid body of the Jewish people, for the Lord chose from these seminaries not a few of His seers and prophets to plead His cause before the nations. Many of the pious and enlightened men, who were called "sons of the prophets," had wives and children, and of such was she who is here introduced to our notice, a widow of one of the sons of the prophets.

Let us visit her abode of poverty. The naked walls, the empty shelves, the miserable table with a wooden bench before it, the straw pallet, the desolate chamber sufficiently show her circumstances. But these are still more plainly declared by the pale and dejected countenance of the indigent widow. She is a daughter of Abraham, and not only after the flesh, for she knows the Lord and is known of Him, who is a Father of the fatherless and maintains the cause of the widow. She is aware that her portion is not in this life but in a better country, that is, an heavenly. Without this animating consciousness she might even have perished in her affliction, for severe affliction had come upon her, one of the severest that can afflict humanity. Her husband, the glory of her house, had been torn away from her by an early death, and the world offered nothing to supply her loss but much to embitter it, for she had also to experience what it is for a poor widow of a pious husband to fall into the hands of merciless men. However fervently he might have commended her on his deathbed to the protection of the Almighty, she was now not only in the deepest poverty, but loaded with debts. How these had been contracted we do not know; but as it is well here to remember the state of the times in reference to those of whom the world was not worthy, so it is enough for us to behold the widow in her embarrassment.

Her creditor was importunate. She had already stripped her house of all that was not indispensable and sold it in order to pacify him; and the sons of the prophets, themselves poor, had doubtless contributed their utmost. Yet all was not sufficient; and unless the whole sum were forthcoming, the inexorable creditor was fully determined to seize and detain her two sons as bondservants for seven years which, according to Israelite law, he had the power of doing. Imagine what must have been the distress of the unhappy mother on receiving a threat to this effect. Her two sons appear to have been the principal earthly supports and comforts left to her and to have them thus torn from her side was grievous indeed. How many nights had she probably spent in weeping upon her wretched couch after receiving such an alarming threat! In truth, her situation appeared hopeless, and she must have sunk under her reiterated trials had not the Word of the Lord supported her and the light of His countenance shined upon her in this hour of darkness.

The dispensations of the Almighty even to His own children are not always joyous; He sometimes severely afflicts them, but His love is always sooner or later manifested thereby. Strange, forsaken, and disconsolate as may seem, at times, the condition of His children, He always accompanies them as their Shepherd and Guide, to whom it is an easy thing to make water flow from the flinty rock and to call forth grapes upon the thorny brier. Such wonders, let it also be remembered, can only be performed in the *wilderness* of His people; and be it ever so dry and dreary, still "all things work together for good to them that love God."

Her Plea to the Prophet

II. But great must have been the distress and anguish of the widowed mother. Though the sons of the prophets had most probably interceded in her behalf, her creditor, who evidently hated the people of God for he oppressed those who were quiet in the land, was only the more importunate. Deprived of every earthly hope, she was now driven back upon Him who is emphatically "the Judge of the widow, and the Father of the fatherless." But many a saint under the law could not approach the throne of grace with that "boldness and access with confidence" which the children of the new covenant enjoy by faith in Christ. "The way into the holiest was not then made manifest"; the veil was not taken away. Hence did many a dark cloud seem to intercept the prayers of Old Testament saints, arising from the consciousness they had of their own unworthiness. When the glory of the divine Majesty, before which the angels veil their faces, discovered to them their own vileness and deformity, they thought it presumption to importune the Almighty about their own insignificant concerns.

What conflict and effort did it then cost the trembling petitioner to penetrate even to the threshold of the sanctuary, while his heart sank within him at the first glance of the Most Holy! But we, brethren, are invited to come boldly to the throne of grace in the name of Him who became man for us. We can say what no ancient Israelite could, Lord! thou hast been "touched with the feeling of our infirmities," having been in all points tempted like as we are, yet without sin. We can exclaim, Abba, Father! hear us for the sake of Jesus, thy well-beloved Son, who is "not ashamed to call us brethren." We know that "we, who believe" in Him, "are justified from all things, from which we could not be justified by the law of Moses."

With what delightful assurances does prayer ascend assisted by such reflections as these! How easily may we now soar above every cloud in the security of this consciousness, for it is our inestimable privilege to know the great work of reconciliation by blood, by the blood of God manifest in the flesh! But the Old Testament saints had recourse to the prophets and employed them as mediators between the Almighty and themselves. Thus did this poor widow hasten to Elisha, as one having nearer access to the Lord than she had and as one who, being endowed with divine gifts and powers, would be able to counsel and help her. With tears and lamentations she appears before him, saying, "Thy servant my husband is dead; and thou knowest that thy servant did fear the Lord: and the creditor is come to take unto him my two sons to be bondmen."

This it seems was all she could utter in her grief and distress. No request is made, but her desire is plainly enough intimated in what she has expressed and in her imploring looks. She was doubtless acquainted with the wonderful event that had not very long since taken place at Zarephath. Such histories, in seasons of calamity and want, tend surprisingly to sustain our wavering faith and to strengthen our hearts. She might have reasoned that if the widow of Zarephath obtained relief, why should she herself be forsaken; and that Elisha would surely not be less able to work similar deliverance in the name of his God than Elijah with whose mantle he was now invested.

Her Miraculous Relief

III. The prophet, pitying at once this pious but afflicted and widowed mother, finds himself at the same moment divinely commissioned to wipe away her tears and to cause her heart to sing for joy; and he said, "What shall I do for thee? Tell me, what hast thou in the house?" She answered, "Thine handmaid hath not any thing in the house, save a pot of oil." Then said Elisha, "Go, borrow thee vessels abroad of all thy neighbors, even empty vessels; borrow not a few. And when thou art come in, thou shalt shut the door upon thee and upon thy sons, and shalt pour out into all those vessels, and thou shalt set aside that which is full." And she went and doubted not, but believed that a preservation similar to that of the widow at Zarephath would be hers. Here we may notice the use and design of such parts of sacred history as these: they are recorded for the purpose of supporting our own faith in God.

With hurried steps the widow hastens home to comply with the directions of the prophet. She collects from her neighbors a great number of vessels for the purpose; she sets them all down in her room; she shuts herself in with her two beloved sons, and now—oh what a holy, solemn moment must it have been—now in God's name she takes her pot of oil; she broaches it and begins to pour the precious liquid into the first vessel which, perhaps, was ten times larger than her jar, but which, to her amazement, is already filled; and in the same manner she fills a second, and a third, and so on. The sons at removing one vessel were obliged continually to have another ready; and thus it continues to flow just as if a fountain of oil had existed in the jar.

At length, all the vessels were filled except the last which was under the jar and which was already filling to the brim, when the mother said to her son, "Bring me yet a vessel!" and he said unto her, "There is not a vessel more." Then, the history says, "the oil stayed"; then it ceased to flow. Full of amazement, gratitude, and joy, she leaves her replenished vessels and hurries back to the man of God, to relate to him, with a throbbing heart, the great and wonderful event that had taken place. Then Elisha said to her, "Go, sell the oil, and pay thy debt, and live thou and thy children of the rest." Happy woman! How gloriously, as in an instant, was her heavy burden removed! She was redeemed from under the hand of the oppressor, and her children, those comforts of her declining years, were not to be torn from her. It must have seemed to her as a blissful dream. But the manner in which her rescue and preservation had been accomplished would set the matter in its true light, namely, as an unequivocal declaration of Jehovah's faithfulness and truth, as a pledge of His fatherly care and protection. It was proclaiming, not by words, but by deeds, "Fear not: I am with thee, the Father of the fatherless, and the Husband of the widow."

Thus are we again shown how wonderfully the Lord can relieve and sustain His people, and how all-sufficient is He after every human resource is expended. But it may be replied that such extraordinary interpositions as these have ceased, and that God now never thus discharges the debts of His children. While we ought not to be overconfident in asserting this, I would ask, is His help really the less marvelous because it is sent to us by ordinary means?

Last Christmas Eve, a poor pious widow, who had several young children to care for, lay sick and helpless upon her bed. In all her neighbors' dwellings, the families, young and old, were literally keeping holiday while this poor widow's heart was oppressed with anxiety and grief. Her couch was watered with her tears; and her children, standing silent and sorrowful around her, had no morsel of bread nor money to purchase it. Her thought was, "O Lord, how mysterious are Thy ways!" and she sighed heavily. Then came Elisha's question into her mind, "What hast thou in the house?" But her answer to herself immediately was, "What have I but a few empty plates and dishes?" This, however, was replied to by another thought immediately suggested to her which was embodied also in Elisha's words, "Go, borrow of thy neighbors empty vessels not a few!" This is not exaggerated; the thought came to her in these very words. But the widow sighed at any idea of applying it to herself. She turned it, however, into prayer, saying, "Lord, behold these my children; in them Thou hast empty vessels, for they are without food and clothing!" And then her heart subsided in another thought suggested to her, "Be not afraid, only believe."

In the self-same moment, the door of her cottage opened, a person entered, and with a friendly salutation laid a present of money upon the table and took his leave. Presently other persons came in, bringing bread and meat, and other sorts of food. The few plates and dishes were now all full, but still the supply was increasing so that the children were obliged to run to their neighbors to borrow vessels, not a few, and none even which they borrowed remained empty. Supplies of linen were also brought, with clothing for the children and even playthings as Christmas presents; but more delightful than all were the friendly countenances and kind expressions of love and cheering consolation with which the gifts were accompanied.

I say that all this happened in a few moments, in such rapid succession, that it appeared as if the persons had concerted together for the purpose; and yet not one of them was previously aware of the other's intention. When all was again quiet and the presents lay spread out upon the table, it appeared to the astonished widow as if the whole had been merely a pleasing dream. Then all that was within her exclaimed, "Surely the Lord is in this place!" and her heart was melted with gratitude and emotion. She now recollected the dying words of her husband, "Be still and weep not; the Lord will be with thee, He will not forsake thee!" "Surely," thought she, "it was the Lord that spoke to me by his lips!" And in the hope of soon meeting him in heaven, she seemed now, as it were, to possess him again and that she could possess her health again, if it so pleased God.

The latter idea had no sooner recurred to her mind, than she at once felt herself stronger and better than she had been for many years. She arose from her bed, praised the Lord with her little ones, and was able to attend public worship the next day and the day following. After this she was obliged again to take to her bed where she still remains; yet, from that moment she has fully known that it would be an easy thing for the Lord, whenever He pleased as by the utterance of a word, to relieve her from all her afflictions. Now, tell me, is not this kind interposition, as well as the event recorded in our text, deserving of our notice? Let such a recent fact then have a place also in our memories, for seasons may arrive in which it will not be without its use.

My brethren, there is a treasury "not made with hands, eternal in the heavens." It is a treasury of all possible good. If a blessing come not from thence upon our basket and store, our plowing and sowing will be in vain, and the sweat of our brow will avail us nothing. Without it, though we eat, yet, as the prophet Haggai says, we have not enough; though we clothe ourselves, there is none warm; and though we earn wages, yet it is to put it into a bag with holes (Haggai 1:6). This treasury is the power, wisdom, and goodness of God our Savior, of whom the psalmist says, "The eyes of all wait upon thee, O Lord, and thou givest them their meat in due season." He possesses the abundance of all things, who speaks and it is done, who commands and it is created. He is clothed with honor and majesty. All power and dominion are His in heaven and in earth. He governs and overrules all. Not a sparrow falls to the ground but with His permission, by whom "the very hairs of our head are all numbered." He leads forth the sun as a bridegroom out of his chamber; He appoints the stars in their courses and calls them all by their names.

He arrays every single lily with more than royal glory and clothes the grass of the field; He gives to the young ravens their food; He crowns the year with His goodness; He communes with the humble and refreshes the weary soul. He is never at a loss, never without means. Every word of His blessing is full of benefits. To this all-sufficient, almighty Father, as manifested to us in the person of Christ, we are directed to make known our every want. Through

Christ are we reconciled to Him and brought into communion with Him. Yes; and thus we may apply to Him in every *temporal* want. Oh, had many among us only taken *this* course, they had not been now in their present perplexity! Had this been done by men in general, the misery of the earth had been unspeakably less.

But then God is so awfully holy, and we are so awfully unholy. This is true. Nevertheless, a way of access to Him is open for the vilest sinner, and that way is Christ. He who comes unto God by this way, with all his poverty, will in no wise be cast out. And then the true believer in Christ, however poor in this world, possesses all things. Take heed, therefore, to be true believers in Christ. Then you will no longer discern, in the Majesty on high, a God afar off, but a God unspeakably near. You will no longer behold Him a consuming fire, but a tender Father to yourselves. Then you will not shrink back, afraid to offer your petitions, but crying, Abba, Father! you will cast all your care upon Him. You will have no more hesitation; you will come boldly to the throne of grace and find your wants supplied.

Our Savior has said, "Ask, and ye shall receive; seek, and ye shall find; knock, and it shall be opened unto you." If you should not find such promises as these fulfilled to you at once, yet proceed upon them as you are here directed; trust in them, and plead them before God. Forget not who it is that has said, "Seek ye first the kingdom of God and His righteousness, and all these things shall be added unto you." And again, "How much better are ye than the fowls!" Plead such divine promises and assurances, and assistance and preservation will certainly be obtained. For heaven and earth shall pass away, but Christ's words shall not pass away.

6

The Shunammite

The way of life is the way of the cross, an afflicted but yet a glorious way. Those who walk in it are never solitary. The Keeper of Israel, with a wakeful eye of fatherly love and faithfulness, ever attends them. Angels are commissioned to bear up their trembling steps. To them has it been promised, "When thou passest through the waters, I will be with thee." Their very tears are noted in the book of remembrance. Principalities and powers in heavenly places are interested about them; and at their departing hour, in whatever painful condition, they are surrounded by heavenly companions, ready to carry them to Abraham's bosom where the Lord is gone to prepare a place for them; so that, plagued as may be our course by sufferings and privations here, happy nevertheless are we, if we have the God of Jacob for our help, and our hope be in the Lord our God. All this will be seen strongly exemplified in the following portion of Elisha's history.

2 Kings 4:8-37

> And it fell on a day that Elisha passed to Shunem, where was a great woman; and she constrained him to eat bread. And so it was, that as oft as he passed by, he turned in thither to eat bread. And she said unto her husband, Behold now, I perceive that this is an holy man of God, which passeth by us continually. Let us make a little chamber, I pray thee, on the wall; and let us set for him there a bed, and a table, and a stool, and a candlestick; and it shall be, when he cometh to us, that he shall turn in thither. And it fell on a day, that he came thither, and he turned into the chamber, and lay there. And he said to Gehazi his servant, Call this Shunammite. And when he had called

57

her, she stood before him. And he said unto him, Say now unto her, Behold, thou hast been careful for us with all this care; what is to be done for thee? wouldest thou be spoken for to the king, or to the captain of the host? And she answered, I dwell among mine own people. And he said, What then is to be done for her? And Gehazi answered, Verily she hath no child, and her husband is old. And he said, Call her. And when he had called her, she stood in the door. And he said, About this season, according to the time of life, thou shalt embrace a son. And she said, Nay, my lord, thou man of God, do not lie unto thine handmaid. And the woman conceived, and bare a son at that season that Elisha had said unto her, according to the time of life. And when the child was grown, it fell on a day, that he went out to his father to the reapers. And he said unto his father, My head, my head. And he said to a lad, Carry him to his mother. And when he had taken him, and brought him to his mother, he sat on her knees till noon, and then died. And she went up, and laid him on the bed of the man of God, and shut the door upon him, and went out. And she called unto her husband, and said, Send me, I pray thee, one of the young men, and one of the asses, that I may run to the man of God, and come again. And he said, Wherefore wilt thou go to him today? it is neither new moon, nor sabbath. And she said, It shall be well. Then she saddled an ass, and said to her servant, Drive, and go forward; slack not thy riding for me, except I bid thee. So she went, and came unto the man of God to Mount Carmel. And it came to pass, when the man of God saw her afar off, that he said to Gehazi his servant, Behold, yonder is that Shunammite: run now, I pray thee, to meet her, and say unto her, Is it well with thee? is it well with thy husband? is it well with the child? And she answered, It is well. And when she came to the man of God to the hill, she caught him by the feet: but Gehazi came near to thrust her away. And the man of God said, Let her alone; for her soul is vexed within her: and the Lord hath hid it from me, and hath not told me. Then she said, Did I desire a son of my lord? did I not say, do not deceive me? Then he said to Gehazi, Gird up thy loins, and take my staff in thine hand, and go thy way: if thou meet any man salute him not; and if any salute thee, answer him not again: and lay my staff upon the face of the child. And the mother of the child said, As the Lord liveth, and as thy soul liveth, I will not leave thee. And he arose, and followed her. And Gehazi passed on before them, and laid the staff upon the face of the child; but there was neither voice nor hearing.

Wherefore he went again to meet him, and told him, saying, The child is not awaked. And when Elisha was come into the house, behold, the child was dead, and laid upon his bed. He went in therefore, and shut the door upon them twain, and prayed unto the Lord. And he went up, and lay upon the child, and put his mouth upon his mouth, and his eyes upon his eyes, and his hands upon his hands: and he stretched himself upon the child; and the flesh of the child waxed warm. Then he returned, and walked in the house to and fro; and went up, and stretched himself upon him: and the child sneezed seven times, and the child opened his eyes. And he called Gehazi, and said, Call this Shunammite. So he called her. And when she was come in unto him, he said, Take up thy son. Then she went in, and fell at his feet, and bowed herself to the ground, and took up her son, and went out.

In this narrative five principal particulars may be noticed: I. The house at Shunem; II. The grateful guest; III. The dying child; IV. Gehazi with Elisha's staff; and V. The raising from the dead.

The House at Shunem

I. About midway between north and south of the promised land and a few days' journey from Jerusalem, there is an extensive plain which reaches from the seacoast to the vine-covered borders of Jordan, presenting here and there a hill and partially watered by the river Kishon. In this tract which for the fruitfulness of the soil, the luxuriance of its vegetation, and the pleasantness of its climate was in former days scarcely equaled in the world, was situated amid groves of evergreen olives and waving cornfields the quiet little town of Shunem, inhabited chiefly by farmers and a place of comfort and simplicity.

Imagine yourselves looking down the street of it and beholding a venerable person with one attendant, just come into the town as a traveler. A rough mantle is girded about his person; but his animated countenance is a striking contrast to his attire, for it is lighted up with benevolence and peace. Respectfully saluted by all who meet him, he returns their salutations with paternal kindness; and having advanced toward a house, rather distinguished from the rest by its superior situation and appearance, we find him received at the door by the mistress of a wealthy family who has welcomed him with unaffected cordiality. That the traveler should have been so well-known in Shunem by young and old to be the prophet Elisha, attended by his servant Gehazi, need not surprise us. He had frequently passed through it on his visits to the seminaries of the prophets, which were stationed in various parts of the country; and whenever the tumult of the world urged him to his sequestered and peaceful retreat on the top of Carmel, he would sometimes have to pass through Shunem on his way.

The inhabitant at whose house he was here welcomed is described as "great" or wealthy, as she was the wife of a substantial Israelite. She was likewise no ordinary possessor of those true riches which neither moth nor rust can corrupt, for we may trust that she was a daughter of Abraham after the spirit and one of those few in Israel who had not bowed the knee to the image of Baal. From the great respect and filial affection apparent in her conduct toward the prophet, we may suppose her to have regarded him as her spiritual father, though we are not informed how she became acquainted with him. But it appears that she was no stranger to him; that he had often availed himself of her hospitality; and that of late, with the approbation of her husband who also feared God, she had prepared a room for his reception provided with a bed, a table, a stool, and a candlestick. Elisha, gratified by their anxiety for his comfort and well convinced of their sincerity, readily accepted this additional testimony of their kindness and in his subsequent visits to Shunem proceeded at once to the little sanctuary prepared for him, which his presence converted into a Bethel. Every care seems to have been taken that the holy man should not be disturbed in his devotions and meditations, for it was perceived that he enjoyed a more wonderful and intimate relationship with Jehovah than others.

This example of the Shunammite pleasingly reminds us of the assurance given by our Lord, "He that receiveth a prophet in the name of a prophet shall receive a prophet's reward; and he that receiveth a righteous man in the name of a righteous man shall receive a righteous man's reward. And whosoever shall give to drink unto one of these little ones a cup of cold water only in the name of a disciple, verily, I say unto you, he shall in no wise lose his reward" (Matt. 10:41,42). What else are we to understand by this declaration, but that whoever respects the divine image in God's children, notwithstanding their humble and unpretending exterior, and whoever shows kindness and love to any one such person for the

Lord's sake, shall participate in the same divine blessings which He is ever pouring down upon the just? What do you say to this assurance?

Does not the Lord highly honor His children by thus rewarding whatever good is done to them as if it were done unto Himself? Does He not express a most tender care over them in thus commending them to the kind reception of the world? Mark then well these words of the Most High. Whoever acts according to them, as did the Shunammite to Elisha, may be assured that the blessing of God will rest upon his house; and that blessing is likely to consist in the most glorious of all gifts, namely, spiritual regeneration, the first germ of which, perhaps, is indicated by such simple instances of love to the people of God. Or, if the person be already born again, his reward may consist in a gift, which, next to the new birth, is most of all to be desired, that of intimate communion with God through Jesus Christ our Lord by a more thoroughly renovated and enlightened conscience. But whoever hates the righteous because they are righteous, let him consider what he has to expect from an Almighty Being who cares for His children with such a tenderness as this; yes, let the very love of Jesus to His people make such a person tremble.

The Grateful Guest

II. With Elisha, now returned again to Shunem and under the hospitable roof of this pious family, time must have passed rapidly, and the hardships of his journeyings have been forgotten in such holy and blessed fellowship. How delightful is it, after having been exiled, as it were, amidst the ungodly of this world, to find ourselves once more in the bosom of a Christian dwelling, where we may refresh our spirits, though but for a few hours, from the vain or vexatious conversation of those with whom business obliged us to intermingle, and where we can again hear the name of Jesus affectionately pronounced together with the sweet and friendly salutations of God's dear children! It is like landing after a long and stormy voyage upon the hospitable coast of a pleasant island. In such meetings somewhat of that felicity is tasted which will be enjoyed in the tabernacles above, in the great and blissful reunion which shall there take place.

Oh, how painfully sensible do we thus become of the immeasurable gulf that exists between the people of the Lord and the most refined and polished circles of the world! We perceive at once that we have withdrawn from the atmosphere of selfishness into that of love, from the element of deceit and dissimulation into that of simplicity and truth. We breathe a different and a purer air and feel with renewed freshness the comfort of belonging to that "little flock," which, like its good Shepherd, is "not of the world."

In the middle ages and in the very center of papal domination, our own neighborhood of the Rhine presented a remarkable and cheering scene. For from Cologne to Mentz and beyond Strasburg, there existed under the denomination of "weavers," most of them being of that calling, a large number of true and enlightened Christians who were obliged to keep themselves concealed to avoid popish persecution. These people were very united among themselves so that they knew one another's names, residence, and circumstances, often without personal acquaintance. In traveling they proceeded from one brother's cottage to another and thus found, wherever they went, a hospitable abode and home, as it were, in their own atmosphere for it was unpolluted by the pestilential air of this world. Oh, that the same primitive relationship existed everywhere among Christians of the present day!For great and manifold are the blessings belonging to such sacred communion. Elisha doubtless regarded it as a matter of gratitude to God, that having so repeatedly to pass through Shunem, he could find there a retreat such as this. The little apartment which had been prepared for him was exactly to his taste, nor would he have exchanged it for a royal residence. In his peaceful chamber and in his secret prayers, we can easily suppose how fervently he commended these his kind friends to God.

The next point in his history at this place is the concern he expressed to see these hospitable friends receive a prophet's reward. He therefore "said to Gehazi his servant, Call this Shunammite. And when he had called her, she stood before him. And he said unto him, Say now unto her, Behold, thou hast been careful for us with all this care; what is to be done for thee? would thou be spoken for to the king, or to the captain of the host?" The prophet having been in credit at court ever since the wonderful victory over the Moabites, his intercession would have been effective both with Jehoram and his ministers. Those great men felt indebted to the prophet, but the prophet felt indebted to these private and humble servants of God. Gehazi is bidden to express the same to the Shunammite before

Elisha, in his own as well as his master's behalf, that no part of the kindness thus acknowledged might appear to be overlooked.

The Shunammite, however, feeling all the obligation to be on her own side, declines receiving any such acknowledgment and considers the privilege of having such a servant of God as her guest an abundant reward for the little trouble she had taken. Of the king or the court, she had nothing to ask as she lived on the most peaceable terms with her own people, feeling nothing of the oppression of those idolatrous times and knowing nothing of disputes or litigations. Having said this, she seems to have withdrawn while Elisha talked over the business with Gehazi. "What then is to be done for her?" asked the prophet. And Gehazi answered, "Verily she hath no child, and her husband is old." Then Elisha, who, doubtless, had laid the matter before the Lord and had now obtained his answer, desires the Shunammite to be called in again. And when Gehazi had called her, she stood in the door, as if kept back by modest diffidence about receiving any reward. He then addressed her with all the dignity and decision of a man commissioned of God, and said, "About this season, according to the time of life, thou shalt embrace a son." The astonished woman replied, "Nay, my lord, thou man of God, do not lie unto thine handmaid."

The prophet having now taken his affectionate leave of the friendly abode, amid mutual blessings and prayers, let us pause for the sake of a reflection or two suggested by the Shunammite's reply, "I dwell among mine own people." She said this with inward satisfaction. God be praised that we can make a similar declaration. Many talk much of being regarded in the highest circles of worldly society; others, that they rank with the master spirits of the age, the men of genius and learning. We do not envy them; but the condition of any Christian brother, residing among real Christians, would indeed be envied by us if we could not enjoy the same condition. We have it, however, and thus we dwell among our own people. We have those about us with whom half a word is sufficient to place us upon the best understanding; nay, with whom words are hardly necessary for such a purpose. Blessed privilege of Christian communion, not to be purchased with the wealth of a world, and that exists only among sincere disciples. It is in *Christian communion* alone that pure love, sincerity, and truth can ever prevail, and that the cup of social blessing cannot be embittered by the thought of separation. Let us learn in *every way* to express fervent gratitude for our own interest in it, and especially *by always endeavoring to draw more closely those bonds of brotherhood in which we are all united in spirit to Christ Jesus.*

But to return to the history which informs us how the word of the Lord, as here spoken by Elisha, was fulfilled: "the woman bare a son at that season that Elisha had said unto her, according to the time of life." Thus did she joyfully experience that the God of Sarah and of Hannah still lived, which she seems to have forgotten at the moment when she uttered her unbelieving remonstrance; "Nay, my lord, do not lie unto thine handmaid." And the God of Israel's deliverance from Pharaoh, the God of Daniel's deliverance from the lions, and the God of the deliverance from Babylon's fiery furnace, still lives. He lives and is "the same yesterday, today, and forever." Were this more steadfastly believed and thought upon, we should see more of the glory of God.

The Dying Guest

III. The history passes over an interval of a few years after which we find the Shunammite's child, who naturally had become the joy and hope of his parents, appointed to be the occasion of a most wonderful event in Elisha's ministry. The happiness of this family at Shunem appears to have been hitherto uninterrupted, and perhaps they had begun to imagine that nothing more would obscure the sunshine of their days when lo, the cloud of a frowning providence hangs over this happy abode. The father had gone out early into his fields to the reapers; and his dear child followed him soon afterward, as it appears, to be with him and to attend upon him. But while he was there "he said unto his father, My head, my head" and the father, not suspecting danger, desired one of the young men to carry him home to his mother. Who can describe the shock sustained by the poor Shunammite at seeing her beloved child thus brought home in a dying condition, for such it proved? "He sat on her knees till noon, and then died." Alas, for the poor afflicted mother! Her only child lies pale and stiff in her arms. He is dead; but can she yet believe it? Does she not call him by his name and implore him again and again to look at her, but all in vain? The beautiful flower is faded, is dead; and the serenity of the happy family in Shunem is departed with it.

But why has the Lord done this? We presume not to pronounce on what particular account it pleased Him to water these plants in

Shunem with such a chilling dew. Perhaps He saw it necessary to convince them that the summit of happiness is not to be found on earth. Perhaps the child had robbed Him too often of their livelier affections, and these he would again reclaim. Or they needed by some deep affliction to be more weaned from the world, to be more habitually sensible that their happiness every moment depended on the grace and mercy of God. One thing, at least, we know, that the affair was to terminate gloriously; that here they were to gather grapes from thorns; that a time was to come when they would kiss the hand that smote them and would joyfully exclaim, Blessed be God, who has led us after the counsel of *His* will, and not after *our own*! When they would be abashed that they had for a moment complained of a providence in which only thoughts of love and peace prevailed. To those who love God, all things must necessarily work together for good.

Elisha's Staff

IV. But behold the brokenhearted mother with tottering steps, bearing her lifeless son into Elisha's chamber! She lays him on the prophet's bed, as if the child were only asleep. She once more gazes at him through her tears and plaintively once more calls him by his name; but alas! a life to her so precious is certainly fled, and she sees nothing but a corpse. Nevertheless she again presses his pale, clay-cold cheek with kisses, and bedews it with her tears. And now, having forced herself away from the chamber of death and locked the door, she dispatched a message to her husband; to whom, however, the messenger was not to mention a word about the melancholy event, but only to request him to send her one of the young men and one of the asses, that she might hasten to the man of God at Mount Carmel and return immediately. Her husband complied, though surprised at her sudden determination as it was then neither new moon nor the Sabbath at which times it may be supposed to have been the practice of Elisha to hold religious meetings in that retirement, apart from the idolatrous neighborhood. She left answer that it should be "*well*"; and as soon as the ass was saddled, she said to her servant, "Drive and go forward; slack not thy riding for me, except I bid thee." So she went and came unto the man of God to Mount Carmel that his prayers might be put up for her at the throne of grace, if peradventure his intercessions might prevail to bring back her beloved child from the dead.

The prophet seeing her from a distance and apprehending that something was the matter, sent his servant Gehazi to meet her. "Run now," said he, "I pray thee to meet her, and say unto her, Is it well with thee? Is it well with thy husband? Is it well with the child? And she answered, It is *well*," which she said either in confusion of mind, or, which is more probable, in very strong faith (see Heb. 11:35). Thus she hurried on toward the man of God, and when she had come to him, to the hill, what a heart-touching scene ensued! She prostrated herself before him and held him by the feet, though Gehazi, presuming that such importunity could not but be offensive to his master, came near to thrust her away. "And the man of God said, Let her alone; for her soul is vexed within her: and the Lord hath hid it from me, and hath not told me." Then, in a few abrupt words which Elisha could well understand and which seem to have been all that her suffocating grief could utter, she said, "Did I desire a son of my lord? did I not say, Do not deceive me?" These two questions told her sad tale at once, and there was stirred up at the same moment in Elisha's heart an ardent desire that God might soon comfort this brokenhearted mother by the restoration of her child from the dead. "Then he said to Gehazi, Gird up thy loins, and take my staff in thine hand, and go thy way: if thou meet any man salute him not; and if any salute thee, answer him not again: and lay my staff upon the face of the child. And the mother of the child said, As the Lord liveth, and as thy soul liveth, I will not leave thee. And he arose and followed her. And Gehazi passed on before them"; but being on so solemn an errand, he was forbidden to speak to, or answer, anyone who might meet him on the way.

Gehazi, having thus hastened forward, arrived at the house and did as he was commanded. He laid the prophet's staff upon the face of the little corpse, doubtless expecting, with the sorrowing domestics, that a miraculous effect would ensue; in other words, that the child would return to life. "But there was neither voice nor hearing." The dead awakes not; and the spectators look down embarrassed.

Perhaps this was an instructive lesson to Gehazi, and it may certainly be such to us. The staves of the men of God are powerless of themselves; and their energy consists in the virtue imparted to them by the prayer of faith in the divine promises, through the mighty name of Jesus. How often have the very powers of hell fled before His weakest dependent servants! How often have mountains of difficulty been removed, and deep waters of affliction been divided, yea, the world itself been obliged to yield through the prayers and exertions of faith! But, where there is nothing of this, it is only "Jesus I know, and Paul I know, but who are you?" Form is in itself but an unmeaning thing to which faith alone can impart energy.

The Child Raised from the Dead

V. Elisha and the Shunammite were now at hand. The prophet had willingly accompanied her and did not need her urgent entreaties. Compassion and kindness would not allow him to remain behind. How naturally would the sight of this man of God attending her, compose her mind with the assurance that all would even yet have a happy termination! How joyfully then ought we to pursue our way, who have a greater than Elisha at our side, even Him, in whom dwells all the fullness of the Godhead bodily, Jesus Christ our Lord!

Gehazi having hastily come away to meet his master and having reported to him that the child was "not awaked," Elisha, followed by the mother, has now entered the melancholy dwelling. Her husband, we may well suppose, having, during her absence returned home, had received them with a burst of sorrow. And we can hardly forbear adding that she, on the other hand, was almost prepared to comfort him with the assurance that "the Lord their God would help them!" Elisha, however, caused the chamber of death to be opened. He entered it, as usual, alone; and requesting everyone to leave him, he "shut the door on them twain," that is, upon himself and the corpse, and prayed unto Jehovah. And now let death and hell arm themselves for the conflict for a greater than Gehazi is here; here is more than a staff of wood and an empty form. Here is faith in the Almighty's word and arm, a faith that can remove mountains with a word or breath of prayer.

On Elisha's first petition the bands of death were not loosed. He then, doubtless by divine direction, extended himself upon the body, and put his mouth upon the child's mouth, and "his eyes upon his eyes, and his hands upon his hands: and he stretched himself upon the child; and the flesh of the child waxed warm." He then rose up from it and walked to and fro with lifted hands and fervent prayers. Again he threw himself upon the body, embraced it as before, breathed the desire of his soul in faith and prayer, and lo, to the honor, not only of his prophetic mission, but of prayer itself, the prayer of faith—he prevailed. The gates of heaven flew open! Oh, the ecstasy of that moment! Signs of returning life appeared; the child, sneezing seven times, opened his eyes, fixed them with a bright and steady gaze upon the prophet, and—lived. Elisha immediately called Gehazi and desired him to call the Shunammite. Almost breathless with joy, the happy mother rushed into the chamber, nothing doubting that she was summoned again to receive her darling. Neither have her hopes deceived her for the prophet advanced to meet her, holding the beloved child by the hand in all the freshness of life and health, and said, "Take up thy son!" No sooner did the delighted mother behold her son, than she threw herself at the prophet's feet and embraced his knees. Hallelujah after hallelujah rose from her innermost soul to the throne of Him who had done such great things for her. She not only recovered her child, but his restoration would serve as a renewed pledge of Jehovah's favor, a living monument of that divine assurance, "Fear not, I am with thee."

And she "took up her child, and went out:" whither, we may well imagine, though we may not follow her. The history here closes her "chamber" door upon her; but as we pass softly by it, we hear sobs within, as it appears, partly of joy and partly of distress, with broken words—words of supplication, of homage, and of grateful praise. Here then let us be content to leave her, for surely she is prostrated with her child at the Lord's footstool, renewing the surrender of her heart to the God of her salvation, dedicating her child to Him as an eternal possession, and casting all that she has before the foot of His throne. How sacred and impressive is such a moment of sacred retirement into which further we cannot intrude! Let us, however, rejoice that the Lord has thus published His name so gloriously abroad in the earth, and that upon those that love Him and whose names are written in the book of life, His mercy endures forever.

7

"Death in the Pot"

W ho are those that shall never see death and yet are dead? The apostle says, "Ye are dead, and your life is hid with Christ in God" (Col. 3:3). How wonderful to have thus outlived yourselves! The Scriptures often speak of those who belong to Christ as crucified, dead, and buried with Him. Turn your attention to Golgotha. What is it you behold there rolling on like a tempest against the Holy One of God? It advances on the wings of night, accompanied by a thousand terrors. The anger of the Almighty is in its train, the acclamations of hell accompany it. Unrestrained it rushes on, and its whole fury is directed against Him whom you see suspended on the cursed tree.

No angel from heaven now stands forth to strengthen Him, no shield from on high to screen Him. He appears forsaken of God and man, and in this dreadful situation, He sees a power approaching Him. It quenches the light of His eyes; it has broken His heart, stiffened His limbs, and, amid the triumphant shouts of hell, rent His body and soul asunder. What power can this be? By what name is this fearful agony of the Eternal Son, this bloody catastrophe and dissolution to be described? It is the rebuke of God; it is death! It is a rebuke, a death, endured by Him who suffered it, not as due to Himself, but to you and me. It is the death of that curse which was due to the sin of the whole world. He bore it as our Mediator; and "we thus judge, that if one died for all, then were all dead: and that he died for all, that they which live should not henceforth live unto *themselves*, but unto *Him* who died for them, and rose again"; which if we do, then are we indeed regarded as having died *in Him*, so that we shall never see real death, as He Himself has declared. Our death is thus complete, that we may now learn to regard our old man as crucified with Him, that the body of sin may be destroyed, that henceforth we may not serve sin; that we may learn to reckon ourselves as dead indeed unto sin but alive unto God through Jesus Christ our Lord; that we may not suffer "sin to reign in our mortal body, that we should obey it in the lusts thereof": that we may be able to join in the triumphant song, "O death, where is thy sting? O grave, where is thy victory?" that we may see the king of terrors prostrated at our feet, and the horrors of death and of the grave crumbled to dust.

2 Kings 4:38-41

> And Elisha came again to Gilgal: and there was a dearth in the land; and the sons of the prophets were sitting before him: and he said unto his servant, Set on the great pot, and seethe pottage for the sons of the prophets. And one went out into the field to gather herbs, and found a wild vine, and gathered thereof wild gourds his lap full, and came and shred them into the pot of pottage: for they knew them not. So they poured out for the men to eat. And it came to pass, as they were eating of the pottage, that they cried out, and said, O thou man of God, there is death in the pot. And they could not eat thereof. But he said, Then bring meal. And he cast it into the pot; and he said, Pour out for the people, that they may eat. And there was no harm in the pot.

Though the present portion of our sacred narrative may appear less attractive and significant than the one last considered, it illustrates the words of the apostle, that all Scripture given by inspiration of God, "is profitable for doctrine, for reproof, for correction, and for instruction in righteousness"; and it conveys truths and reflections which acquire a double interest from the times we live in. It shows what God is to His children in seasons of difficulty and distress: and do I err in supposing that such exhibitions are at present peculiarly adapted to our soul's wants?

Let us then here notice, I. The dearth in the land; II. Death familiar among the heirs of heaven; and III. The Lord's hand not shortened.

The Dearth in the Land

I. It is on the way to Gilgal, a city which we have before had occasion to notice,[1] that the man of God is next observable. That town

---

1. See chapter 5, I. Also compare Krummacher's *Elijah the Tishbite*, chapter 21, I.

was situated in the vale of Jordan, not far from Jericho. Here, as has been mentioned already, there was a seminary of the prophets in the midst of a population deeply sunk in idolatry. It was from this place we attended the Tishbite to his triumphal coronation. Since our last visit, oh, how again does the land mourn! The beautiful country can hardly be recognized, so desolate is it now become. At that time, as far as the eye could reach, nothing but golden cornfields waved around us; we were met in all directions by ponderous wagons, groaning under the rich treasures of the harvest, while the vines and pomegranates bent beneath the weight of their luxuriant burdens. The blessings of affluence and peace everywhere abounded, and in the pleasant fields and vineyards, the shouts and rejoicings of the reapers scarcely ceased by day or night.

But behold now, how great a change! Blight has overspread the fields; the meadows are parched; the sickle rusts on the cottage wall; and a great part of the population are enduring the miseries of famine. All this appears the more strikingly to have been a visitation of divine chastisement, because such calamities were rare in that most fruitful and blessed of all lands. Even the sons of the prophets, whom Elisha was visiting, shared largely in the general distress.

The prophet, had he so pleased, might have remained at Shunem where his wealthy friends would gladly have entertained him; and under their hospitable roof he would have experienced little or nothing of the difficulties of the times; but no such considerations could influence him; his post was at Gilgal; both his duty and his heart bound him to the sons of the prophets.

A good shepherd does not desert the fold when trouble comes; he rather finds a pleasure in sharing it with his flock, be it even unto death. Those only can evince such cheerful, undissembled constancy, who have the Spirit of Him who said, "I am the good Shepherd: the good Shepherd giveth his life for the sheep. But he that is an hireling, and not the shepherd, whose own the sheep are not, seeth the wolf coming, and leaveth the sheep, and fleeth: and the wolf catcheth them, and scattereth the sheep." Oh may the love of *this* Shepherd destroy in us that desolating abomination, selfishness!

Elisha arrives at Gilgal and finds a gloom spread over his little community. Their stores, at no time superfluous, were now entirely consumed; their gardens were stripped, and their purses empty. They were indeed oppressed with want, and their wealthier idolatrous neighbors would be more inclined to ask, "Where is now thy God?" than to extend to them the hand of benevolence. They must have been dejected and distressed; and in what respect then, it may be asked, had they any advantage over the ungodly? Had they not to suffer the same want, and was not the same trouble allotted them?

Yes, the children of God are often more afflictively dealt with than the children of the world; and relief is sometimes found sooner by the latter than by the former. Where then, is the difference between those who love God and those who are still alienated from Him? Verily the difference notwithstanding is immeasurable; and one and the same calamity is quite different in the effects of its visitation upon the godly and upon the ungodly. While the latter often become by it more hardened in their sins, the former are chastened and corrected by it, as by the hand of fatherly love. It obliges them to have more entire recourse to the Lord as their Shepherd; to obey and to trust in Him of whom they felt not their need sufficiently in the day of their prosperity; and then, how great is the gain to have thus experienced the blessedness of abiding entirely in Christ; to have the confession again and again wrung from us that we are only worthy to be buffeted by the world, and that we are deprived of every refuge but the free grace and mercy of God. Oh, how sweet are the fruits thus produced by sanctified affliction! Therefore it is not because we are "condemned with the world," but because we are beloved of the Father, that we are appointed to share in public calamities.

With Elisha's arrival at Gilgal we behold, however, a reviving spectacle in the sons of the prophets gathered about him, as a father with his children. As such he converses with them, comforting and strengthening their hearts, and they eagerly listen to every word he utters as their divinely inspired instructor. How inwardly happy are they in his presence! He is a bright star of promise in the night of their affliction. The gloom of sorrow disperses before his words, and every eye again sparkles with joy. Yes, my friends, days of sorrow are not without much that is pleasing and sweet. They are cloudy indeed, and dark, but they resemble those lowering moist days which unbind the frost and make the waters flow. At such times the spikenard of the divine promises sends forth its perfumes. Then do we first seriously listen to the voice of the venerable comforters of ancient times; and how beautiful do their feet then appear upon the mountains! Many sacred truths, which in more prosperous seasons we had but half learned, are now brought into use and found invaluable. Our spirit thus can rejoice while our outward man is depressed.

Elisha's presence and consolations having banished solicitude from the minds of his friends, his cheerful voice is heard desiring his servant to set on the great pot and seethe pottage for the sons of the prophets. Then, as savory esculents were no longer easy to procure, one of the disciples went out into the field to see if he could discover some vegetable that might be eaten. But has God reserved any such thing for His servants in His vast domains? Surely He will provide and show where the provision is to be found. Yes; the man comes home laden with a certain fruit, having the form of an egg; he has gathered his lap full. The fruit is shred into the boiling vessel of pottage, none suspecting that these gourds of the wild vine contained any harm. How strange! and yet God permitted it; yes, He permitted deadly poison to be ignorantly gathered and mixed up as food for His servants! And why? Because His name is "Wonderful," as we have again occasion to acknowledge when we here see the "end of the Lord," whose ways are goodness and truth.

Death Familiar among the Heirs of Heaven

II. The pottage is prepared and brought to table, and the brethren, cheerfully and without suspicion, sit down to their repast. And have they no warning from on high? None: the Lord permits them to begin their meal. But while eating the deadly mixture, they become sensible of its pernicious qualities. They rise from the table in anguish and cry, "O thou man of God, there is death in the pot!"

It was indeed a heart-rending spectacle. They had seated themselves at their simple meal, so happy and joyful in God, so full of fervent gratitude for renewed supplies of food; thanking the Keeper of Israel for His bounty and faithfulness; and now, all at once, behold, death looks them in the face. What a dreadful change! What a sad interruption of their cheerful confidence and faith in Jehovah! It might well have shaken the strongest faith; though when the Lord afflicted His people in such mysterious ways, it is generally to draw forth from them Job's sorrowing declaration: "Though he slay me, yet will I trust in him." But it is sometimes to prepare an occasion for the triumphant display of His grace and willingness to save and to open a channel for those tears of godly shame which generally flow after seasons of distrust and discontent.

Here, then, we behold disciples of Elisha and, for aught we know to the contrary, servants of God, indiscriminately exposed to a violent and sudden death. But we have here no discovery of strong faith except in the prophet Elisha. We see only the common feelings of nature alarmed and in dreadful commotion. How blessed then is it to be armed against any sudden invasion of the king of terrors! to have put on "the whole armor of God, that ye may be able to withstand in the evil day, and having done all, to stand!" And do not the promises of God in Christ Jesus teach us that the chambers of death itself are only chambers of repose, and thus show us death itself only as a friend?

Our great Forerunner ascended visibly to heaven in His human form that our hopes might have a sure foundation, leaving us the cheering assurance: "I will come again, and receive you unto myself; that where I am, there ye may be also!" It is not, therefore, against death that we have now need to arm; but it is against sin only, that comprehensive evil, which consists in slavery to the world, the flesh, and the devil. And we should be the more concerned about this because death, which is always an awful thing to nature, becomes indeed awful, unless we are thus determined warriors against sin. Yield then to the Redeemer the most unlimited possession of your body and your soul.

Our death is a call from God. No one dies by chance but always at the moment appointed, neither sooner, nor later. Our days are all numbered. "Thou hast appointed" to man "his bounds that he cannot pass" (Job 14:5). Real Christians, therefore, may well leave this matter with God. For no accident can befall them till the Lord's appointed time arrives. And when it arrives, it is to them as a Father's messenger calling them into His more immediate presence. Death is even numbered among the possessions of the children of God, so that the apostle writes, "Death is yours" (1 Cor. 3:22). It is as Samson's slain lion.

When Jacob saw the wagons which Joseph had sent to carry him to Goshen, "the fainting spirit of Jacob revived." This effect should be experienced by the true Christian when he contemplates his last hour, for to him "the day of death," as Solomon speaks, "is better than the day of his birth" (Eccles. 7:1). It is the ascension day of believers, the commencement of their happier life. To them "to live is Christ, and to die is gain" (Phil. 1:21).

Ill then does it become our sons of the prophets to raise such a cry of terror. Dread of this kind should be reserved for other occasions, as, for instance, when a scheme of human wisdom would commend itself to us as independent of the atonement of the Son of God and would point out a way to heaven in another direction than that of Golgotha; when a theology without Christ, without a priesthood and a sacrifice would assume an *evangelical* disguise; or, with open front and shameless audacity, would offer itself to our acceptance either by books or from the pulpit; then we may well start back with horror and cry, "There is death in the pot"—for then, indeed, has poisoned food been placed before you, even wild gourds planted by the great destroyer of souls. He who is seduced to partake of these *"dainties,"* eats and drinks in *that* death, against which there is no antidote. Alas! that even the pulpit as well as the press should have furnished such subtle and deadly poison and in such abundance; but so it is; therefore take heed of their highly garnished productions. Alas! how many of our seminaries also provide nothing better for the nurture of the rising generation! Where in them is to be seen "the nurture and admonition of the Lord"?

The peril which now threatened the sons of the prophets was undoubtedly great and to all human apprehension desperate; and the danger to which their faith was exposed was even greater than that which threatened their lives. For had they not implored the divine blessing on their food? Had they not implored it in the company and by the mouth of one of God's most eminent prophets? We may be sure they had. What then were they now to think? Yet the Lord's thoughts were not as their thoughts. His were "thoughts of peace, and not of evil, to give them an expected end" (Jer. 29:11). This appalling incident was only to commend to them His saving power and mercy.

The greater the apparent difficulty, the greater and more glorious the deliverance. The prophet has received his instructions, and he knows that God will support him. If anyone has cause to rejoice, it is Elisha. His embarrassment was not trifling when the hilarity of their social meeting was so suddenly and unexpectedly interrupted by their alarming cry. Yet his anxiety, instead of repelling him from God, served to direct his thoughts immediately upward. He poured out his alarmed spirit in fervent cries to Him who was able to save from death, and an answer of peace was instantly returned that the brethren should not die, but live. That they should live, not to be justified in their distrust of God, but to find reason with shame to lament it. God had yet work to be done by these prophets in Israel and would not suffer their violent removal to become a triumph to Satan and his idolatrous adherents.

Elisha calls for a handful of meal. Who would have imagined that so unpromising an expedient should have conquered death and deprived hell of its triumph? But the prophet prescribes it in the name of the Lord; and how potent will the most insignificant means become when thus employed! Then a cruse of salt is sufficient to remove from an entire district the horrors of a desolation that has prevailed for many years. Then a piece of wood can make the bitter waters of Marah sweet and wholesome. Then can the anointing with clay impart sight to the blind, and that of oil restore health to persons sick unto death. The healing power of every medicine depends upon the presence of one single ingredient, the blessing of God. If this be present, it matters not how insignificant are the means.

The Lord's Hand Not Shortened

III. The children of the prophets did not stumble at the inadequacy of the remedy demanded by Elisha; they well knew that God often works by weak instruments. He who despises the day of small things is not fit to build that temple of the Lord which began in humble majesty. The Lord of that temple was crowned with thorns and sent forth fishermen and publicans to be the preachers of His kingdom. The meal was soon provided, and Elisha cast it into the pot without pomp or ceremony, in the fullest reliance upon Him who works alike by things great or small. He then says to his servant, "Pour out for the people, that they may eat" and they hesitate not, but eat in faith. Faith is never put to shame. Those only are made ashamed who trust in their own strength; but faith shall see the glory of God. The disciples ate, and there was no harm in the pot. The pottage was savory and good, and the poison they had already swallowed was rendered perfectly innocuous. Thus a handful of meal in the hand of the Almighty sufficed to disarm death, to disappoint hell, to preserve the salt of the earth, and to sustain His church in the world. Let none be afraid who have the God of Jacob for their help. He who hath "all power in heaven and

in earth," and "worketh all in all," can render everything sub-
servient to His pleasure.

Thus did the sons of the prophets at Gilgal experience what was
afterward expressly promised by our Lord to His immediate followers: "If they drink any deadly thing, it shall not hurt them" (Mark
16:18), a promise which was doubtless fulfilled. Spiritually also is it
fulfilled every day to those who are living by faith in the Son of God.
How many, alas! are poisoned to eternal death by a book, a system,
or an error! But while the lusts of the flesh and of the mind are kept
mortified through the Spirit in the exercise of lively faith, such fascinations of the world have no power to inflame them. "Resist the
devil, and he will flee from you." Temptation is thus overcome and
made a subject of praise and thanksgiving to God. There is then no
"death in the pot."

Oh! the blessed security of the children of God against whom
every deadly arrow is blunted and every sword thrust aside!
Whatever would hurt or destroy them shall turn unto their salvation
through prayer and the supply of the Spirit of Jesus Christ. The world
is to them but as a refiner's crucible. Even Satan's power and devices
are overruled by Him who is our Wonderful Counselor.

The decree is gone forth in behalf of the spiritual church, the
faithful people of God, yea, in behalf of the very weakest of the flock:
"All things are yours; whether life, or death, or things present, or
things to come, all are yours" (1 Cor. 3:21,22). All things work
together for their good. And shall those who are thus wonderfully
protected be anxious and perplexed? Shall they suffer their hearts to
be oppressed by any care? Let them blush at such a thought. Is it not
written, "He that toucheth you toucheth the apple of his eye?" (Zech.
2:8). Away then with all vain fear; the fear of losing a little worldly
convenience in the service of the "King of kings." Let no such things
be once mentioned in the kingdom of grace; for the grace of that
kingdom can render every deadly thing, except sin, healing and
wholesome.

8

The Man from
Baal-shalisha

Martin Luther remarked to a person who called upon him with melancholy intelligence, "The gospel is good news, and is certainly true; but I know of little or no good news in the world besides." The first and chief announcement of it is the love of God; and it is cheering and consoling to observe the workings of this love among His children, as we shall now have an opportunity to perceive. Its ways are, indeed, often wonderful and shrouded in darkness; but let us remember the words of the prophet, "There shall be a covering over all that is glorious" (German version of Isa. 4:5).

2 Kings 4:42-44

> And there came a man from Baal-shalisha, and brought the man of God bread of the firstfruits, twenty loaves of barley, and full ears of corn in the husk thereof. And he said, Give unto the people that they may eat. And his servitor said, What, should I set this before an hundred men? He said again, Give the people that they may eat: for thus saith the Lord, They shall eat, and shall leave thereof. So he set it before them, and they did eat, and left thereof, according to the word of the Lord.

As our history advances, the character of Elisha's life and times exhibits more and more typically the features of the New Testament. The event now to be considered forcibly reminds us of similar ones recorded by the evangelists; not that it equals those in grandeur, for it is in comparison but as a single stalk to the full sheaf; still, if we carefully and devoutly attend to it, we shall find much to reward and edify us. Let us notice, I. The man with the loaves; II. Elisha's command; and III. The confusion of Gehazi.

The Man with the Loaves

I. The scene of these events is still in Gilgal and among the sons of the prophets whose difficulties were not yet at an end. Hitherto, indeed, had the Lord helped them and gloriously supplied their wants from day to day. Though the morning might be often ushered in with sighs and weeping, the evening as often closed with gratitude and joy. Yet they, as children of God, neither had nor needed any better provision for the morrow than what was secured to them by their faith in Him. Food was always supplied to them as they wanted it; but, as they had often nothing in store, occasions for "taking thought" must have been common among them. At length, however, they were more impressively taught what hand it was that fed them and that the Lord would provide.

They were now again in trouble. Their last morsel was consumed, and there were no signs of more so that want began to stare them in the face. Did they turn away from it to the prophet? His calm appearance would indicate that he is "not careful to answer" distrustful thoughts "in this matter." Was patience among them exhausted? Did murmurings arise? Natural enough might it have been for one to sigh out, "Alas! when is this misery to cease?" And for another to exclaim, "We have escaped poison, only to die of hunger"; and for a third to look as if the bitter question were already upon his tongue, "Of what profit is it to trust in God?"

How then would we, my brethren, undertake to allay discontent like this? Shall we agree with it and say in the same strain, "It is not worth our while to hope or trust in God? It is true, 'he spared not his own Son, but delivered him up for us all'; yet can he give bread also; or will he provide flesh for his people? 'He feeds the young ravens when they cry'; but from us, who possess his love, and to whom heaven with all its joys stands open, he withholds these common mercies, and we perish, we perish!" Shall we say this? Shall we doubt concerning Him by whom the hairs of our head are all numbered, whether our wants are known to Him, or whether He cares for us in temporal trials and difficulties? It would be well sometimes to put such questions as these to our discontented and needlessly anxious brethren who, though "of more value" to their heavenly Father "than many sparrows," can yet repine as though they had no confidence in Him.

Is it not discontent and arrogance to expect the Lord to give us a stock in hand instead of our being satisfied with present supplies and trusting in Him for tomorrow? "As thy day, so shall thy strength be," whether for life or for death. What though here in Gilgal they seemed reduced to the last extremity? It was not really so, for the Lord can provide. A knock was soon heard at their door, and on its being opened, a countryman entered bearing, as firstfruits, twenty small barley loaves which he lays upon the table together with a scrip of corn which it was then the custom to parch and eat. The pious countryman had brought these presents to Jehovah's prophet, probably because, according to the law, such firstfruits belonged to the Lord and to His priests; and the ten tribes being then no longer permitted worship in the temple at Jerusalem, he believed that in thus bringing the firstfruits to Elisha, he had dedicated them to Jehovah. Thus were the sons of the prophets again taught not to distrust the love and faithfulness of God.

Events like this at Gilgal are not of rare occurrence in Zion. Many among us have received similar and even more surprising help. So many anecdotes of the kind have been furnished from among ourselves and been related from our pulpit that I am almost afraid to add to them for fear of their becoming commonplace. Nevertheless I will venture to mention one more, which, though it contains nothing remarkably striking in itself, serves to show that the Lord is magnified even in small things. Last Christmas Eve a pious mechanic said to his apprentice, "Tomorrow is Christmas Day, and we have nothing in the house and no money to get anything for dinner. The article we made for Mr. M____ is at the silversmith's to be mounted, and he I am afraid has been too busy to have finished it; and if it is not sent home today, the gentleman who has ordered it will give us scolding enough, but no money. Run and see if it is ready." The boy did as he was directed, though his master thought it would be in vain to go. But before the boy came back, the pious master had shaken off his despondency and was able to trust in God, fully assured that the Lord would provide in some way or other. No sooner had he thus thought than the door was opened, and the gentleman who had ordered the article entered, and said, "Well, is it ready?" "Yes," replied the man, "though, I fear, not mounted; the boy is just gone to see." "Well," rejoined the customer, "if he brings it, send it me directly; if not, let me have it after the holidays; but I will pay you for it now." So saying, he threw down two dollars upon the table and went away. He was hardly gone out of the house before the apprentice returned in great dejection and with a sorrowful countenance said, "Master, we must go without victuals tomorrow, for the work is not finished."

"That is unfortunate," replied the master; and then, taking up a paper with a cheerful countenance, he showed the astonished boy the money he had just received. "Master, where did that come from?" asked the boy. "Where," said the master, "should it come from, but from God who reigns above?" Then, relating to the boy what had happened, he exclaimed, "And does not our faithful God and Lord still live? Surely the Lord lives, and he knows full well where poor Jacob lives."

Yes, my friends; this happened last Christmas to that same poor Jacob, who, a fortnight ago, shook off the dust of this earth from his feet. I could relate many similar occurrences, all of which have taken place in our own parish; and one in particular which happened within these few days. For was not that of the letter last week an extraordinary affair? The letter contained a dollar with these words, "I know not how it is, but I am irresistibly impelled to send you this money. My own necessities are extreme, but I am not permitted to keep it. Take it then, and it must be so." And nothing could have been more opportune than was this dollar. But enough. There would be no end were we to relate the many similar instances with which we are acquainted.

"What part of Germany are you from?" said a celebrated professor lately to a young clergyman who had called upon him. He mentioned several places he had visited and among the rest, *Wupperthal*. "Oh," said the professor, sarcastically interrupting him, "that is a place where fine marvelous stories are related!" Yes, we praise God that our valley is not so barren of *facts* related in these "marvelous stories," as is probably the experience of that professor; and these stories will one day surpass in importance the annals of the most renowned wars and victories, for what are they but fragments of the history of Jehovah's love and relationship with His people and so many additional proofs of His condescension, faithfulness, and power?

The God in whom we believe is a living God; and we experience Him to be such. There are many in the present day who, because they like to live "without God in the world," think of Him as only the Being who, having first set in motion innumerable worlds, now calmly contemplates their revolutions but neither directs nor controls them. This is the most comfortless and absurd of all ideas. They indeed assign to *heaven*, to *nature*, and to *fate* their several imaginary parts, but God with them is imagined out of His own world. How infinitely more pleasant and cheering is the steady light reflected from the Scriptures which directs us to a God of life and activity, a just God and a Savior, upholding all things by the word of His power! Not a lily breathes its perfume that is not clothed by His hand; not a sparrow finds its food, that is not fed by "your heavenly Father." "The eyes of all wait upon thee, and thou givest them their meat in due season. Thou openest thine hand, and fillest all things living with plenteousness." He not only created the sun and the stars but daily leads them forth like a flock and constantly preserves their never-dying fires; He causes the dew to descend upon the tender herb and neither slumbers nor sleeps; He in due season whispers to the swallow and to the stork, "Arise, and go hence!" He controls every power, and Him the whirlwinds and lightnings obey.

He is the life of every living thing without whose secret influence bread would cease to nourish, water to refresh, medicines to heal, and by whose all-pervading Spirit it is that we breathe this vital air, that the blood flows warm in our veins, that the hand moves and the mind retains its power of thought. Yes, the views afforded us by the Scriptures concerning the government of God are such that we must necessarily conclude were He for a moment to withdraw His superintending care, all things would return to their original confusion and emptiness, and the lamp of life would go out in darkness and nothingness.

This account of the intimate connection between God and His creatures is the true one, for He has Himself delivered it to us in His Word. He is the life of all that lives, not less so of the worm in the dust than of the seraph before His throne. All things exist by Him from moment to moment; His kingdom rules over all. Yea, "the preparations of the heart in man, and the answer of the tongue, is from the Lord." "A man's heart deviseth his way: but the Lord directeth his steps." Over the movements of our inmost soul He presides; "The king's heart is in the hand of the Lord, as the rivers of water: he turneth it whithersoever he will."

There is nothing we do that is not under His control. "O Lord, I know that the way of man is not in himself: it is not in man that walketh to direct his steps." Laban, when seeking the life of Jacob, was in a moment disarmed of his rage and constrained mildly to declare, "It is in the power of my hand to do you hurt: but the God of your father spake unto me yesternight, saying, Take thou heed that thou speak not to Jacob either *good or bad*." (Lutheran version, "*otherwise than kindly*"). Esau, burning with anger, laid wait for his brother, but when they met, he ran toward him and fell on his neck and kissed him. Balaam was resolved upon cursing Israel, but when he opened his mouth for the purpose, lo, he was constrained to bless them altogether and to predict Israel's prosperity. Saul, when he at length found David whom he considered as his mortal enemy standing before him, instead of showing the fierceness of his revengeful jealousy, exhibited all the gentleness of the dove; and instead of denouncing death against him, he accosted him as a beloved son, "Is this thy voice, my son David?" and was far from offering him the smallest injury.

Thus the Lord controls the most secret impulses of the human heart and governs there, as everywhere, in the most unlimited sense according to the counsel of His own will. How consoling is this truth! But it is only so to His faithful people. It is no comfort to the enemies of God to be told that they are thus dependent on the power of the eternal Majesty. None but His children can find reason to rejoice that Jehovah is the living God, for His providence is always working blessings for them; and indeed, what blessing is there that it does not include? In its bosom they repose, as watching over their existence and directing their steps; and from the shadow of its protecting wings they can never for a moment remove.

It is as a bounteous Provider, supplying their tables and preserving them from hunger, whose honor is engaged not to suffer them to want "any good thing." Our heavenly Father, by His beloved Son, requires all His children to cast their care upon Him, assuring them that though a mother may forget her sucking child, He will never forget them. He is their faithful and watchful Guardian, as "a wall of fire round about *them*," their "shield and exceeding great reward."

All this we may well consider Him to be who is almighty and

omnipresent, who controls all the power of the enemy, whose voice "breaketh the cedars," and "divideth the flames of fire." He can impart a healing balm to every flower that adorns the path of life and can extract the poison from every noxious weed. He is a Comforter who is always present at the fittest moment, mixing with every pain the comfort of salvation. As an unwearied Friend, He is with them day and night, ruling over the present and anticipating the future, arranging everything as His love may deem most advantageous, skillfully administering to them pleasure and correction, and watching over them with a constancy and tenderness infinitely surpassing all human love.

Elisha's Command

II. The man from Baal-shalisha must have been a most welcome visitor not merely on account of the value of his gift, but because, as the firstfruits of a new harvest, it was a joyous intimation that Jehovah would again smile upon the afflicted land. His arrival in Gilgal with the bread, like that of Joshua and Caleb with the grapes of Eshcol in the Hebrew camp and the dove with the olive branch in the ark of Noah, must have chased the gloom from their desponding minds and opened the future to their view in bright and promising prospect.

Thus in our days of spiritual dejection and barrenness, we breathe more freely and indulge a more cheering hope, if we meet with a person whose life manifests a healthy, glowing, and joyous faith. The exalted piety of such a person affords us clear evidence that heavenly grace is not withheld; we seem to recognize in it the first indication of a general pentecostal visitation; we indulge the hope that our community may soon be the scene of a revival, the bare thought of which raises the very soul and brightens the dim night of our earthly existence with a cheering dawn. As the miner when he discovers after much toil and labor in subterranean darkness the smallest particle of gold regards it as a favorable sign so that his hopes are raised and he joyfully exclaims, "This will no doubt lead to greater treasures," so is it with us in the spiritual kingdom. The news of a single conversion among the heathen fills us with delight, for it serves to open to us the meaning of prophecy and indicates, like a streak of early light, the nearer approach of morning. A single believing Jew, taking up the cross indeed and addicting himself to the ministry of the saints, serves to give a more cheering aspect to his whole nation; and the new birth of such a person is like a powerful breathing upon the thousand-stringed harp of the promises, awakening its tones to louder and livelier strains.

As the twenty barley loaves lay upon the table, we may imagine with what complacency the younger members of the family would look first upon *them* and then upon the *giver*, as ready to embrace him and give vent to the fullness of their thankful hearts. The elder ones, also, would be pleased to acknowledge that it was long since such beautiful bread had been seen in Gilgal. It has been even supposed that such bread had never before been set before them. It is true, it was not from that table in the kingdom of God at which men sit down with Abraham, Isaac, and Jacob; but to these sons of the prophets it would appear to resemble it much more than ordinary bread. The only alloy to their satisfaction was that the loaves, being neither large nor very many, would soon be consumed. One or other of them may indeed have been disposed to think, "If God intends to relieve us, why not at once, rather than by halves?" Thus discontented and presumptuous, we are a people whom God can rarely please. We find nothing more difficult than to suspend our judgment till His purposes are ripened; for, if our desires are not instantly gratified to their full extent, we become distrustful of His power, goodness, and faithfulness. Were He to remove the veil from our eyes and show us the gifts designed for us, how should we be abashed and ashamed of our lack of faith and of our low-thoughted cares and presumptions!

As Elisha surveys the loaves, he would doubtless consider them as sent by the Lord and as entrusted to his hand for the sustenance of his poor brethren. But will they suffice to relieve the cravings of more than a hundred persons? Undoubtedly they will, for the Entertainer is Almighty. It depends not on the quantity of the food; its nourishing quality consists on His blessing. We have not to learn the power of the bread, but the power of Him who gives it and bestows it daily upon us. These we may easily conceive would be the thoughts of Elisha, which would encourage to further cheerful confidence in God. Entering, therefore, magnanimously into the spirit of their divine Provider, he commands his attendant to take up what is before him and "give unto the people that they may eat." It was spoken in faith, purely in the name of God and in God's stead.

This circumstance may remind us of the late pastor Henke who once acted in a spirit similar to that of Elisha. It happened that a Christian friend called upon the worthy man who at once invited him to stay and dine, though he knew that he had nothing to set before him. At noon the servant passed several times through the room in order, if she could do it unobserved, to call her master out. The pastor, however, not perceiving her intention, only reminded her that it was time to lay the cloth. The servant went away embarrassed, but soon returned and requested him to come out for a moment. "Sir," she said with a sorrowful countenance, "you have desired me to lay the cloth for dinner, but you have forgotten that there is scarcely a piece of bread in the house, and you have sent, as I heard you declare, your last farthing to a poor sick person." "Ah," replied Henke, smiling, "is that all you have to tell me? Lay the cloth just as usual; the dinner will be in time enough if it comes when we are seated at table." The servant, not a little astonished, did as she was instructed. The pastor and his guest took their seats, and the good man, with a cheerful countenance as at other times, offered up a prayer in which he spoke much of "the fowls of the air," and "the young ravens." As he pronounced his "Amen," a ring at the bell was heard. The servant flew to the door, and what did she discover? A basket with handsome provisions which a neighbor had been irresistibly prompted to send. With the utmost placidity as if nothing extraordinary had happened, the pastor directed the whole to be arranged upon the table; then turning to the servant, he inquired with a smile if there was "anything in the entertainment to find fault with?" These are delightful instances of trust in providence, but we are not to ape them. It is easy to order the table to be prepared; but that of itself is not sufficient. Remember Gehazi with Elisha's staff at Shunem. Yet have you Elisha's or even Henke's faith? Then hesitate not; for a royal Provider will supply you.

Gehazi's Confusion

III. "Give unto the people, that they may eat," is Elisha's command to his servant; but Gehazi replies with a look that seems to say, Surely you cannot be in earnest. He counts their number—a hundred men, besides women and children, and all so hungry that these twenty loaves would scarcely satisfy ten of them. The servant, shaking his head, asks, "What! should I set this before an hundred persons!" And he utters his question with a tone and manner that seems to insinuate that the prophet must be dreaming or had issued an absurd command. He viewed the matter with carnal eyes and attempted to gauge his master's thoughts by his own mean and groveling conceptions. His scruples remind us of a person who should take up a cannon ball, try how far he can hurl it, and then gravely declare to an intelligent soldier that it can never be thrown to a distance. For Gehazi had just in this manner forgotten what it was that gave energy and impulse to his master's command. That command was supported by a faith that could remove mountains, by such a reliance on the promises of God as overcomes all difficulties.

The energy of the Holy Spirit was in the order, yea, the power of the Almighty Himself. How then could the people be otherwise than filled! But of all this Gehazi was too ignorant. He understood the command, "Give to the people, that they may eat," as if it were nothing more than what might have proceeded from his own lips. He did not consider that such words spoken by Elisha were essentially different because they had been spoken in the name and with dependence on the word of God and therefore could do wonders. How presumptuous then were his unbelieving thoughts! It was his duty silently to obey and to distribute the bread; whether the people were to be filled or not was no affair of his; he was only required to perform the duties of a servant, but he acted as if the miracle depended on himself; and how often are we disposed to act in the same spirit!

When our Lord sent forth His disciples, saying, "Go, heal the sick, cleanse the lepers, raise the dead, cast out devils," how unbecoming would it have been for them to have replied, "Lord, our power and skill do not extend to such things." The commands of the Son of Man were as good as promises; that is, what He desired them to do, He purposed to do by their means. In like manner, there is much enjoined us to do which, were we to undertake it in our own strength, would come to nothing. We are commanded to overcome death, to tread spiritually upon serpents and scorpions and all the power of the enemy, to resist the devil that he may flee from us, to lift up our heads in the greatest affliction, to rejoice evermore, never to be cast down, always to be holy as our Father in heaven is holy, and many other wonderful works. How are these great and yet positive commands to be received? Surely they are to be received like those which were given to the apostles when our Lord said, "Go, and heal the sick." For they are commands full of encouragement and promise; and if this thought only take possession of the whole man, we become animated with strength and courage, with peace and joy, for we can then lift up our heads and triumph over death, and the world, and every foe.

Elisha, in no wise embarrassed by the remark of his unbelieving servant, repeated the command with increased emphasis, "Give to the people, that they may eat"; and he added, "For thus saith the Lord, They shall eat, and shall leave thereof." And now the servant, having begun to distribute the bread as he was desired, beheld it multiplied in his hands. Every one partook of as much as he required: "they did all eat and were filled," filled likewise, we trust, with gratitude to God. Yes, and there was still bread left in abundance upon the table. But it may be said, "This was out of the course of nature." Be it so: it is not more incomprehensible than is the growth of the tree in the garden or than that a single grain of wheat cast into the earth should return a hundredfold. The same almighty and creative power is displayed in the latter case as in the former.

Let this miraculous transaction serve to strengthen our own faith, my brethren, as we trust it did that of the sons of the prophets. And you, in particular, who may be languishing under complicated wants and miseries the end of which you cannot see; if the Lord be yours, "be careful for nothing"; for, as the Lord liveth, "he careth for you," and will relieve all your necessities. Fix your attention more than ever upon the great conclusion which you may obtain with infallible truth from the still greater argument of the apostle: "He that spared not his own Son, but delivered him up for us all, *how shall he not* with Him also freely give us all things?" (Rom. 8:32). In this and in the following verses he breaks out into great rejoicing. His heart seems full, while he realizes with one glance all that is treasured up in Christ for the children of God; and at this view he appears to rise above the world and mortality. He beholds his enemies vanquished at his feet; he sees a righteousness of overwhelming brightness and finds himself possessed of a fullness of gifts and blessings the extent of which he is incapable of estimating; and under a protection so secure, he seems to have nothing more to do upon the earth except to triumph and give praise.

Whence then does the apostle derive this superlative delight? Not from himself, but from a fountain that is daily and hourly open to ourselves. Christ is that fountain of blessings. All, all is traceable to the love of God in Christ. Neither let us overlook that the apostle speaks not only of himself, but of brother and sister in communion with him and intimates that if they cannot all break forth into the very exaltations with him, it must be ascribed not to any deficiency of their privileges, but to their want of faith. The first and last truth in which he exults is incomparably glorious and great. It is, "God is for us." In this we perceive the whole sum of the apostle's privileges and power; here is his rock and his fortress. The Lord is on our side; He bears us on his heart; He graciously undertakes for us; He encompasses us with his love. This is, indeed, a truth in which we may well rejoice. But, can it be so? May sinful and helpless man really boast that God is on his side? The Word of God here assures that he may; "He that spared not his own Son, but delivered him up for us all," attests it and attests it irresistibly.

We are primarily and ultimately directed to the love of God in delivering up His only begotten Son who was from eternity with the Father in heaven "His best Beloved," "the brightness of his glory, and the express image of his person." How astonishing the fact of His having been sent to be the propitiation for our sins! Behold here, how eternal Love has triumphed! Behold the Son of God as an infant in the manger, veiled in our nature, divested of His glory, destitute and exposed to a thousand dangers, unnoticed and unknown by the world, yea, an object of fiercest enmity and most barbarous persecution. Why was all this? It was because only at such a price could we be redeemed from merited condemnation. Yes, God for this purpose "*delivered him up.*" The expression denotes a forsaking, a sacrificing. The same word is used in Matthew 10:21 where it is said, "And the brother shall deliver up the brother to death"; and in this sense of death it is employed in the passage before us. And then, He delivered Him up "*for us all.*" "*For us*" means "in our stead"; and thus our thoughts are at once transferred from the manger to the cross.

Oh, what an affecting transfer! But the Scripture must be fulfilled; "Awake, O sword, against my shepherd, and against the man that is my fellow, saith the Lord of hosts." The Man of gracious lips was permitted to exclaim, "My God, my God, why hast thou forsaken me!" The Man who went about doing good was nailed to the cross, and His compassionate soul was "exceeding sorrowful, even unto death." If we are sensibly affected while thinking on the sufferings of God's beloved Son, *what* must we think of the love of God toward us in thus not sparing Him, but delivering Him up in our stead! For He did deliver Him up. Oh, unfathomable love! Oh, unutterable mercy!

The apostle, having thus set before us the love of God, draws from it wonderful, delightful, and incontrovertible inferences, under which we may reduce every anxious care, and out of which we may form another Eden in this vale of tears. His first and grand inference is, "How shall He not with Him also freely give us all things?" Admirable is this inference and beyond all contradiction. The truth of it is certain and plain even to a child. Was His love to me such that He gave His own Son to suffer death upon the cross for me? Then He certainly will not refuse me inferior blessings. For all things in heaven and earth are as nothing compared with this unspeakable gift. How inconsistent is it to doubt the goodness of God as to the supply of our daily wants! You seem thus to say, "God has indeed given me his Son, so far, I admit, his love extends; but it is not so evident that He will give me clothing, food, and shelter." How absurd and blind are such reflections! What! shall the grace that confers upon you its crown and heaven itself fail to supply all your wants upon your pilgrimage?

It is with reluctance I enter upon the refutation of such unreasonable thoughts, lest by so doing I should awaken a suspicion that they rest on some foundation. O be wise, my brethren, and consider how infinite that love must be which places underneath you its everlasting arms. And, whenever doubts and fears arise, flee to Bethlehem, behold the young Child lying in the manger, contemplate the brightness of the love which there shines upon you, and ask yourself the question propounded by the apostle, "He that, for our sakes, spared not his own SON, how"—answer you angels, you men and devils, join all your sagacity and say—"How shall he not with him also freely give us all things?" The apostle draws another inference from the love of God. It is, "Who shall lay any thing to the charge of God's elect? It is God that justifieth." The inference here is likewise sound and unquestionable. Such was the love of God to us that He gave His Son for us under the law that He might fulfill it; under the curse that He might sustain it. And the Son of God has actually fulfilled for us the law and endured for us the curse.

If therefore, we believe in Jesus Christ with the heart unto right-eousness, God will judge us according to the merits of His Son; and then, unto the last breath we breathe out of heaven, nothing, be it what it may, can deprive us of the right thus exultingly to inquire, "Who shall lay any thing to the charge of God's elect?" Yes, who shall accuse them? Shall Satan? He is "cast out." Shall the angels? Here is a righteousness that will eclipse their own. Shall our fellow men? We should be sorry to find them at the last day our accusers; but they would be found liars. Shall conscience? It is become "the answer of a good conscience toward God." The Supreme Judge has already pro-nounced us justified by a faith which works by love; and "being justified by faith, we have peace with God through our Lord Jesus Christ." "It is God that justifieth."

The apostle draws another inference. If, he argues, God be for us, if He spared not His own Son but delivered Him up for us all, "Who can be against us?" How evident is this inference also, and how incontrovertible! As he pronounces the word, "Who," he looks all around, as though he would address the inquiry to heaven, earth, and hell. The most appalling objects may present themselves to his view, but at these alarming objects he is neither to despond nor to be made weak. He exclaims, "If God be for us, who can be against us?"

Seeing, then, that for us also God has given His only begotten Son, what shall prevent us from breaking forth into the same spiri-tual joy? Let us but be conquered by the same love that conquered Paul, and our place of defense is as "the munitions of rocks." We are then in a citadel whose walls are fire, whose gates are decorated with the spoils of a thousand vanquished foes, and whose foundations are in the holy hills. The saints in this security are proof against all assaults. Here the weakest shall be as David, who, amid all the assaults of his enemies, lived in it uninjured and then closed his mor-tal life, as he did his Psalms, with triumphant hallelujahs! In such a stronghold does every true believer dwell. The love of God in Christ is their defense and forms with all the other divine perfections an insuperable barrier around them. Here we may be alarmed, but not conquered; attacked, but not overcome. "We are kept," says the apos-tle, "by the power of God through faith unto salvation," and if so, then "God is for us, and who can be against us?"

In the strength of these three important inferences let us learn to continue on our way in holy fear and consistent obedience. Are we disquieted about our temporal existence, let us, for a moment, thoughtfully retire and quell the tumult of our hearts with this divine suggestion; "He that spared not his own Son, but delivered him up for us all, how shall he not with him also freely give us all things?" Does a sense of sin, of sin constantly repented of and struggled against, depress us, let us call to mind the infinite love of God. He has delivered up His own Son for us. "Who shall lay any thing to the charge of God's elect? It is God that justifieth." Does fear lay hold upon us at the sight of the many enemies and difficulties we have to contend with, let us recollect that God has given us, in His precious promises, sufficient warrant to exclaim with exultation, "If God be for us, who can be against us?" Hallelujah! Amen.

9

Naaman

Anxiety as to "what shall be on the morrow" occasions more than half the troubles of life. Visit any abode of affliction among the poor or the rich, and you will find that its distresses arise oftener from anticipations of the future than from the exigencies of the moment. Hence the prevalent custom in all ages and nations of seeking for tokens of security from misfortune. Hence the almost universal recourse to astrology, oracles, priestcraft, false visions and dreams, and even to birds, whose settlement upon the housetop has been imagined as valuable a prognostication as was the arrival of Noah's dove.

Signs of this sort are of little account. Nevertheless, one sign there is which is infallible; and they to whom it belongs may well rejoice at it and may learn to cast every anxious care away. What can this be? Is it wealth? Far from it! Remember the man described in the gospel who pulled down his barns and built greater. Is it honor and fame? These quickly fade like a green bay-tree. Is it talent and learning? These cannot avert distress, or death, or the wrath of God. Is it political distinction? He who pours contempt upon the great ones of the earth that honor Him not is able also to destroy both soul and body in hell. Is it our own supposed rectitude? That will prove a miserable covering when tried by the measure of the righteousness of God. Is it even Christian knowledge? Judas Iscariot possessed this when swift destruction came upon him.

The true token of happiness is different from all these and is referred to in Psalm 86:17, "Show me a token for good." It is not an exterior but an interior sign; yet it always shines forth in the life and conversation of the outward man. It is natural to none, for it is a wound inflicted on the heart by the grace of the King and is the invariable result of self-knowledge. No herb, no balm produced from this earth can heal it. The publican exhibited it when he smote upon his breast; and the thief upon the cross, when he cried, "Lord, remember me"; and the woman who was a sinner, when she washed the Savior's feet with her tears and wiped them with the hairs of her head. All with whom it has been well in time and in eternity have had this infallible mark, which, in other words, is a heart truly broken up and humbled by the deep consciousness of sin. Those who have it feel self-condemned and themselves deserving the curse of a righteous God. This constitutes the wound.

Of a truth it is an unsightly token, but it is of inestimable value; and though but little esteemed by the world, it is the only prognostic of true happiness. To this the Scriptures testify. But it stands not alone; it is associated with another, namely, with the mark with which the Lord distinguishes His people for their preservation. That mark is the determination not to know anything in comparison of Jesus Christ and Him crucified. Where these are found together, the wound and the mark, conviction of sin and faith in the Lamb, the contrite heart and reliance on the only Sacrifice, there the good sign is complete and only there. It does not dazzle like this world's honors, like the golden chain, the star of nobility, or the badge of royalty; but how gloriously shall the splendor of this sign one day outshine all these! In the world it confers neither dignity nor rank; but the angels of God behold it with joy and love those who possess it, knowing themselves appointed to be their ministering servants. God be thanked that there are everywhere among us some whose hearts bear this token, compassed as they may be with many infirmities.

That delightful part of the narrative of Elisha's history on which we are about to enter is a practical commentary on David's words, "Show me a token for good." God grant His blessing to our meditations!

2 Kings 5:1,2

Now Naaman, captain of the host of the king of Syria, was a great man with his master, and honorable, because by him the Lord had given deliverance unto Syria: He was also a mighty man in valor, but he was a leper. And the Syrians had gone out by companies, and had brought away captive out of the land of Israel a little maid; and she waited on Naaman's wife.

Events of Elisha's life now come before us which still more strikingly bear a New Testament character. Here the breaking down of the partition wall between Israel and the heathen is anticipated, and several other things of an evangelical description.

By way of introduction to what this part of the narrative has to offer, we shall consider, at present, the new personages here presented to us: I. Naaman the Syrian; II. That humble instrument for his salvation, the little Israelitish maiden; and we pray that, under the divine blessing, this alone may serve not only to gratify, but to benefit us.

Naaman, the Syrian

I. The history turns our attention to Damascus, an ancient city, the capital and residence of the monarchs of Syria, situated in a fertile region northwestward of Hermon and Lebanon. Let us leave the boundaries of the Holy Land to contemplate for a while the deathlike shades of that heathen country. Thick darkness surrounds us. On every side the altars of idolatry are multiplied. Not the faintest ray of pure light, of the knowledge of the true God, relieves the awful gloom that covers this benighted people.

We might almost imagine them separated from the land of divine revelation, of seers and prophets, by oceans or immeasurable deserts instead of that mere ridge of mountains which divides Syria from Canaan. But a more formidable and impassable barrier was their national hatred against the laws and customs of Israel, their ancient and hereditary enemy. The pride of these heathens caused them to shut their eyes to the light of Judah and to extinguish on their very frontiers any spark of heavenly wisdom that would have passed to them from thence. Yet the Almighty graciously designed to cast the torch of His truth into the very heart of this fenced country and to establish beside the altars of their dumb idols a new altar to the glory of His name, JEHOVAH. Wherever He has purposed to enlighten, who shall disannul it? His command, "Let there be light," scatters the thickest darkness. His grace and power and His omnipotence, go forth together, and who shall withstand them?

God is not a God in heaven only, He is also a God among men

and will be known as such; He will be recognized as a God who resides and governs in the midst of us; and, great in the smallest things, His guiding hand directs the most minute affairs. For this reason His works of grace proceed commonly through the intervention of human means; and He conceals His own sovereign control under the concurrence of a variety of apparently accidental and trivial circumstances. Nevertheless, He shows by the event that all was divinely arranged and thus displays to us not only His work, but Himself as the all-governing, omnipotent, omnipresent Jehovah. These remarks will be confirmed by the present history.

On the throne of Syria was seated the warlike Benhadad, the same who, in the lifetime of Elijah, had led the battle against Israel and who commanded in person on the bloody field where Ahab, whom God had rejected, fell, transfixed by an adventured arrow. Among the assemblage of grandees whom that mighty heathen prince had gathered about his person, there was one particular favorite whose talents had raised him to the right hand of his king, and the renown of whose deeds had made him the idol of the people. His name was not less descriptive of his person than of his official relations. He was called *Naaman* which signifies *well-formed, beautiful*; a designation which afterward indeed became a reproachful contrast to his figure and appearance. At present he was arrayed in the doubtful and perishable glory of earthly greatness; his brow was decorated with laurels gained upon the battlefield, his breast glittering with the insignia of royal munificence and favor.

The public voice proclaimed him the greatest commander of his age, and his acts were probably celebrated in popular songs. For the rest, Naaman was a heathen, born and educated in all the idolatrous blindness of his people; he had often, indeed, been providentially conducted into the land of divine revelation but had remained insensible to its light. Hitherto he had only visited this people, from whom his healing and salvation were to proceed, in the hostile attitude of a warrior, like too many in our day who can tolerate and delight in any but those who, having access to the tree of life and possessing the true riches, are the only people who can render them the services they stand in need of. Happy is it for us that "it is God who worketh in us to will and to do of his own good pleasure," that the will itself is vouchsafed of God as an earnest of its accomplishment. Happy is it for us that the grace of conversion not merely solicits and invites, but that it operates with divine energy, both seeking and making its subjects. Who would be saved were it otherwise?

Naaman, likewise, was to experience this gracious power. That God of whom he was at present ignorant had great designs concerning him, however unfavorable appearances might be and however conflicting the elements that opposed. The Lord governs in the human mind with the same almighty sway as in the kingdom of nature. He not only calls forth the stars in the canopy of heaven but the very thoughts of our souls, and can bid them come and go at His pleasure. All hearts are in His hand. Obedient to His will, the vast universe holds on its course; and man, the child of dust, with every insect and atom, are under His control. Such a connection banishes, indeed, the proud idea of national and individual independence; yet renunciation of all self-sufficiency in the creature tends but to our greater tranquillity. The only thought that can enable us to take a cheering survey of the world and its affairs is that all things are sustained and guided by the hand of almighty power and infinite wisdom. What would become of the world if its affairs were ordered by the will of man and not by the will of God!

At the period at which we next behold Naaman, a dark cloud had obscured his glory. Although he was the same distinguished hero as before, he was no longer an object of envy. Alas! the bitterness of gall had been infused into his cup of joy, his glory was corroded by a canker which in an instant had brought down this man of prosperity and grandeur to a level with the most pitiable of the sons of men. Naaman was now a leper! He was afflicted with that dreadful and disgusting disease which was employed to represent to Israel the most abominable thing under heaven—sin, and the healing of which was typical of salvation in Christ, the greatest of all blessings. His body, from the crown of his head to the sole of his foot, was one entire ulcer; his skin a lacerated, suppurating, inflamed sore. His comeliness was changed to disgust and horror, and his breath into that of deadly pestilence. Such was now the situation of a man who so lately had been raised to the pinnacle of glory and earthly felicity. Who is there, however mean and wretched, that would exchange situations with Naaman?

How often we are inclined to think, "Such a one is reposing in the lap of prosperity; what a rich, what a great man is he!" But did we only know the misery that is often concealed beneath such splendor, we should be far from envying men their earthly distinctions. Be contented then with your temporal condition, however unpromising it may appear; a glittering exterior can add nothing to your happiness. Cease to covet anything allotted to others. It is the peace of God alone that can impart real happiness; and to him who possesses this, a plain morsel of bread is sweet, and a cottage is as happy an abode as a palace.

The Little Maid

II. We may easily suppose that for the recovery of so important a man as Naaman, no efforts were left untried. The king, who had found him the most powerful supporter of his throne, would certainly command his most skillful physicians to attend him, and they no doubt would zealously use every means in their power for his relief. But no means proved successful for the relief of Naaman. The mysterious and inveterate disease of leprosy appears never to have yielded to medical treatment. Accordingly the Scriptures represent it as a plague, which, having been inflicted by the immediate hand of God, could only be removed by His immediate interposition. Diseases of the kind are not uncommon; and they serve to check the pride of man, not only by rebuking for sin, but also by circumscribing human science and wisdom within the limits of a becoming humility, for they serve to keep alive our consciousness of entire dependence on the Almighty and to guard us against the erroneous idea that the preservation of our lives is in our own hands. What a signal discomfiture has the science of this world lately sustained in its conflicts with that devastating pestilence, which, issuing from the east, overspread a great portion of the world and which still continues its ravages! As Christians, we cannot but acknowledge this as a timely and salutary rebuke to the growing pride of human intellect, for, in truth, its boastings had attained a height that knew no bounds. Science, which in its inflated pride had usurped the throne of the Godhead, has been obliged to confess by the mouth of its most distinguished representatives that it is unable to detect and eradicate this disease; and human art, which had arrogantly professed to do all things and assumed the lofty air of a worker of miracles, has here sustained a signal defeat.

We have now to consider how the afflictive visitation upon Naaman was likewise sent in goodness and mercy. God was gracious to this heathen captain. But was it because Naaman first loved God? Certainly not. It was because God would herein display His goodness and mercy. Naaman had evidently lived after the flesh and had sought his own glory in valor and war. But God delighted not in the strength of the battle, neither took pleasure in the prowess of sinful and mortal man. The only account therefore that we can give of His favor to Naaman is that "He will have mercy on whom he will have mercy."

But how shall such mercy be brought near to him? What way of approach is there to the man who has not the faintest conception of the living God, is ignorant of His Word, and spellbound in the mazes of his erroneous and superstitious faith? Fear not, for with God all things are possible. Who would have expected that the leprosy should have been appointed as the first link in that chain of events by which such a display of divine mercy was to be effected? The second link is one which we should be still less likely to have thought of. During the continuance of the war between Benhadad and the king of Israel, the Syrians had invaded the Israelitish borders in marauding companies and had carried away (probably from some village) a little captive maiden, who appears to have been thus utterly separated from her parents, and, having been made a slave, was providentially brought into Naaman's family, and waited on Naaman's wife.

Here a mysterious hardship seemed to have been permitted by the "Keeper of Israel"; but we are sure to err when we form a judgment on the ways of God without waiting to see the end of His providence. This event, which appeared to originate in the mere will of man and to be the result of discord and confusion, was the commencement of a plan which, through the wise dispensation of God, was to command the admiration of future ages. For it turned out to be only an additional illustration of the fact that precisely when God's care of His people is thought to have come to an end, it unexpectedly receives a new and glorious confirmation. For yet a little while and you will perceive how admirably this mysterious dispensation will unfold itself in the recovery of Naaman and, for aught we know to the contrary, in the salvation of his soul and of the souls of many. Certainly such mercies of God are never displayed entirely in vain. Yes, the development of this mysterious event will be such as to give sufficient cause to the little maid, whose fate now appears so deplorable, to cast herself adoringly before the Eternal, and to kiss the hand that withheld its succor in the hour of her captivity; to call forth from the afflicted Naaman the grateful acknowledgment that in this child a kind angel had been sent to Damascus for his relief; and to extort from the whole city the confession that "The Lord he is God, and none else."

So that we likewise must be filled with admiration and be constrained to confess with lively and renewed conviction that we have abundant reason calmly to repose in the government of the Most High, whose counsels, though mysterious in working, are glorious in their final accomplishment.

Blessed is he whose God is the Lord, and who possesses the assurance that the events of his life are ordered by unerring wisdom and goodness. Such a person may assuredly reckon that when things seem most dark and inexplicable, the Lord of all will sooner or later certainly appear for him. For the words of the psalmist are everlastingly true, that "Good and upright is the Lord: therefore will He teach sinners in the way. The meek will He guide in judgment: and the meek will He teach His way. All the paths of the Lord are mercy and truth unto such as keep His covenant and His testimonies" (Ps. 25:8-10).

10

The Little Maid from a Foreign Land

The Lord, whether He seem to have forsaken us or to have arrested us with a feeling of His displeasure, has doubtless in each case the design either of leading us to repentance or of confirming us in it. He would divest us more and more of self; He would make us more thoroughly sensible of our entire dependence on Him and on His grace. Like considerations may serve not only to reconcile us to many of His mysterious dealings with ourselves and others, but even to make us gratefully admire and adore the wisdom and goodness which He displays therein. Our present subject happily tends to the same result.

2 Kings 5:3

> And she said unto her mistress, Would God my lord were with the prophet that is in Samaria! for he would recover him of his leprosy.

Our thoughts tarry with growing interest at Damascus on account of Naaman, whom providence had now so specially taken by the hand. No sooner do we witness with painful sympathy the decay and expiration of all his worldly glory, than another of infinitely greater brightness appears to dawn. And how remarkable was the commencement of this mercy! Bands of the Syrian army had made incursions upon the Israelitish frontiers, had attacked and plundered some unprotected place, and had carried off a little Jewish maiden, probably to sell her in Syria as a slave. Who would have imagined that such a scene of calamity was the introduction to a process of divine mercy toward Naaman and his country? In what degree it was such will presently appear.

Damascus

I. We may first turn our attention to a heathen marketplace, that of Damascus, where it is very possible that our little maid was exposed for sale. But be that as it may, whether with a multitude of other unhappy people violently torn from their homes and driven like cattle to the market this child was also appraised and sold, or whether she was handed over at once as a present to Naaman's wife, of two other things we cannot well doubt, namely, that she must have suffered extreme anguish and that the particular providence of God was in this event. There must have been a time when her young heart was well nigh broken, when she thought upon her father and her mother, and her distant and beloved home. She falls, however, into the hands of Naaman's wife, and how but by the providence of Him who called the universe into being? This child proves to her mistress as a messenger from heaven, and not to her mistress only but to Naaman; and hereby events transpire which were to interest his household, and his prince, and the Syrian nation, and king Jehoram, and all Israel; yes, and ourselves also. Such divine disposals beginning often in sorrowful events and often in little things, it behooves us seriously to consider. What is here presented to us may serve to shed a light on what is dark in our own experience and may furnish us with the reason why the Almighty, instead of granting directly the blessings we may have implored and the assistance we may have earnestly desired, has appeared to shut up our path and to appoint to us sorrow upon sorrow.

The Man and the Maiden

II. The captain of the host of Syria sits in his chamber, oppressed and dejected by an incurable disease, and thinks of anything but recovery, or of its probability, or of its means so near at hand. But now, in another part of his mansion there resides a little captive Israelitish maiden employed in "waiting upon Naaman's wife."

Were we to be banished for a time, like this Hebrew maiden, to the privations of a foreign land and condemned, as are many of our distant brethren and sisters, to stand isolated in our faith in the midst of a cold, unbelieving, benighted world, oh, how would those privileges rise in our estimation to the enjoyment of which long possession has almost rendered us indifferent! While not a few are ready to envy us the pleasant opportunities of brotherly communion that have really befallen us, and are thinking that our spiritual profession must be ever fresh and green, amid the streams of refreshment and encouragement which surround us, alas! What is our interior condition! O that we did not ourselves so frequently trouble a spring from which we might draw such abundant supplies of spiritual profit and delight! Did we love one another better, my brethren; were we more firmly united, more unanimous and mutually intimate; were we more confidential with each other, more unreserved and open, than we too generally are, how unspeakably should we gain in substantial joy and blessing! I beseech you, if you value these things at all, think oftener of the apostle's words; "If there be any consolation in Christ, if any comfort of love, if any fellowship of the Spirit, if any bowels and mercies, fulfill ye my joy, that ye be like-minded, having the same love, being of one accord, of one mind; in lowliness of mind, let each esteem other better than themselves."

Whether the little Hebrew maiden was particularly well-informed and instructed we do not know; but she brought with her sufficient light to cheer the dark and dreary path of the disconsolate. It must, at least, have been known to her that God was not only the God of the Jews, but also of the whole earth. She could not, therefore, have doubted that if Naaman humbled himself before Jehovah, he might experience that divine favor was not limited to the borders of Canaan; hence she said, "Would God my lord were with the prophet that is in Samaria! for he would recover him of his leprosy"; and who can say to what other and greater blessings?

The wish of this child was uttered in perfect simplicity and evidently without the remotest suspicion of the great results it was to originate. But the information was instantly communicated to Naaman himself. And how much had that little, lowly daughter of Abraham already accomplished by her pathetic exclamation! In a moment did she thus revive the hopes of the afflicted pair and introduce into this house of heathen gloom the first ray of cheerfulness. Those who had so lately contemplated death and who had only dreamed of separation and the grave are now suddenly awakened to anticipations of prolonged life and future felicity.

We also may remember a similar and more delightful period in our own lives when a ray of gospel truth first cheered our minds after we had gone on restless and dejected under a sense of our estrangement from God, the words, "Come unto me, all ye that labor and are heavy laden, and I will give you rest," or some other such cheering invitation, having first made known to us One that could help us, and One alone. And have we been deceived or disappointed? Blessed is he who has found himself where the footsteps of Jesus are heard and where all may obtain counsel, consolation, and relief. O go unto Him all you that stand as it were far off from Him! Let those who desire the healing of their souls immediately have recourse to Christ. He, and He alone, can effectually recover us from the leprosy of sin. In Him, and in Him alone, is our peace, security, and life. In Him, as in a living temple, dwells the all-sufficiency of the Godhead bodily. What though it be awfully proclaimed from this mystical temple, "Whoever forsaketh not all that he hath, he cannot be my disciple!" let us but enter; and within we shall read the words, "Here is peace; here the weary find rest and refreshment"; and from a thousand pillars that stand as firmly as the everlasting hills, do those indelible truths shine forth; "I am thy God: I have loved thee with an everlasting love, and all that I have is thine." Amen.

11

The Journey to Samaria

How unspeakably consoling are those words of our blessed Lord, "THE SON OF MAN is come to seek and to save THAT WHICH WAS LOST!" (Luke 19:10). He here represents man as a sheep wandering without a shepherd in the solitude of a waste and howling wilderness which, finding nowhere a hospitable shelter, is exposed, weak and defenseless to the ravenous wolves, and ignorantly pursues the path of death. Or, we are reminded of a ship foundered in the mighty billows and "lost" to all hope of recovery; or of a person who has borrowed a large sum of money and who, when the time for repayment arrives, has not a farthing left and is obliged to part with his house and all that he has—his comfort, his credit, his strength, and, perhaps, his life. Examine yourselves and see if your own spiritual circumstances do not answer to this descriptive word "lost"; and if they do, then mourn and lament, but yield not to despair, for it was "to *seek* and to *save* that which was *lost*" that "the Son of man" came.

Sorrow and humiliation for sin are indispensably requisite to all who would enter the temple of the New Testament. Do we wish that Jesus should befriend us, we must plead that we are "lost"; and should we even have good qualities and good works whereof to boast, we must on no account make them our plea. For the Lord might answer us, "I came not to call the righteous, but sinners to repentance." Let others boast of the sincerity of their repentance, the fervor of their piety, the purity of their desires, or whatever else they please; our plea must be, "Lord Jesus, we are lost and ruined, therefore have mercy on us!" This appeal, humbly urged, will never meet with a rebuke. "The Lord abideth faithful; he cannot deny himself"; and He declares that

107

the humbled and the lost are the objects of His saving mercy. To save *them*, yes, to seek them out, He declares to be His peculiar office, the real end of His mission into our miserable world. Thank God, He came to seek *us*, and that we had not first to seek *Him*; for had this been the case, who would ever have come to Him? We are not merely lost as travelers, who, by deliberation and the help of guideposts, can regain their right road; but we are lost as a piece of silver is lost, which of itself will not return into our purse and must be carefully sought. Blessed are we that He, who alone can *save*, condescends also to *seek*. And this is beautifully exemplified in what follows concerning Naaman the Syrian.

2 Kings 5:4-7

> And one went in, and told his lord, saying, Thus and thus said the maid that is of the land of Israel. And the king of Syria said, Go to, go, and I will send a letter unto the king of Israel. And he departed, and took with him ten talents of silver, and six thousand pieces of gold, and ten changes of raiment. And he brought the letter to the king of Israel, saying, Now when this letter is come unto thee, behold, I have therewith sent Naaman my servant to thee, that thou mayest recover him of his leprosy. And it came to pass, when the king of Israel had read the letter, that he rent his clothes, and said, Am I God, to kill and to make alive, that this man doth send unto me to recover a man of his leprosy? wherefore consider, I pray you, and see how he seeketh a quarrel against me.

The termination which this mysterious history was likely to take now begins to show itself. Three points claim our attentive consideration: I. Naaman's preparation for his journey; II. His passport; and III. His arrival in the Holy Land.

Naaman's Preparation

I. The pathetic sigh of the Israelitish maiden, "Oh that my lord were with the prophet that is in Samaria!" produced its effect. It is surprising what important results may ensue from a passing and accidental word, be it spoken by whom it may, if only accompanied with the divine blessing. How could it have entered the mind of this little foreigner in Damascus to attach such importance to a wish thus uttered by her simplicity! Yet what a succession of glorious events gradually proceeded from it. And why did they proceed from it, but because the great Being, who governs all things, *designed* that thus it should be? Through His own overruling wisdom and goodness it was made a means of shattering the strongholds of heathenism and of wresting from Satan a portion of his power; and, indeed, who can say in how many other ways this apparently trivial event was to effect good in the world even unto this day! It may serve, at least, to remind us how valuable is the least connection with anyone who is at all connected with that church of God which is appointed by Himself to be a blessing in the world. His servants are the salt of the earth, and their very words are not uttered in vain. How agreeable will be their surprise when the Lord shall hereafter discover to them the beautiful plants that, under His blessing, have sprung up in stillness and obscurity from the good seed which they, by their words and actions, had unconsciously scattered! Then they will perceive that they have not lived in vain with regard to others, and that "their works," which no stream of time can sweep into oblivion, "shall follow them" into eternity.

On Mount Caucasus in Georgia there is a people, anciently known by the name of Iberians, who in the early part of the fourth century, when all around them was spiritual and moral darkness like the shadow of death, became possessed of the blessings of the gospel in the following remarkable manner. The Iberians having been successfully at war with a neighboring people, among whom Christianity had gained some ground, brought away a young captive Christian maiden and sold her into slavery. The child was purchased by a reputable family, who as little suspected, as did Naaman's wife, the value of the purchase they had made. For the maiden was a vessel of divine mercy, and profusely as her tears might have been shed in secret, she found consolation in her Savior and quietly and willingly performed all, and even more, than was required of her. By her obliging disposition and great fidelity which were rare qualities among the Iberians, she soon acquired the confidence and affection of those around her.

It one day happened that, according to the custom of the country, a sick child was carried about the neighborhood from door to door in hope that someone might be able to suggest a remedy for its disease. But none could render the least assistance, and most people wondered that any hope of the child's recovery should be entertained; so that the poor parents with their dying infant proceeded on their

melancholy round with increasing despondency and fear. At length
it occurred to them to show the child to the amiable stranger; they
thought it possible that in her country a cure for its complaint might
be known with which she might be acquainted; and as no other
resource appeared, it was resolved upon as a last resort.

The bed was immediately carried to the house where Nunnia, the
Christian maid, lived as a domestic slave. On hearing their desire, she
remarked with some embarrassment that she was but a poor girl and
quite unable to advise them; but, she added, with a smiling countenance, I could direct you to One who is not only able to restore the
child to health, but who, were it already dead, can even recover it to
life. The afflicted parents eagerly inquiring who the person was and
where He might be found, she replied, "He is a great and mighty
Lord, who fills the throne of heaven, but He willingly humbles
Himself to those who seek Him, and He is all compassion and love."

They implored her to fetch Him. The maiden immediately retired
to bow her knees before her Lord and Savior Jesus Christ, to whom
she prayed, "Manifest thyself, O Lord, for thine own glory; show thyself, and grant thy help!" And as she returned to the child with the
joyful assurance in her heart that the Lord had heard her petition, lo,
the child opened its eyes, smiled, and was restored! In a transport of
joy the happy parents returned home with their treasure and related to everyone they met what a great and glorious event had taken
place.

But to Him who had wrought this miraculous cure, the honor was
not ascribed; it was given exclusively to the little slave whom they
now regarded as supernatural being. The report flew quickly
through the country and soon reached the ears of the queen who, not
long afterward herself becoming sick, thought immediately of the little slave. She sent messengers to request that she would visit her; but
Nunnia declined the invitation, for she was greatly distressed that
they should persist in ascribing to her an honor that belonged to her
Lord alone. The queen, however, determined to visit her in person
and ordered herself to be conveyed to the house where Nunnia
served. The maiden was greatly affected at seeing her. She prayed
again, and the queen likewise returned home in health.

Miraus, the king, was overjoyed when he saw his beloved consort
return in health and made instant preparations to send the richest
and most costly presents to her who was thought to have performed

so great a miracle. But the princess dissuaded it, assuring him that it would afflict the mysterious child, for that she despised all earthly wealth and could only be rewarded for her services by their worshiping her own God with her. The king was not a little astonished; but the circumstance made, for the present, no further impression upon his mind.

Upon the whole, it appears that the flash of celestial light which these two extraordinary cures had brought into the darkness of Iberia produced at this period no lasting effects. It happened, however, not very long afterward, that the king being on a hunting party and following his game with unusual ardor, lost himself in the depths of a wood. In this situation he was surprised by a dense fog, which quite separated him from his train, and every effort to extricate himself only served to entangle him more in the solitary wilderness. Evening approached, and his embarrassment became extreme. He sounded his horn, but the answer he received was from the echoes of the surrounding cliffs, which increased his feeling of loneliness. It was now he remembered what the foreign maiden had said of the power of her great, invisible King, whose throne and habitation were on high, but who was everywhere present with those who sought Him. If this be true, thought Miraus, what is there to prevent His appearing for *me*?

As the thought arose, he bent his knee in the solitary wilderness and prayed, "O Thou whom the stranger calls her God! Jesus, if Thou art, and art almighty, O show it now, and recover me out of this perplexity! If Thou openest for me a way of escape, my heart, my life, and all that I have shall be Thine." The words were no sooner uttered than the dark mist began to disperse, the heavens appeared serenely blue, and the astonished king, having proceeded a few steps, regained his track, and recognized the place where he was. He returned home in safety, but deeply affected. He related his adventure to his queen, and they no longer doubted that the God of the little slave was the living and true God, for they had experienced and felt Him to be so.

The next morning they repaired to Nunnia, for they thought that she before all others ought to hear what great things had come to pass. With considerable emotion the king related also to her the wonderful event, and then both the king and the queen kindly took the maiden by the hand and entreated her to tell them more of Jesus.

From that moment the royal pair were seen sitting like teachable children at the feet of the lowly slave, and Nunnia proclaimed to them with unaffected simplicity all that she herself knew of her Savior and of His wonderful works. They listened to her words with avidity, and their hearts melted and burned within them.

Nor was it long before a still more interesting sight presented itself; for both the king and the queen thought that they could not confer greater benefit on their people than by proclaiming to them the blessed gospel which informed them of God as having been manifest in the flesh. The king therefore preached to the men, and the queen to the women and maidens; the Lord blessed the message, and the people received the good word with gladness. Jesus entered the hearts as well as the habitations of these savage hordes, and a new creation sprung up in the gloom of their moral desolation.

On the ruins of their idolatrous altars were erected cheerful Christian edifices, which loudly resounded with the praises of Him who also here had searched for His own sheep and sought them out. Among the descendants of this people in our days, the Spirit of life has again begun to breathe. Active and anointed messengers have again displayed among them the standard of the cross, and the most gratifying proofs are increasingly exhibited, that the grace which planted this vineyard in so wonderful a manner fifteen hundred years ago has not departed from it.

What think we of this occurrence? Is it not delightful and encouraging? How striking the resemblance it bears to the history of Naaman! Yes! Jesus is "the same yesterday, today, and forever." How easy is it for Him to accomplish His purposes by the smallest as by the mightiest agents! And how well does He know when and where to find His sheep! "For though thy people Israel be as the sand of the sea, a remnant shall return." "I will call them my people, which were not my people; and in the place where it was said unto them, Ye are not my people; there shall they be called the children of the living God."

But, to return to Damascus. When Naaman had heard the declaration of his little slave, he resolved on following the hint which had been given him and soon received permission and encouragement from his king to undertake the journey. If Naaman *asked this* permission he did right; though in our visiting the *spiritual* springs of Israel, it is not necessary for us to confer with man or to be troubled about the approbation or disapprobation of "those that are without." The king having been informed of what the little Israelitish maid had said, replied, "Then go thither! Go to Samaria!" The preservation of a life so valuable as that of the distinguished commander of his armies was all-important to him. Could he have entertained a hope that relief might be obtained from the physicians and priests of his own country, the jealous monarch would not have ceded to the hated Jewish people the honor of the cure. Now, however, he not only does this, but more; he even offers the invalid a letter of recommendation under his own hand.

This royal document was immediately written and sealed. It was addressed, "To Jehoram, king of Israel," and was as follows: "Now when this letter is come unto thee, behold, I have therewith sent Naaman my servant to thee, that thou mayest recover him of his leprosy." It must be admitted that this epistle was worthy of its author, as evincing the great blindness of his heart. He imagined that if anyone in Israel were possessed of miraculous powers, it must be the king of Israel himself. As if the Almighty judged as man judges, or had any respect of persons in dispensing His gifts and graces; or, as if He imparted supernatural powers as an abiding possession, to be controlled and exercised at human pleasure. Oh what folly and absurdity are uniformly exhibited whenever the ungodly and profane adventure to meddle with "the things of the Spirit of God!"

The sick man, after thankfully receiving the royal letters, hastened to make the necessary preparations for his departure, in a manner that became his rank. His most splendid equipages were prepared, and his officers ordered to accompany him with a numerous train of domestics on camels. Money was likewise abundantly provided. He took with him the large sum of ten talents of silver, or about sixteen thousand dollars, besides six thousand pieces of gold of which the greater part appears to have been intended to enrich the man who should effect his cure. For the same fortunate individual the ten splendid changes of raiment appear to have been intended. Thus royally equipped, he took the direct route to the land of promise, the land of his hopes.

From all this pomp it would appear that the ideas of Naaman were not much more enlightened or spiritual than those of his royal master. He, likewise, expected to find in the prophets of Samaria little more than a kind of magicians and enchanters, similar to those of the heathen world. Of a God who dispenses blessings and commands them to be dispensed without money and without price, he had not the slightest conception. And, indeed, it is not natural to the corrupt heart of man to guess at the noble principles of real religion. That persons should be most welcome to the throne of grace who feel themselves most poor and destitute, and most willing to obtain what they desire without any desert on their part, is incomprehensible to "the natural man."

How difficult is it to us, even when renewed by grace, to sacrifice to this truth our legal conceptions, our ideas of service and reward! Alas! how often do we approach the Lord, like Naaman, laden with imaginary gifts or else with vows to present them! How frequently, how imperceptibly do we again fall back upon the foolish thought that not until we can reckon upon something of our own are we at liberty to enjoy the consolation of the divine promises! We do not then prostrate ourselves before God and present our supplications like Daniel, for the sake of His mercy we profess indeed to depend on the merits of our great Surety, but we depend, in fact, on the notion of our own acquirements, subtle as may be the covering that conceals such a notion from us. Yet why do we do so, when it is not only our privilege to ask and to receive "wine and milk without money and without price," but this is even enjoined upon us as a duty? Such is the arrangement before the throne of Jehovah. Oh, let us conform to this blessed regulation!

His Passport

II. Naaman commenced his journey under the patronage and with the passport of his lord; which at every stage would secure him an uninterrupted passage and the greatest attentions. For our comfort we possess a similar safe conduct, though of infinitely greater value and of a more exalted description. It is the same that was given to the sick man in the gospel, to whom Jesus said, "Go in peace." And of which the disciples were the subjects in the request made by Jesus to His enemies, "Let these go their way."

We too, brethren, are set out upon a journey; we are continually and rapidly advancing in it. Whether we know and wish it or not, our progress is without intermission or pause. This journey commences with our life, and the hour of our death is the last stage of it. We do not, it is true, recline in a carriage, neither do we perform it on horseback or in a ship; but the wings of time, on which we repose, move with a far more vigorous and rapid speed. Every stroke of the clock warns us of our progress. Every movement of the pendulum proclaims with a solemn sound, "Travel onward!" How lately did our road lie through the smiling fields of spring! It seems but as yesterday. Now, the roses have faded; and soon the leaves will wither and fall rustling to the earth. Then snow succeeds, and before we are aware, the lovely flowers of spring will again shoot forth; thus time rolls on. And how long will it be before we fade like the leaves, for all flesh is as grass! The grass withers, the flower fades, and whither are we traveling but toward that eternity into which all the streams of life are successively discharged. But eternity is distinguished by two provinces of very different natures, separated by an impassable gulf; the one a lake of fire, the other a paradise of bliss; the one, heaven, the other, hell. In the one or in the other, all will be landed. The last wave of time casts us upon the shores of the one province or the other.

Now, it may fare ill with us on our pilgrimage. We may fall into the hands of formidable enemies; we are liable to be attacked and subdued, and to suffer imprisonments whose horrors are not to be described. For do not thousands daily become entangled with the delusion of sin, and are they not more and more encompassed by its fatal snares, till in its horrible embraces they are overtaken by eternal perdition and death? Remember Ahab, Judas, and Herod. How many of the same spirit do we everywhere behold! How many who willingly take upon them the yoke of Satan and become quite involved in self-deception and falsehood, as if they had sold themselves to do evil, as if they had voluntarily consigned themselves to that everlasting torment which is prepared for the devil and his angels!

Think of the wretched beings over whom Jesus so pathetically pronounced, "Woe! woe!" Thousands fall into the hands of Moses, by whom they are accused; the accusation is heard before the highest tribunal; each delinquent is condemned, and his name written in the book of cursing. Thousands are cast by an alarmed conscience into the furnace of despair, and despair is the stigma of the reprobate. Thousands, at the command of the Judge, are dragged by the last enemy, the king of terrors, to eternal desolation; alas, who can conceive to what misery and torment? And thousands in their last extremity will cry, "Lord, Lord, open unto us!" But they will be doomed to hear the answer, "I know you not: depart from me, ye workers of iniquity!"

These are dreadful miseries, horrible events. What are all the afflictions of earth compared with them? What is loss of fortune? What the loss of health, or of the world's esteem? To languish in bodily pain, what is it, when compared with such spiritual evils? They are all too insignificant to be mentioned in comparison. Job, Lazarus, and Bartimeus, in their misery, were a thousand times more enviable than the rich man clothed in purple, or than Saul, Herod, and many others in their robes of state. But it may be anxiously inquired, Is there no escape from these horrors? Yes, my brethren, many escape them. In what way? They possess a passport. He who travels without one will doubtless one day be arrested as a transient or criminal. A passport, if it be genuine, is a great protection on a journey, but false ones here are of no avail; they lead to certain and greater disgrace and ruin. Yet many, alas! make use of them, and many, it is to be feared, even among ourselves.

Some make out their own passports, which contain much self-applause. "We are," they say, "not bad people; we give to the poor, we do what is right!" and there is no end to these self-deceptions. Others obtain their passports from the world, in which they are described as excellent people, held in general estimation. But where did the world obtain its authority for furnishing passports? Its seal is neither legal nor valid. And even though you should possess a passport written by the children of God, testifying of you that you are members of the same kingdom; place no dependence on it. How often have they been mistaken in their testimony and through shortsightedness or ignorance given false certificates!

Your credentials must come from far higher authority, even from Him who once said to the hostile multitude, "Let these go their way"; and to the woman, "Go in peace." Yes, this woman received the true passport, the only one that is valid under all circumstances and in all contingencies; and it is possessed by the very least of those who belong to Christ.

Nothing of the kind could have been granted as a matter of course to anyone of our fallen race; for we are all by nature children of wrath. But the Son of God had compassion on us, He became our Surety, having undertaken to save that which was lost, and to present us holy and unblamable and unreprovable in the sight of God. He "hath redeemed us from the curse of the law, being made a curse for us: for it is written, Cursed is every one that hangeth on a tree." Thus "by the obedience of one shall many be made righteous"; He having not only rendered it possible for Grace and Mercy to sign their passport, but for the divine Holiness and Justice to subscribe it with a firm, unwavering hand. For Mercy alone would never have signed it. God then, and God alone, issues the passport, even the God of mercy and truth; and He does so on the ground of the meritorious obedience of our atoning Mediator.

From having thus alluded to the Christian's spiritual passport, it may be further worthwhile to glance at a few of its contents. It describes the name of anyone who is its owner, to be such as no man knows, save he that has it; and his age, as not comprehensible within the chronicles of this world. It speaks of God as our Father, and of Jerusalem above as the mother of us all. It speaks of some wilderness of Mount Sinai as the place of our natural birth, and of Zion as our spiritual residence; of our rank as priestly and royal; and of our profession as that of spiritual combatants, benefactors, healers, and children of song. It speaks of our fellowship with the Father and with His Son Jesus Christ, by our having been made partakers of the Holy Spirit. It speaks of the object of our pilgrimage as the enjoyment of things which God has prepared for those who love Him; of our being borne occasionally as on an eagle's wings, and clothed with the garments of salvation; of our speaking the language of Canaan, and of our being fair and comely in the sight of God; of our having the eyes of our understanding enlightened; of our ear as opened daily to divine discipline; and of our tongue as loosed to confess the name of Jesus, and to praise the Lord.

If we inspect it once more, in order to notice how far it is valid, we find it is valid to the heavenly city, where there is no night, and where there is no need of the sun, neither of the moon, to enlighten it; where every tear is wiped from all eyes, and men hunger no more, neither thirst anymore. Better is it that our right hand should forget its cunning than that we should forget this city of God. Our passport thither implies also a command given to ourselves to go forward in seeking it; and a command to all creatures, and all events, to cooperate for our advancement thither; a command to the angels to take charge concerning us; and a command to all adverse powers in

the world to "let these go their way." To every bearer of this important document, it is expressly enjoined, "Be of good courage, fear not;
go in peace." The angels obey its commands with delight; and the
powers of the adversary from necessity. Foolish then, indeed, is that
person who can possess it, and yet not anoint his head and wash his
face, and leave worldly anxiety and sorrow behind him.

Many a one is, indeed, provided with this document of heavenly
credentials, though hardly at present aware of it. Or he carries it
about with him sealed, and thus is but little acquainted with the
pleasant nature of its contents. Such are bidden to "give all diligence
to make their calling and election sure," which if they do, then, however their passport may be for the present concealed from themselves,
its value is not impaired, but it will still secure to them a safe conduct. Nevertheless, the consciousness of its possession and the ability
to decipher it are invaluable blessings, which we should daily aspire
to attain.

His Arrival

III. At the end of one or two days' journey, our traveler came in
sight of the mountains of Israel. In what a different light did he now
behold them stretching out before him, from what he had done on
former occasions, when at the head of his trained legions and mounted on his warhorse, he had proudly contemplated them at a distance
in order to select the height on which to unfurl his victorious banner.
In proportion to his confidence of obtaining a cure, would be the
home feeling, yea, the tender affection, with which he would now survey the country, opening like a place of refuge to his view. Beyond
those hills he looks for the realization of all his hopes, and his heart
bounds thither much swifter than his wheels can carry him. He is
now, moreover, likely to raise a standard upon Israel's hills, which shall
bear the inscription, "Jehovah is my help." Now also a battle is to be
fought; but the gods of Naaman will fall in the encounter, and he
himself will become a captive to the Lord God of the whole earth. He
will now, as formerly, not retire empty from the field; but his conquests
shall be imperishable in their consequences. As at other times, the
song of victory and triumph shall be raised, but it will be such as the
angels of God can join. Of all this Naaman has at present no idea. A
fountain of bodily health is all he seeks and all he hopes to find. But
God has greater designs toward him.

His route conducts him for some time along the foot of lofty mountains to the lake of Gennesaret; then he passes Capernaum and Bethsaida and enters the plain of Jezreel. And now Samaria, the lofty residence of the king of Israel, soon becomes visible. This was the place of his destination, and surely on such an occasion as this, even the heart of Naaman could not have been without strange emotions as he approached it. Naaman, upon his arrival in the city, "brought the letter" of Benhadad "to the king of Israel." Whether his having "brought" it implies that he did so in person, though a leper, we are not told. But of this we are certain, that his unexpected visit and the contents of the letter gave no little concern to the king of Israel; who read in it as follows: "Now when this letter is come unto thee, behold, I have therewith sent Naaman my servant to thee, that thou mayest recover him of his leprosy." The king, indignant at this strange communication, tore his royal robe and exclaimed with vehemence incomprehensible, at first, to all around him, "Am I God, to kill and to make alive, that this man doth send unto me to recover a man of his leprosy? wherefore, consider, I pray you, and see how he seeketh a quarrel against me."

But what unnecessary alarm, and what groundless uncalled-for passion, as if he were required to perform the miracle! Nevertheless, even here there is something commendable. For Jehoram himself is indignant at being thought to arrogate the place of God; whereas through ages past unto the present day, how many who have professed and called themselves Christians have everywhere virtually done this and are doing it still! This remark deserves the deep consideration of all who profess either spiritually to kill or to make alive. And what else but the latter of these alternatives are we ourselves doing, if we practically renounce our dependence on the grace of Christ and can think of no homage but that which is claimed by our own self-sufficiency?

If the letter of Benhadad manifests the blindness of a heathen, the burst of feeling from Jehoram strikingly shows some influence of the light of truth which still shone in Israel. For he is not only sensible that the leprosy, as inflicted by the special visitation of God, can be removed by nothing but divine interposition, and that its cure would be as life from the dead, but though in imitation of his fathers he was addicted to idolatry, he is convinced in his heart that Jehovah is God, and that in His sight, there is no offense of greater magnitude than to deify the creature by investing it with the honor due to God alone. Therefore he is seized with instantaneous consternation at a request seeming to be addressed to him, which he is thoroughly convinced should be addressed only to the living God.

We may perhaps be surprised to meet with so much true Israelitish sentiment and feeling in Jehoram; but it is not difficult to account for it, if we consider how much light yet remained in Israel, and how readily even bad men can avail themselves of such light to serve their own purposes, or when these are not counteracted by it. In the present case, it shed some of its rays around one who was still a miserable being; a striking instance of whose perturbable state of mind is further seen in his causeless and distrustful apprehension of renewed hostilities on the part of Benhadad; an apprehension which, at least, should not have so unnerved a man who had witnessed such wonderful proofs that there was for Israel a Keeper who never slept, and who could deliver the prey out of the mouth of the lion.

But Jehoram's consternation was likewise evinced in the embarrassment which he betrayed, perhaps in the very presence of the afflicted Syrian, as if in Israel a leper had never been healed; as if in the whole history of that people no instance of Almighty help could be found to justify the hopes of Naaman; also in his having so entirely forgotten that there was a prophet in his own dominions, of whose wonderful powers he had himself received ample demonstration. So that what little light he showed as a son of Israel was merely accidental, and such as it was not in his power entirely to quench; while in every other respect he was a contemptible character, an apostate without faith, and altogether devoid of elevated desires and real dignity.

If Jehoram's unholy embarrassment at the request made by the Syrian moves our pity or indignation, let us turn it against ourselves. For how frequently do we, in like manner, and upon the most insignificant occasions, become disturbed so as to betray the honor of God, and of the kingdom to which we belong! At the smallest misfortune or the most trivial difficulty, we can suddenly disquiet and demean ourselves, as though our faith in the Lord and in all His promises had been but fancy and delusion. Ought not our spiritual character to be above permitting us, even under the most mysterious dispensations, to sink down thus into practical unbelief, so as to bring into discredit with others, our high calling and holy profession?

Instead of so readily speaking about the unpleasant things that have happened to us, ought we not much rather to be animated with devout zeal, to show forth more faithfully the salvation and lovingkindness of our God? Ought we not infinitely prefer becoming a reproach and the offscouring of all things, rather than bring a reproach upon that kingdom whose citizens we have professed ourselves before the world?

We have every day experienced mercies and blessings unspeakably great and far outnumbering whatever cross incidents may have befallen us, and we ought so to remember them as, at least, to put all our complainings to shame. And then what is any one of those cross incidents which thus astonish and confound us, but things equally ordained by the only wise God and brought about by His mysterious providence, all for our final benefit and for His glory? Yes, every such thing is made to harmonize with His own gracious designs.

But what was Naaman now to do? For this afflicted man, who had arrived so elated with hope, finds that his fair prospect has suddenly vanished away. Jehoram can no more assist him than could Benhadad and the Syrian physicians; but he confesses his inability to serve him or to recommend him to anyone who can. What a distressing situation for Naaman! And yet all this was just as it should be; for now is the way prepared in which the Lord will magnify His name and display His power. The moment is arrived in which Elisha can appear and manifest gloriously that Jehovah is God, and not Baal, nor any other. Verily, the whole world can find no assistance except from the God of this despised and unassuming man. Now, as a last resource, all hopes are directed thither, and in him Naaman shall rejoice, to the honor of that God whom Elisha worshiped.

When the world has exhausted its consolations and resources, then it becomes manifest that the house of Israel is not so utterly worthless as is too generally suspected. How welcome, at such times, are the love and the faithfulness of a believing Christian! How seasonable his consolations, and more precious than gold and much fine gold! Where the resources of human art and succor terminate, there the efficiency of real Christianity commences. Here the sun of worldly glory sets, there the consolations of God spring up as light in the darkness. When the mighty upon earth are constrained to confess, "We know of no remedy," the servants of the Most High can lift up their hands unto God in the heavens, and can draw down that help which the world cannot give, and for any affliction, for any plague or trouble, can obtain the healing balm of divine truth and an everlasting cure. The resources from which they derive such help are never exhausted, for "their help is in the name of the Lord, who hath made heaven and earth!" He is their "refuge in times of trouble," whether their own trouble or that of others. God acts by their means, and they act by Him. He is the Fountain of Israel, and they are the channels through which His mercies flow.

12

The Beggar

"He that humbleth himself shall be exalted," is the standing law of God's kingdom. If we now attend seriously to the sequel of Naaman's history, we may become, by the divine blessing, the more disposed to obey that law.

2 Kings 5:8-10

> And it was so, when Elisha the man of God had heard that the king of Israel had rent his clothes, that he sent to the king saying, Wherefore hast thou rent thy clothes? let him come now to me, and he shall know that there is a prophet in Israel. So Naaman came with his horses and with his chariot, and stood at the door of the house of Elisha. And Elisha sent a messenger unto him, saying, Go and wash in Jordan seven times, and thy flesh shall come again to thee, and thou shalt be clean.

Three particulars here claim our attention: I. The interposition of Elisha; II. The journey to Jericho; and III. The prophet's directions.

The Interposition of Elisha

I. The aspect of things for Naaman was at present not very cheering. Could then the hint of the Israelitish maiden have been only a delusion? Had imagination raised up visions which sad reality was to dispel? Naaman had reached the end of his journey, but hitherto it appeared to have been performed in vain. Is then Samaria as Damascus? Is there no help in Israel? Was the leper's last hope to be given up? Not so. Here was only one of those many instances in which it has been "good for a man to wait and quietly hope for" the

123

Lord's mercies. The more desperate the case appeared, the more sig-
nally was it to display the Lord's power. The world with its wisdom,
its skill, and its expedients was first put to shame; and the reason is
obvious; for the giving of divine relief, after every human means had
failed, would the more evidently redound to the glory of God and to
the consequent benefit of man.

The news of the celebrated stranger's arrival in Samaria and of the
scene that had taken place in the palace quickly spread throughout
Israel and soon reached Elisha's humble dwelling at Jericho. When
he heard of the reception given by the king to the afflicted
stranger, he was not a little affected by it. He was devoted to the
honor of Jehovah, and thus to see it clouded could not fail to pain
him at the heart. Could the king already have forgotten that there
is a living God in Israel? Could he thus expose Israel to the scorn of
the heathen, as if here also the fountains were dried up, as if all truth
had failed?

The zeal of the prophet does not pine away in musings but displays
itself in action. He instantly sends a messenger to the capital with
orders to appear before the monarch, and to say to him in his name,
"Wherefore hast thou rent thy clothes? let him come now to me, and
he shall know that there is a prophet in Israel!" What great
words! How sublime this interposition of the man of God! He comes
forth from his seclusion, like the sun, breaking through the dark
clouds. He assumes, indeed, a high and lofty tone, but it is warranted.
It is no idle boast. Let others rend their garments at will; but for Israel
on such an occasion to do so were unworthy. The kingdom of
Jehovah is not a realm of poverty.

How noble and public-spirited was the feeling of the man of God!
Wave proudly aloft, banner of Zion. There is no shade like yours.
Come hither, come hither, all who need counsel and help. What a
whole world cannot furnish we here possess. Is it wisdom that you
seek? Do not doubtfully inquire what it is, and where it is to be
found. It is found already; its fire is in Zion. Is it peace? Do not tear
your clothes as if peace were unheard of in Zion. Seek it on her rich
pastures. Here its streams murmur, and its gentle breezes blow.

Is it righteousness? O take courage, though you have not yet
attained it in your spiritual bondage. In Zion a heavenly righteousness prevails, the righteousness of God, and you may be clothed with
it as with a robe of light.

Is it strength, to triumph over the cares of life and the fear of death, that you desire? The inventions of human wisdom cannot impart it. But fear not, there is still no reason for despondency. Come to Salem, and we engage that whatever opposes you shall be vanquished at your feet. Yes, search out your innermost needs, express your most hidden desires however great or many they may be; give vent to them all; within the boundaries of Christ's kingdom we promise you their most ample gratification and fulfillment. Here there is an end of poverty; here heaven pours out its fullness. Here is the termination of every grief. Then "let him that is athirst come." "Wherefore do ye spend money for that which is not bread? and your labor for that which satisfieth not? hearken diligently unto me, and eat ye that which is good, and let your soul delight itself in fatness."

The Journey to Jericho

II. Elisha's messenger arrives in Samaria, hastens to the palace, and discharges his commission. Jehoram receives the communication with pleasure. It relieves him from a secret embarrassment, and he therefore readily endures the pungency of Elisha's words. He causes the sick commander to be informed that in Jericho there dwells a prophet to whom he might go. No guidepost ever imparted more welcome information to a bewildered traveler. Naaman's joy must have been indescribable. The message surely sounded to him like the oars of an approaching boat to a shipwrecked mariner; like the voice of help to one who has fallen into a deep pit. "Yes," would he recollect, "it was of *a prophet* that the little maid in Damascus spoke!" And his sensations at this moment would resemble those of the eastern sages, when, on issuing from the gate of Jerusalem, they beheld themselves still guided by the star which was to conduct them to the object of their desires and expectations. His cheering prospects, which had been so obscured and clouded, would assume at this happy intelligence their former freshness, and his confidence of recovery would be now more ardent and consoling than before.

If God send us forth and guide us on our way, let the direction seem ever so strange and bewildering, we cannot but reach in safety the place of our destination. A hundred times will our prospects darken before us and around us, but a hundred times will they reopen with increased brightness. A hundred times will our hopes appear to have expired, but as often will they revive and brighten up with fresh

gatherings of glory. And having finally overcome the difficulties of
the wilderness, we shall serve God in His holy mountain; and then
will the confession of Joshua be ours, "There failed not aught of any
good thing which the Lord had spoken" concerning us (Josh. 21:45).

Naaman had no sooner received the welcome tidings of Elisha's
message than his retinue was immediately on the move. His
camels and horses were harnessed in haste, the chariots were led
forth, and the splendid eastern procession, now departing through
the streets of Samaria, was once more the attraction and renewed
talk of its inhabitants, many of whom perhaps expressed their doubts
whether the prophet would heal him. Naaman trusts that he will;
and probably he never returned from the victorious battlefield with
half the interest with which he now advanced toward Jericho. The
distance was speedily traveled, nor was Naaman long in discovering
the humble abode of the prophet; for surely there could not be a
child in Jericho who had not heard of Elisha, or who did not mention his name with veneration and love. His memorable miracle of
healing the waters was enough to acquire him the gratitude of the
whole city.

As Naaman proceeded toward the prophet's dwelling, he was likely to be greeted with many a joyful assurance, that if he came to seek
from the man of God the cure of his disease, he had not undertaken
such a journey in vain. Surely his feelings of impatience to gain an
interview with this wonderful man would be very great. At length
the chariot stops before a lowly habitation, which is pointed out to
him as that of the prophet. But was this the residence of the man
who was to do him a service, which he had sought in vain from all
the world, from all the most distinguished physicians and priests both
far and near? Little probably had Naaman learned that power may be
clothed in the simplest attire, and that it is only emptiness or impo-
tency that needs to decorate itself with pomp and parade.

There were also many other things with which he was equally
unacquainted; but they will gradually come under his observation and
will accomplish a strange revolution in his mind. If the meanness of
Elisha's dwelling had alarmed the pride of Naaman, his extraordinary
reception proved to him in the highest degree vexatious and
offensive. The noble leper had doubtless imagined that the moment
his splendid equipage should halt at this humble door, the prophet
would be out to receive him and submissively offer him his services.

But everything turned out differently from what the hero had expected, and contrary to the style and manners of his country.

The prophet was well aware what person was waiting at his gate, but was not the least elated by it. Yet, as if the communication made to him had respected the most ordinary and unimportant event, he remained undisturbed in his humble dwelling. All he did was to send a servant, probably Gehazi, briefly to inform Naaman what he must do in order to be cleansed of his plague. This procedure appears the more extraordinary in Elisha, because everything like haughtiness and reserve was altogether foreign to his character and his calling as a representative of divine grace and goodness.

But Elisha was perfectly master of what he did, and his whole proceeding, though in appearance indicating self-sufficiency and even pride, only attested a high degree of spiritual wisdom and prudence in the service of the Lord his God. The noble stranger was, at the very outset, to be made to feel that he had not now to do with a Syrian magician or an idolatrous priest, but with the servant of a Majesty which has no respect for persons, and in whose presence all human conceptions of great and small, high and low, dwindle into nothing. He had to learn that the distinctions which very properly exist in this world are as nothing in the eyes of Him before whom all alike are sinners, devoid of that glory which alone has merit in His sight; that splendid rank and high sounding titles, though justly numbered among the things that give importance to dust and ashes, are but as a vapor in the estimation of Him, neither constitute any claim to divine favor; that he must not therefore expect to be regarded of God as superior to the meanest, but be contented to accept the help of Jehovah, simply on the ground that He is a God of mercy to miserable sinners.

Of this and similar truths Elisha doubtless wished, in the most impressive manner, to convince his noble guest; and therefore it is that we see him, with holy self-denial, laying aside his obliging affability and assuming a demeanor toward the stranger which seemed rather to say, "Draw not nigh hither, put off thy shoes from off thy feet!" which was characteristic less of the mild benignity, than of the dazzling majesty of Him whom the prophet was called to represent among men. But in how estimable a light does the man of God appear on that very account! Can all the preachers of the gospel in modern times venture to survey themselves in this living mirror?

Alas! how frequently does pastoral deportment in the present day seem to justify the supposition that the Lord, whose interpreters and representatives we are, judges "with man's judgment"; that He has given a preference to rank, station, and wealth; and that He stands nearer to the noble, the dignified, and wealthy than to those of low degree. But, in truth, the ministers of Christ in general, are now too little regarded by themselves or by others as the representatives of Jehovah and of *His* mind. And this is the well-merited reward of our love of worldly preeminence. Even those in whose presence we obsequiously lower the standard of truth, despise us in their hearts, much as they may value and compliment us as "well-bred" and "gentlemanly." Oh may the "Lord of all" mercifully interpose to restrain this contemptible spirit on the part of His poor servants, and to establish them on the foundation of the apostles and prophets from whence the fascinations of dignity and rank would be viewed as a vapor!

Doubtless there was nothing that Elisha more fervently desired than that it might be granted him to place what we may call the *beggar's staff* in the hands of his noble visitant. Neither could this desire be prompted by any other motive than love itself; for he was perfectly acquainted with the promise in the seventy-second Psalm in which the Lord promises to answer the cry of the poor and needy. Oh blessed state of poverty and need, contradictory as such an exclamation may sound! For though everyone is poor by nature, yet it is not everyone who *knows* it, or desires to know it. For very few are humble enough to live habitually by grace; to rest habitually on the merits of another; to be led along by the hand of divine mercy.

Pride and self-love are our greatest obstacles. Poor and needy as we are, we are not easily made sensible of our real condition. Providence may visit us with chastisements, and misfortune upon misfortune may come upon us, but we are often more ready to repine and despond than to imagine that such visitations are "for our profit" and improvement; and how often do we still remain unhumbled under them? Instruction, education, example, correction, and punishment may do much for man, but they can never make him truly humble in spirit. A whole array of Scripture passages, exhortations, and philosophical evidences of transgressions, judgments, calamities, and I know not what besides, will of themselves produce no effect to the purpose.

The Lord will often rather break than bend. The change so

devoutly to be wished is the work alone of Him who "giveth repentance unto Israel." And to be clothed with this humility of spirit is better than to be arrayed in princely garments. But how is it effected? Sometimes by alarming convictions of the strictness, extent, and spirituality of the divine law. Hereby the man becomes sensible that his *quantum* of supposed virtue falls far short of what he is bound to pay. He therefore forms resolutions and purposes of amendment; for he is now awfully persuaded that the divine commandments *must* be kept! That without obedience there is no holiness, and that without holiness there is no happiness.

But, alas! the more earnestly he endeavors after all this, in his own strength, the more overwhelming are his discouragements. For experience now teaches him that he is retreating instead of advancing; that he sinks deeper every day, becomes poorer instead of richer, and accumulates debts instead of discharging them. His awful apprehensions are increased; he renews his exertions; but repeated shortcomings confirm his conviction that he is *bankrupt*; that he has nothing wherewith to pay. Yet he hears the gospel of peace proclaiming, "Believe on the Lord Jesus Christ, and thou shalt be saved." He hears the simple message of the cross, and a beam of hope pierces the gloom of his despondency. He sees himself cast upon Christ as his only hope; and at length he falls down and humbles himself before the throne of grace. The consciousness of being a helpless sinner, and that there is salvation only through the precious blood of Christ, is now that *beggar's staff* in his hand which God alone can give.

This humble state of mind cannot long remain concealed from the world. It is a spectacle of joy in the presence of the angels of God; and it becomes a spectacle of wonder and praise, as also of reproach and scorn, to men. To real Christians it is an unspeakable joy that another brother is born to them, that their Lord still works mightily, that His Spirit breathes upon the dry bones, and that His kingdom prospers. The angels again rejoice that their King displays more and more the exceeding riches of His grace, and that they can thus welcome another fellow-heir of glory. In the Scriptures we nowhere read that there is "joy in heaven" over men's acquisition of gold, or nobility, or splendid appointments, or crowns of worldly praise. But the humility and change of mind of which we speak are an occasion of joy to the whole kingdom of God; while the devil only, and his agents, are abashed at the sight—a glorious testimony to the value of Christian humility.

But it is not others only to whom it is the occasion of joy. The subject of it himself soon feels the comfort that attends it; and irksome and revolting as he thought it beforehand, it is now his welcome element. For it is the very element of heaven, the element of benevolence and love. And as God's children kindly welcome him as a brother, so God Himself regards him as no more a slave but a son. He bids him to "be careful for nothing," but to "cast all his care on Him who careth for him." He assures him of His everlasting love; and that He will never leave him nor forsake him.

Here then is the true *honor*; here are "the true riches"; here alone is happiness. Little as it is thought of by the world, all the true nobility that the world ever knew have been characterized and distinguished thereby. Abraham, and a train of successive prophets, and the apostles have been clothed with it. The best fathers of the church and the best reformers were most remarkable for it, and "counted it all joy." And shall not *we* highly prize and seek after that which will rank us in the same class with *them*? Of what *real* value to me are all other distinctions, however imposing? These may any day belong to traitors and infidels, and they perish with the using. Not so that clothing of humility which is never put on by the ungodly. With this beggar's staff we may courageously pursue our path to heaven, where it will become as a palm of victory in our hands. What multiplied motives have we for not being ashamed of it here!

But we are not beggars at your door, O miserable world! From you we desire nothing. Keep what you have. Your poverty can afford us no pleasure. We prostrate ourselves before another gate; and oh, how great and glorious are the benefits we there receive! "As having nothing, and yet possessing all things." To those to whom it was once said, "Thou art wretched, and miserable, and poor, and blind, and naked," it is now said, "All things are yours."

The Prophet's Directions

III. We are next to consider Elisha's prescription to his noble patient. He sent unto him saying, "Go and wash in Jordan seven times, and thy flesh shall come again to thee, and thou shalt be clean." This was, in truth, a most unexpected and singular direction; it amazed Naaman in the greatest degree and once more darkened his hopes of returning felicity. But who can mistake the highly typical character of this advice? Against the spiritual leprosy, sin, we can only prescribe in a similar manner: a bath, a washing, a baptism; not, however, in the waters of an earthly stream, but in that "fountain opened to the house of David for sin and for uncleanness." Here it is absolutely necessary that all polluted sinners must wash; otherwise, as Job says, "thou shalt plunge me in the ditch, and mine own clothes shall abhor me" (Job 9:31). "If I wash thee not," said the Savior to an apostle himself, "thou hast no part with me" (John 13:8).

Read this declaration with a threefold emphasis, and the one thing needful will be distinctly perceived. Place the accent first on the word "I"; "If *I* wash thee not:" CHRIST must do it. Wash yourself as you will, and with what you will, if Jesus does not wash you, you are still unclean in the sight of God. Try the cleansing efficacy of your own supposed meritorious services; they may gain you applause before the world; but do not hope for the complacency of the Most High, if you are too proud to pass under the cleansing hand of Jesus. A good name among men has its value; but if your desires extend to heaven and the world to come, then dwell seriously upon the words, "If I wash thee not, thou hast no part with me." "If I WASH thee not." It matters little what Jesus may have done for you besides, unless He has WASHED you. You may say, "He *teaches* and *instructs* me"; but Judas Iscariot might have said the same, and yet he perished. You may even have directed *others* to Him as the fountain for the house of David; but have you been washed in that fountain *yourself*? Without this you remain a sinner; and "the wages of sin is death."

But wherewith, or by what means, is this washing and cleansing brought about? The apostle answers this inquiry and exclaims, "THE BLOOD OF JESUS CHRIST, his Son, cleanseth us from all sin." The church triumphant "have washed their robes, and made them white IN THE BLOOD OF THE LAMB." To all whom God "justifieth," it is triumphantly proclaimed, "Ye are come TO THE BLOOD OF SPRINKLING!" He who heartily welcomes and wholly values the sufferings of Immanuel as his only dependence and his only foundation, that person wears garments purified with the blood of Christ, and is free and cleansed from his foul and native leprosy. Would *we* enjoy such a happy condition? We then must come by faith to "the blood of sprinkling," that we may be "washed, sanctified, justified, in the name of the Lord Jesus, and by the Spirit of our God." For "there is *now* no condemnation to them that are in Christ Jesus, who walk not after the flesh, but after the Spirit." Nothing of the kind any longer clings to them. All the sins of their past lives are fully atoned for, rebuked, punished, remitted; blotted out of the book of God's remembrance and cast into the depths of the sea, so as to be no more found; yes, all this was done in the divine foreknowledge long before those sins were committed.

And does the blood of the Lamb purify? It also furnishes goodly raiment, adorning, and honor. He who with heart-purifying faith receives as placed to his account the atoning sufferings of Christ, that person is also allowed to receive and to put on the merit of Christ's glorious obedience. And he shows that he has done this by bearing in his changed character the Savior's image. Yes; and it is on this account we triumphantly testify that as justification emanates from the blood of Christ, so, with equal truth, does sanctification likewise devolve through it. For, live only and entirely by true heart-felt faith in your once-suffering, bleeding, dying Savior, and the germ of "the virtues of HIM" in your renewed nature will, BY THE GRACE AND POWER OF HIS SPIRIT, spring up, unfold, blossom, and bear fruit in your disposition, life, and conversation. Then the love of Christ thus dying for you will be like a precious oil to nourish and kindle up the spark of your little love into a flame, and true humility within and without will be the pledge of your exaltation unto victory. Live, I say, by faith in that merciful, that dying love, and it will make you merciful, and forgiving, and conscientious, and patient. You will then have no desire for the vain pleasures of this world, but you will have calm courage and confidence whenever trouble or death may come. "Keep," then, "the faith" we here speak of, even faith in the atoning blood of Christ; hold it fast; for the more tenaciously you abide by it, the more will you find that word of Scripture true, "the blood is the life."

Well, therefore, may the church triumphant in heaven be represented as singing the song of Moses, AND OF THE LAMB (Rev. 15:3). For whatever they *are* in moral excellence, whatever they have been enabled to do on earth in fulfilling the law, whatever they now *have* and *enjoy* in heaven, they owe it all exclusively to "Him who hath loved them, and washed them from their sins in His own blood."

"Worthy then is the Lamb that was slain!" This is their song before the throne; they know nothing of their own merit. Yes, this is

that whereby alone they received, or ever *could* receive, their wor-
thiness to obtain that world; and thus it came to them, as children
receive a birthright inheritance, without the least claim on the
ground of their own personal desert, yet no one interposing, or dar-
ing to interpose, a protest against it. They had to pay down
nothing for the purchase of it; they had only to part with their
dreamy and delusive notions of self-righteousness, their pride, and
their lusts. These they were willingly obliged and constrained to sacrifice to the honor and love of the truth. The whole foundation of
their glorying was laid by Another, and no part of it by themselves.

And this having been once laid for them, was laid forever, as sufficient as it is everlasting. It needed no addition of man's device nor
ever will. O precious blood of the Lamb of God! Wonderful, all-pow-
erful, all-efficacious atonement! Let the world, if it please, tread it
under foot; let those who are "doing despite unto the Spirit of grace,"
let them, if they will, "count the blood of the covenant an unholy
thing"; it shall, nevertheless, be my strength and my song in this frail
tabernacle, this house of my pilgrimage; and I will commend it while
I live; I will praise the Lord for it as long as I have my being; yes, for
the everlasting covenant of it, as all my salvation and all my desire.
For where had I now been if Christ had not died for me? But His
atoning death swallows up my death in victory. It destroys "the body
of sin" in me, which is the *real* "body of death," "that henceforth I
should not serve sin." Thus from the blood of sprinkling I come forth
"*a new creature*"; "a new creation."

Triumphing in Christ alone, I pluck the palm of victory from the
grave itself and from the hand of hell. But who can worthily praise
the Lord for this grace of atoning blood and for its unfathomable
power and efficacy! A single application of which is sufficient in a
moment to make crimson sins white as snow; yea, it makes me *the
righteousness of God* in HIM, even in Christ Jesus; and by virtue of it
I become at length "blameless and harmless," "without rebuke," and
"without fault before the throne of God"; yes, and raised to privileges
of adoption and sonship which Adam in paradise never knew.

This atonement, moreover, covers my guilty head with "a crown
of life," and brings me "into the holiest at once"; it gives life to that
love which, being "made perfect," is the earnest that I shall "have
boldness in the day of judgment," and shall "not be ashamed before
the Lord at his coming"; but shall be welcomed to everlasting rest

under His shadow "at his appearing and his kingdom." O invaluable and wonder-working atonement of blood! Who can ever worthily praise and bless the Lord for this! O that I may never lose sight of it! Especially in that hour, when this mortal life, and, with it, all this world to me, shall sink away in dimness and night from these dizzy and death-arrested eyes! O Thou who art FAITHFUL AND TRUE, grant that then, when eternity is opening to my mental sight, when its dawning brightness shall make all the guilt of my past life, all the blackness of my ingratitude, seem revived before me in more appalling vividness than ever, O then, then, yea, and now, against that day and hour let me be strong in faith, in hope, and in love! Thus, when I walk through "the valley of the shadow of death" I shall fear no evil. A believing view of You as having by Your death reconciled me to God and much more as saving me by Your life, shall command me to overcome all fear. Let then the remembrance of Your atonement by Your precious blood be ever present to my thoughts, to the belief of my heart. According to my faith, my hope, and my trust, so let its efficacy abide with me, and its presence for my every need be realized by me. Let the lintel and the sideposts of my earthly tabernacle be sprinkled and sanctified by it continually. Yes, let Your blood of atonement be sprinkled upon us all, to "purge our conscience from dead works, to serve thee the living God." Let it be upon us all unto reconciliation and life eternal. Amen.

13

The Way of Recovery

Speed in this wilderness is the gift of God alone. Whether He grant it, or whether He allow the believing pilgrim to halt disconsolate on His way, the mark is at length attained. "The name of the Lord is a strong tower: the righteous runneth into it, and is safe."

2 Kings 5:11-14

> But Naaman was wroth, and went away, and said, Behold, I thought He will surely come out to me, and stand, and call on the name of the Lord his God, and strike his hand over the place, and recover the leper. Are not Abana and Pharpar, rivers of Damascus, better than all the waters of Israel? may I not wash in them, and be clean? So he turned and went away in a rage. And his servants came near, and spake unto him, and said, My father, if the prophet had bid thee do some great thing, wouldest thou not have done it? how much rather then, when he saith to thee, wash, and be clean! Then went he down, and dipped himself seven times in Jordan, according to the saying of the man of God: and his flesh came again like unto the flesh of a little child, and he was clean!

How interesting and instructive are these few verses! The heart of Naaman is here laid open to us. And what one thing can be more like another in all its essential features, than is "the heart of man to man"? While, therefore, we are considering the conduct of Naaman, some of us may unawares discover our own character. Naaman's remarkable displeasure, together with the judicious and well-timed remonstrance addressed to him by his faithful servants, will form the two subjects of our present meditation. May this be accompanied with the divine blessing! Amen.

Naaman's Displeasure

I. "Naaman was wroth!" In a moment he feels himself insulted by the prophet's message to him. His thoughts seem to have been, "This is too much! To make so long a journey, to spare neither labor nor pains, to be put off from one to another, and at length shifted to this contemptible expedient of going and washing in Jordan seven times! Truly it was worthwhile to travel so far into this land of wonders for such an experiment! What do they mean? Do they suppose that the captain of Syria is to be thus trifled with?" Thus is he incensed in his splendid chariot, as though he would again grasp the sword. He is deeply mortified; he believes himself, perhaps, intentionally deceived; his reflections goad him toward despair at seeing, as he supposes, all his hopes wrecked at the very mouth of the haven.

The anger of this troubled warrior is a spectacle of itself. How unreasonable was it, and how dangerous to him who indulged it! It had almost turned him away, with the whole burden of his misery, from the threshold of recovery and health. And who were the objects of his displeasure? Perhaps not even the little Israelitish maid was excepted; for her hint had proved to him, as it now seemed, a piece of mere folly. And what could he think of king Jehoram, who had sanctioned his application to Elisha? Or what of the citizens of Jericho, who had confirmed him in his vain, insubstantial hopes? But, lastly, he was angry against the prophet himself, by whom he might regard himself insulted and mocked. And yet had Naaman persisted in these proud notions, so as to have returned in anger to Damascus without a cure, there to have fallen a victim to his terrible malady, whom would he really have had to blame but himself? The rod of destruction to all his hopes would have been made up of his own pride, his own presumption, his own preconceived opinion, his carnal mind. The remedy is before him. Why does he not accept and welcome it? Simply because it is indicated to him in a different form from the one in which he expected to meet with it.

"Behold," he says, as the chariot is turning to depart, "I thought, he would have" done this and that. But if there is one thing in the world more pernicious than another, it is oftentimes that disposition which the expression, "I thought," as here used by Naaman, betrays. Our great adversary easily avails himself of the high opinion we have of our own judgment, to construct out of it the most formidable barrier between sinners and their salvation. Many have gone so far as to yield to a certain conviction that they are sinners, but, at this point, their own suppositions will begin to intervene; the sum of all which is, that they arraign the oracles of God at the bar of their own shallow reason and judge concerning divine truths and commandments as they would concerning the traditions and commandments of men.

But what desperate temerity it is thus to venture upon the dread ocean of futurity in the frail and treacherous ship of mere human understanding! Upon a mere opinion will no prudent merchant venture his capital in any speculation. He must have some reasonable certainty respecting a favorable result. And yet to risk the happiness of the soul upon the doubtful security of an opinion, how easily is this done, and how lightly accounted of by many among us, though a fearful retribution will certainly one day overtake it! Those who at present *will* think independently of the word of God, will have a miserable recollection of it in that day when all *their* thoughts shall have perished. It will be the misery of disappointed miscalculations. Imagine only the agony of their self-reproach, the soliloquy of their disappointment. "I thought it would be well with me after all. I thought that sin was not a thing of so much importance. I thought that God would forgive me. I thought that punishment in a future state was doubtful; that what was believed concerning the devil was merely imaginary; and that strict notions about religion were but state contrivances. I thought that I was as likely to be right in *my* opinions as others in *theirs*; but, oh dreadful delusion! I find it now to be far otherwise, my own *thoughts* have fatally deceived me!"

And what was it that Naaman here thought? He had indulged narrow and haughty ideas of his own, the fallacy of which he soon experienced. "Behold," said he, "I *thought*, He *will surely* come out to *me*!" As if he had said, "A person of my rank does not every day stop at his door." He evidently expected deference to have been paid to his station and quality; and he was chagrined at a reception which seemed to lower him to the meanest common applicants. His high thoughts of himself encountered most unexpectedly a check and mortification so that he at once shrunk aside with disgust into the conclusion that the prophet was destitute of power.

This was a hasty conclusion indeed; hasty, indeed, and extraordinary, but not uncommon. What is the ordinary reception which a *faithful* preaching of the gospel meets with from the world? Is it any better than Naaman's notions of Elisha at Jericho? The gospel, in respect of its faithful application to the conscience, knows no distinction of rank or station, of education or moral worth, but addresses itself to all, indiscriminately, as fallen children of Adam, born in sin, shapen in iniquity, unworthy of the least of God's mercies, and at best but unprofitable servants. Thus it directs everyone to depend for salvation on free grace alone. But on this very account does the world often reject and set it at nought; and why, but because *their own thoughts of themselves* are very different? Nevertheless, as the word of God is true, *their thoughts of themselves* are a perversion of all right thinking.

And what else were the thoughts of this blind Syrian, who thus further expresses himself; "I thought he will stand, and call on the name of the Lord his God, and strike his hand over the place, and recover the leper." Yes, there we have it! He had brought with him ideas, formed not from divine truth, but from heathen falsehood; or to speak more plainly, from the natural imaginations of the corrupt heart of man. He had probably imagined that a kind of exorcism was to take place at once by Elisha's calling on the name of his (Elisha's) supposed national and local god, with a solemn approach to the diseased man and a mysterious waving of the hands over his sores and ulcers; with other such-like pomp of heathen ceremony.

But now, when nothing of all this his expectation was realized, but everything of a contrary and humiliating tendency, his hope of supernatural relief vanished at once. Like a man who thought himself imposed on and even insulted, he seemed to give his last hope to the winds. How pitiable was his delusion! Had he laid aside his own opinions and prejudices for a moment, the very simplicity and absence of all show in Elisha's procedure would have led him to a very opposite conclusion, for it would have forced upon him the joyful conviction, "This man cannot possibly be a cloud without water; surely he must have the aid of divine power; he is calmly confident of the issue of his message to me; he would not risk his high reputation by giving instructions so direct and unambiguous, as, 'Go, and wash in Jordan seven times, and thy flesh shall come again to thee, and thou shalt be clean.'"

But Naaman sits entrenched behind his own opinions, measuring what is divine by an earthly standard and little considering that what is merely human calls for the aid of imposing circumstance and appendage only because it is poor and insignificant in itself; while that which is divine, being sufficiently great and important of itself, would seem more or less deteriorated by any addition of external decoration.

Yet, how many are there who still participate in the wrong sentiments of Naaman! And as they hold his sentiments, so are they involved in his fate as uncured lepers, though, alas! in a much more melancholy degree. Their unblessed opinions dim their vision with a servile covering of worldly elements, so that they blink in the very dominions of light and truth and grope in darkness at noonday. Hence it is the same to them as if there existed no word of God; for their minds are perverted by notions utterly foreign to every divine communication and to all the Lord's doings as set forth in those sacred writings, for the very style and tone of which they show a cordial disdain. As little do they recognize the great and glorious agency of the Most High in all the features of nature and of human affairs; thus because nothing of what they see, in the one or in the other, accords with their own preconceived notions of divine interposition. So they practically disown the God of revelation, of providence, and even of nature itself. Their own thoughts, opinions, and sentiments, go to destroy everything that is great, divine, and blessed in the world, and deify, on the other hand, a philosophy or a vulgar sentiment that is as vain and worthless as it is outwardly imposing and plausible.

Therefore must all who would persuade themselves that they "have chosen the way of truth" be ever jealous of any imagination or opinion that tends to flatter the pride, vanity, or indolence of our fallen nature. Preconceived opinion, as, for instance, respecting the humble manner in which the Christian revelation was first ushered into the world, is the nurse and mother of infidelity. The corrupt inclinations and self-flattering prejudices of mankind form the very pillars of Satan's empire. By their means it is that he governs the world; while wherever men begin to question the infallibility of their own conceptions, there is his kingdom shaken. And if we proceed a little further so as to become convinced that the manner in which God should reveal Himself to His sinful creatures can be learned only *from Himself*, we are not far from the kingdom of God. For those who inherit that kingdom are of childlike docility; neither do they presume to understand before they have been instructed. But there are multitudes in our day who deny truth to be truth because they have determined what is truth before they have become acquainted with it.

The Remonstrance of His Servants

II. Naaman's unexpected reception from Elisha was not the only or the chief cause of his extreme vexation. The unpromising appearance of the remedy which the prophet had prescribed had still more to do with it. Elisha had bidden him, "Go, and wash in Jordan." "In Jordan!" thought the indignant captain: "are not Abana and Pharpar, rivers of Damascus, better than all the waters of Israel? may I not wash in them, and be clean?" And, indeed, we must admit that he was right, if the two rivers he refers to were to be regarded in the same light in which *he* regarded them. For to this day are the waters of Syria esteemed more wholesome and strengthening than most of those in the promised land.

But who had bidden the stranger to compare the *physical* properties of Jordan with those of the rivers of Damascus? He did not reflect that in his favor on that occasion there was a divine promise attached to the waters of Jordan. The assurance had been given him in the name of the Almighty that by this water he should be cured of his leprosy; therefore a healing power had been, for the present case, imparted to it, surpassing all the *physical* powers of other waters. Yes, it stands to reason that the special blessing of God can render the meanest appointments the most salutary; a barley-loaf better than a sumptuous entertainment; a shepherd's rod in the hand of Moses more powerful than an imperial scepter; and any condition of poverty superior to the greatest abundance.

What were all the medicines in the world compared with the brazen serpent in the wilderness after the Lord had said, "He that looketh upon it shall live"? What the largest possessions of corn, wine, and oil in comparison with the widow's handful of meal in a barrel and a little remnant of oil in a cruse after the Lord had pronounced concerning these, "They shall not waste nor fail"? Verily, the worth of everything depends upon its being associated with the divine blessing. The scanty pittance and the hard couch of God's poorest children are infinitely preferable to the fine linen and sumptuous fare of those who, not seeking in the first place the kingdom of God and His righteousness, have no divine promise recorded in their favor, that all needful earthly things shall be added unto them.

"Judge not," then, like Naaman, "after the outward appearance." He considered the water of Jordan simply as the water of Jordan, without reflecting on that divine blessing which, like the angel at Bethesda, would descend upon it. Hence to wash in that river appeared too simple an operation to warrant any hope of essential benefit. Had Elisha commanded something uncommon or ceremonious and difficult, this would have raised the warrior's hopes. But the simplicity of such a prescription, so widely different from his own ways of thinking, seemed to leave him no prospect but that of a miserable death. He therefore indignantly orders his charioteer to drive off: "he turned and went away in a rage." Impatient of delay for any further inquiry, he will have his orders instantly obeyed, his servants mounted on their camels, and his whole train on the march.

But do we not feel as though we could have seized the bridles of the horses and have closed the gates of Jericho to prevent the departure of this deluded stranger? Should we not have shed tears of compassion at beholding the unhappy man turning away from the very door of mercy and ready to carry home to a deathbed his burden of loathsome disease and wretchedness? With such a burden he would certainly have returned as he came, had not the providence of God mercifully interposed to rescue him from the delusive imaginations of pride and prejudice. And this is just what the great Author and Finisher of our faith has done for recovering many a proud person from the leprosy of sin. And how necessary have such interpositions been! The bare consciousness that we have the leprosy of sin, or even the superadded wish for recovery, is insufficient of itself to persuade us heartily to accept the appropriate and divinely appointed remedy. In the very sight of the manger and the cross, if left to ourselves, we should still turn aside, and in the darkness of some self-flattering way of our own, we should miserably perish.

Naaman, if he would be cured, must be healed of his own proud delusions; the mighty captain and counselor of Syria must listen to humble and humbling advice. Now, observe how beautifully God's providence wrought for the accomplishment of this merciful purpose. He suffered him previously to discover the evil passions of his own proud spirit, to make him sensible that this, as well as his body, needed a cleansing from Jehovah. Nor does he miraculously prevent him from actually commencing his return homewards, but leaves him to act according to his own free will.

There was something also humiliating in God's choosing as the further instruments of His merciful intentions toward Naaman, the inferiors and servants of this great man. He had already moved off from the humble dwelling of Elisha, who probably remained quietly in his prophet's chamber, imploring that the eyes of the infatuated man might be opened; when some of Naaman's attendants, who viewed the matter with more simplicity of mind, came up and accosted their master in his chariot, and with equal respect and earnestness entreated him to comply with the directions of the prophet and at least to try the prescribed remedy.

From their apparently familiar and affectionate address, "My father!" (though it may have been only an Eastern compliment), we may not unreasonably conclude that Naaman was an affable and benevolent master. Certain it is that many are affable and benevolent in their ordinary conduct, till a proposition is made to them of similar import to that, "Go, wash in Jordan, and be clean" and then, alas! how soon will what appeared to be a lamb be heard to speak as a dragon! Should, however, the result be more favorable, it is a pleasing sign of the influence of divine grace. And doubtless it is only under such influence that the "Fountain opened for sin and for uncleanness" will be cordially and thankfully resorted to.

We may observe in the words of Naaman's servants the beautiful simplicity of good common sense. "My father, if the prophet had bid thee do some great thing, wouldest thou not have done it? how much rather then, when he saith to thee, Wash, and be clean!" Truly, they were right. Had Elisha prescribed the achievement of something great or extraordinary, though it were a pilgrimage through the Arabian Desert or to the top of some lofty mountain, or a fast of many days, or a costly sacrifice, how buoyant had been Naaman's hopes and how ready his compliance! But to wash in Jordan, and this seven times, appeared to him so perfectly futile that he could not imagine any healing, much less that of the incurable leprosy, attainable by so insignificant and meaningless a ceremony.

The reasoning of Naaman's servants will admit of further consideration for Christian use. How difficult do men find it implicitly to acquiesce in the gracious liberality of the New Testament economy! The very facility with which the blessings of the Christian covenant may be attained becomes an offense. To be thrown entirely upon a single resource, "the simplicity which is in Christ," is a matter of stumbling to the pride of human nature. Hence the necessity of constantly watching to stand fast in the faith of that great truth which serves to sustain, purify, and animate the very life of *all* Christian obedience; namely, that "by grace ye are saved, through faith, that by the grace of God we are what we are"; and that the propitiation of Christ, the Son of God, who freely laid down His life for us, is the everlasting basis of all spiritual healing and reconciliation. The invitation of the gospel therefore is, "Come and purchase, without money and without price!" Thus the way of faith is one of humiliation and self-abasement from beginning to end, and "eternal life is the free gift of God through Jesus Christ our Lord." For "whosoever will," behold "all things are ready," and "let him take the water of life freely." Here is Mary's "chosen" and "good part" without Martha's "cumbrance and trouble about many things."

Choose the same then, dear brethren, for yourselves! Walk not after the imagination of your own hearts which will certainly deceive and disappoint you at last, as many have experienced already. Be willing to go into total poverty of spirit, for to this is attached the healing and satisfying blessing of the kingdom of heaven. In the way of our own preferences we may imagine ourselves free, but we are here in the very worst state of slavery; we may imagine ourselves honorably employed, but we are bringing forth fruit unto death; we may believe that we are keeping all the commandments of God's law, while it has undoubtedly many things against us, which if not timely remitted by the only method wherein we are authorized to expect it, will amount to its awful curse and to our final rejection.

If, on the other hand, for Christ's sake, we renounce and let go at once our own imaginary glory, then we acquire in its stead a glory that fades not away. If we deny every false claim of self and "yield ourselves unto God as those that are alive from the dead, and our members as instruments of righteousness unto God," having His will for our will and His glory for our only glory, then indeed we are counted as the children of the King, yea, as one with Him.

Spend not then any longer your "money for that which is not bread, and your labor for that which satisfieth not" but hearken diligently to the voice of the Good Shepherd and feed upon that which is good; yea, "let your soul delight itself" in its abundance and shine in the garments of salvation and robe of righteousness prepared for you by the King of the freely invited guests. Here is the divine blessing; here is the love of God; here is the kingdom of heaven opened through the precious death of Christ to all believers. Blessed are they that practice His commandments, that they may have right to the Tree of life and may enter in through the gates into the city. For without are—"whosoever loveth and practiseth untruth."

Turn, therefore, to this "Stronghold, ye prisoners of hope," all ye who value your immortal souls. Be enslaved no longer to any *self-flattering* imaginations of your own. Truly in vain is salvation hoped from the multitude of such hills! Come and receive it as a free gift from the hands of divine mercy which "giveth unto all men liberally, and upbraideth not," and which expects nothing in return except the grateful love and reasonable service of a devotedly obedient heart and life.

14

The Cure

"They that be whole need not a physician, but they that are sick! I came not to call the righteous, but sinners to repentance!" Thus spoke our blessed Lord to the self-righteous scribes and Pharisees. If He is the Good Physician, who is found among the sick, why does He seek them except to heal them? If He is the Friend of publicans and sinners, for what purpose is it but to call them to repentance and to separate them from sin forever? He came into the world to save sinners, and every miracle of mercy that He wrought showed that His design was that sinners might be *saved*; that is, not only pardoned, but *transformed* into new creatures by the renewing of their mind so as to become devoted to God. Pardoning grace is always sanctifying grace. Of such things we shall be at least reminded in this concluding portion of Naaman's history.

2 Kings 5:14,15

> Then went he down, and dipped himself seven times in Jordan, according to the saying of the man of God: and his flesh came again like unto the flesh of a little child, and he was clean. And he returned to the man of God, he and all his company.

The narrative now takes a favorable turn, and Naaman obtains the object of his wishes. Let us praise God for it; for we should have regretted to this day had the leper returned uncured when an effectual remedy had been divinely pointed out to him. And yet he had very nearly foregone the benefit of it; so destructively may anyone stand in his own light, when he presumes to judge of divine things by his own imagination and arbitrarily undertakes to determine how the finger of God shall be recognized. Let us now observe how the Syrian was first cured of his folly, and then of his disease.

How Naaman Was Cured of His Folly

I. He had gone, as we have already noticed, to a dangerous extreme. His rage had well nigh turned him back to Damascus, there to end his days in misery; to regard the honor of Jehovah, the God of Israel and of the whole earth, as a mere creation of the fancy, and the Lord's prophets and servants as fanatics or impostors. But no! this shall not be. The Lord God of all grace and mercy most providentially here interposed and stopped the wheels of Naaman's chariot. It is not Elisha who appears as the instrument for this purpose. He knows that a net of providence has encompassed this Syrian, and serene at his struggles, the prophet remains tranquil in the devout retirement of his chamber.

God never lacks agents for His own purposes. The words with which Naaman's servants now accosted their master deserve to be always remembered, and therefore we repeat them once more. "My father, if the prophet had bid thee do some great thing, wouldest thou not have done it? how much rather then, when he saith to thee, Wash, and be clean?" Naaman had no sooner heard this artless address than he became of another mind. He perceived at once that such counsel was good.

He was conscious that he would have been ready to follow any more difficult method of cure; why then not at least try one that was easier? Might it not, also, have now occurred to him that perhaps the simplicity of this prescription was intended for the very purpose of displaying the power and mercy of the God of Israel? Be this as it may, the remonstrance of his servants was overruled to accomplish wonders. The hint of the little maiden, which had appeared but as a faithless beacon, now again shone forth as a beneficent star. The strangeness of Elisha's conduct is at once forgotten, and the thought that Abana and Pharpar, rivers of Damascus, were better than all the waters of Israel withers at its root. The hurricane of Naaman's passion is stilled; he orders his chariot to be turned once more, and the cry of the cavalcade is, "To Jordan! to Jordan!"

Though he might have spared himself some additional misery had he thus yielded in the first instance, yet this interlude of rage and dismay could be overruled for good. For if he were really healed after all this sinful murmuring, raging, and reviling, no exhortation would be necessary to convince him that he owed his cure to a God of long-suffering and tender mercy. His heart and conscience would preach loudly and eloquently enough, and humility and contrition would ensue of course.

It is a great thing when a man becomes heartily willing to acquiesce in the simple arrangements of God for the cure and recovery of the soul. But without the divine agency no one ever evinces this state of submission. It presupposes that denial of self to which only the influence of the Holy Spirit can dispose us. To carnal and proud reason the simple way of faith has ever appeared foolish, degrading, and inadequate; and to the self-righteous mind, superfluous. If, therefore, you are induced by a feeling of misery and need to accept and welcome "with all readiness of mind" the healing and cleansing of the Savior as your only refuge, a new heart has been divinely given you, and a new spirit been put within you.

The company arrives at Jordan. Naaman alights and proceeds toward its bank with what feelings we can better imagine than describe. It was surely the most eventful moment he had lived to see. Above the waters of this stream his last hope trembles; will they be its grave, or will they impart health and happiness? The issue to this leper in body and mind is life or death!

Let us recollect the mysterious significance of the leprosy in Israel. That singularly dire and loathsome disease was plainly appointed to be a special emblem of sin; and we can hardly find an emblem more striking and significant. Its incurableness by ordinary means served to indicate our radical native corruption, that iniquity of spiritual constitution in which, through the fall of man, we are "shapen" and "born." Its contagiousness set forth the evil influence of one sinner upon another, even when the general conduct is outwardly decent and correct.

The disgust belonging to it was to remind us how abominable is all sin in the sight of Him who is of purer eyes than to behold iniquity. He who was visited by the plague of leprosy was excluded from the camp and separated from the people of Israel; the spiritual meaning of this is very obvious. Such a person dared not approach the sanctuary even at a distance; by which we may be reminded of the sentence of the Judge, "Depart from me, ye cursed, I know you not." But if a kind of white leprosy covered the whole man, from the crown of the head to the sole of the foot, then, singularly enough, the priest pronounced the leper clean (Lev. 13:13). So "where sin hath abounded, grace did much more abound!" If, however, the smallest appearances of ulcer or raw flesh was discoverable, there was no hope of being pronounced clean (Lev. 13:14,15). Thus, as long as the life of any one besetting sin is allowed to rankle, the spiritual leper is not likely to have it pronounced by our eternal High Priest, "Go thy way, thy sins are forgiven thee."

When any Israelite leper was cured by extraordinary divine interposition (for it does not appear that a cure of this disease was ever wrought in any other way), then was he to show himself to the priest outside the camp; and the latter was to take two birds, alive and clean, and cedar wood, and scarlet and hyssop; and the priest was to command that one of the birds be killed, and the other be dipped in the blood of the slain bird over running water, and then permitted to escape (Lev. 14:2-7). This escaped bird was symbolic of the leper who had been cleansed, who through the death of the former was pronounced free.

The leper was also to be sprinkled seven times with the bunch of hyssop that had been dipped in the blood of the bird that was killed over running water. The meaning of this rite was familiar to David, who, implying that he himself was a spiritual leper, energetically prays, "Purge me with hyssop, and I shall be clean: wash me, and I shall be whiter than snow." The same leper was also, after seven days, to have some of the blood of a sacrificed lamb put upon the tip of the ear, the right hand, and the right foot. The spiritual signification of this was, "Thine ear has not listened aright, thy right hand has been a right hand of iniquity, thy foot hath slipped from the way of life." All required atonement.

The same members were afterward anointed with holy oil, the remnant of which was poured upon the head of the cleansed person, which was symbolic of the Holy Spirit's anointing of the redeemed unto new obedience of life and to the high spiritual privileges of adoption. After the performance of these ceremonies, the sick man was again received into the camp on the attestation of the priest that he was perfectly clean. And although the scales of the leprosy had not entirely disappeared, yet no one might presume any longer to consider him as impure whom the priest had pronounced clean. The consolatory nature of this latter ordinance is too evident through its thin and transparent veil to require any further explanation.

The above ceremonies, however, were not resorted to in the cure of Naaman. As a heathen, he was not amenable to this peculiar law of Israel, and the Lord could dispense with His own Levitical institutions whenever it seemed good in His sight. Nevertheless, the command given to Naaman, with respect to seven times in the matter of washing in Jordan, accorded with the sprinkling of the Israelite leper *seven times*; and even the *dispensing with* all other Levitical ceremonies in *Naaman's* case had a meaning in it.

How His Disease Was Healed

II. It is easy to imagine Naaman's agitation of hope and fear, when, separating from his attendants, he descended alone to the bank of the river and dipped his feet in Jordan. It was an eventful moment. The question at issue was whether Jehovah was the true God or not; whether Elisha was His true prophet or not; whether Canaan was the land of His people or not; and whether the stranger was to raise to Jehovah a song of praise or to return to the heathen world, there to disparage and insult His name. Could anyone of all his train have been entirely insensible to the importance of that moment? Would not a deep and anxious silence prevail among them when their master entered the river and commenced the experiment; when he dipped once, but without effect; a second time, and the leprosy was not departed; again, and again, and again, but the result was the same? Still he was not disheartened, for the prophet had prescribed "seven times." The sixth time was at length completed, and now he prepares for the last trial, the one on which all depends. What must have been his feelings! Did he not hesitate to make the seventh plunge? It was the last resort; a thing which none are willing to essay because, should it fail to answer expectation and hope, it brings forth despair.

Imagine Naaman's reflections on this occasion: "If the waters now refuse their aid, Woe is me! my fate is decided, my hope expires, my death is certain! Yet, here I cannot remain, for the prophet said, Wash seven times. Well then, once more, in the name of God and of the prophet!" And now he dips again beneath the flood. An anxious murmur runs through the attendant assembly. "Now we shall see," they observe to each other; "now is the moment come." Naaman would doubtless remain under the water as long as his breath permitted him; and, while there, with what anxiety would he look for once to the God of Israel's help and from his heart implore, "O Jehovah, God of Israel, help; and if thou art He, now show thyself; heal a wretched leper; in pity, in mercy heal him!" Surely his very soul would thus cry; and what was the result? "Before they call I will answer."

While yet under the water he might have been conscious of a change, yes, of a surprising vigor infused into his limbs, of new life streaming through every vein, and of a joyful feeling beyond even that of returning health. In a paroxysm of transcendent delight he rises out of the water, and a burst of acclamation greets him from the shore. For lo, he is healed! Oh, unheard of occurrence! Who among them had ever witnessed such a sight as this; the leprosy suddenly departed from their master; his countenance glowing, and his eyes glistening with the brightness, and vigor, and cheerfulness of youth; his scaly covering left beneath the flood, and his wasted flesh again restored, fresh and healthy like that of a little child, and pure from the crown of the head to the sole of the foot! Oh, what a solemn and joyous moment! Enough to call forth the feeling from every heart, "How awful is this place!" Enough to extort from everyone the confession of astonishment, "Here is more than Baal and his priests!" Enough to constrain all to admit, "The Lord, he is the God! the Lord, he is the God!" The scene of Mount Carmel was here renewed, but it smiled with evangelical glory.

Now view the waters of Jordan as typical of the blood of Christ, and you may discern a process which must be repeated on all of us. In this healing and miraculous flood, we must all bathe or die and perish in our sins. In the cleansing and atoning efficacy of that precious blood, we behold the last, the only resource for sinful man. Why then do we neglect to apply in earnest to this fountain of living waters? Why accumulate vows and resolutions of self-amendment, only to break them? Why drudgingly follow a self-righteous course of action, which, after all, is but a shining impurity? God invites and commands us to approach Him, to draw nigh unto Him with implicit faith in the blood of His Son. To this we must conform with all our heart and soul, or we are accounted rebels whatever may be our supposed excellence. Till then, we must not think that we are obeying the will of God. We are leprous in His sight; and thus we must feel our absolute need of that cleansing from all sin, which is by the blood of Jesus Christ alone, and by none of our own deservings. We must be fully conscious of our own unworthiness and give ear to the word which commends Christ to us as our wisdom, righteousness, sanctification, and redemption.

The lily is not the less beautiful for being decorated by the hand of God Himself nor is the person who is restored to health censurable for ascribing it all to God. He alone is the health of our countenance, and our salvation is of Him through Jesus Christ alone; and those only who thankfully and obediently recognize this are the true subjects of God and of His dispensations. Believe then, and acquiesce in the declarations of His word, "Without me ye can do nothing"; and again, "For by one offering He hath perfected forever them that are sanctified"; and again, "There is therefore now no condemnation to them which are in Christ Jesus"; and again, He bore "our sins in his own body on the tree," and blotted out "the handwriting that was against us"; and again, "Ye are clean through the word which I have spoken unto you: abide in me, and I in you"; and again, "By him all that believe are justified"; and again, "God hath made him to be sin for us, who knew no sin; that we might be made the righteousness of God in him!"

Let us submit to the gospel of the blessed God. Let us renounce self, whether it be our own supposed powers of reasoning, our own opinions, or self-righteous efforts; and rendering due honor to Almighty God, His will, and arrangements, let us esteem that heavenly wisdom which by this vain world is accounted foolishness, as infinitely superior to all human wisdom and human excellence. Is not such an estimation perfectly correct? For if the Bible be the Word of God, as it assuredly is, then implicit submission is due to its every dictate; and it enjoins us to wash in the blood of Christ, to bathe really and truly in it, to let our every hope be derived from it, and this that we may be saved. If we refuse, then we must abide by the two tables of that law, which, however we may expect to work our commendation, works wrath. We shall certainly obtain no justification from the law of Moses. It will surely judge and condemn us, as men uncircumcised in heart.

Naaman, who must have been now transported with delight from his miraculous cure, might well congratulate himself upon having renounced his own notions in time, and submitted to the seemingly absurd directions of Elisha. Yes, and if he could now appear in the midst of ourselves, how animating would be his address to every doubting, hesitating, self-righteous person among us! "Children," he would say, "trust in Jehovah's word. It is a rock. Judge not of His counsel by the opinions of men. Follow it fully and implicitly, and let experience tell the result. Whatever He commands and ordains, perform it and submit to it with all humility of mind, with all simplicity, and without dispute. Does what He has prescribed appear too easy? Why should you desire difficulty? Does it appear too simple? Why should human arts be employed? Does it appear dangerous? The responsibility is His. Does He counsel you to a simple method whereby you may become enlightened, and clear-sighted, and healthy, and clothed, and in your right mind, and rich, and free, and triumphant, and righteous, without spot and without fault before his throne? Enter then in at this strait gate, by believing 'on Him who justifieth the ungodly.'" Does not Naaman know these things *now*? And would he not, were it possible, thus plead with you?

But let us still consider him as he came up out of the water. What a miracle of sudden renewal does he stand on the shore! Surely here is a renewal of *mind* as well as of health. The benighted heathen, the blind worldling, the hitherto unsubdued and guilty hunter of men, now looks like an Israelite, an humble Israelite, a servant of Jehovah the living and true God. And, if we are right in such a conclusion, on what foundation then was it that this change rested? Certainly on no other foundation than the atonement of the Lamb slain in the purposes of God before all time. Without this there had been no cleansing in Jordan. In whatever way the healing power of God displays itself among men, the atonement of our Surety alone is its instrument. Indeed this keeps down sin from breaking out into a flame which would consume the world.

How Naaman really acted when he came up out of the water we are not informed; but we think we behold the deeply agitated man as he approaches the land bending almost to the ground in lowly adoration, throwing himself silently upon the earth, and devoutly kissing the sacred soil with tears of gratitude to God. His feelings must have been too strong for utterance. "O what a God you are!" must surely have been the language of his soul; and who among us can refrain from joining in such an exclamation?

Review, for a moment, the whole guidance of this stranger and then judge if any providential guidance of man has ever appeared more beautifully connected or more wisely concerted. It was necessary that Naaman should first resort to all human remedies and prove them worthless. He was directed to Israel, not by any dictate of science, but by the simple word of a captive child in slavery. He had witnessed the royal and idolatrous Jehoram rending his garments in despair of helping him and had heard him acknowledge that God alone could cure a man of his leprosy. He had to experience self-humiliation at the prophet's door and there to receive advice which his natural and proud, reasoning heart would reject as foolishness so as to see no alternative left but that of returning home to die of his disease. And now, at the very moment when his spiritual leprosy exhibited itself in a most dreadful eruption, when his intemperate rage boiled within him, ready to rave against Jehovah and His anointed prophet; when he was, perhaps, on the point of swearing irreconcilable hatred to the God, the religion, and the land of Israel; precisely then did the moment of his recovery arrive. For by all this had a way been prepared for the healing of his body and, as we may trust, of his soul also. For everything had been so ordered, that after his cleansing, it would hardly be possible for him to avoid making two reflections: the one, "It is Jehovah, the God of Israel, who has healed me"; the other, "He has healed me, an unworthy, miserable sinner, by the purest mercy."

Let us then suppose the happy man prostrate in the dust, perfectly restored, his spirit filled with contrition and adoring gratitude. And may we not suppose that the attendants likewise were so affected by this glorious manifestation of the living God that they could not refrain from bowing the knee before Him? Surely the silent bank of the Jordan now presented a scene sufficient to make its very waves to leap once more at the name of the Rock of Israel and to draw down the adoring attention of the angels of God.

Naaman, having probably rendered his first tribute of homage to the God of Israel, arises from the dust, changes his dress, springs into his chariot with youthful alacrity and, after turning in amazement once more toward the river with his heart gratefully raised to the God of his health, gives commandment to return back to Jericho. "Back to Jericho!" is the joyful exclamation, and forthwith the whole company moves forward. A finer triumphal procession had seldom been witnessed in Israel. It is indeed not Naaman's, but God's. Naaman is but the mirror in which the glory of Jehovah's mercy was reflected, a living epistle to proclaim the triumphant kindness and love of God. Such was Naaman now, and such was he desirous of proving himself. Therefore he seats himself as conspicuously as possible and seems to say, "Read in my very countenance, in the soundness of my flesh, and in the cheerfulness of my looks, the truth that Jehovah is merciful and gracious, long-suffering, plenteous in goodness and truth, keeping mercy for thousands. And what, indeed, must have been his feelings? He has entered upon a new world; a new life is opened to him. His dungeon walls of ancient darkness have fallen down, and the empire of truth has opened to him its pearly gates. He has found the living God. He has been visited with the benign light of his countenance. And what a fund of inexhaustible treasure did he find in finding God! This was to find eternity in time and a heaven in the valley of the shadow of death; to find old things passed away, and all things become new.

Surely we may contemplate his altered condition with spiritual joy. Its aspect is now evangelical and like a well-filled leaf from the book of life. From devout attention to it we may learn more than from all the volumes of the learned of this world. In it we may see the question of the existence of a living God decided by a most convincing demonstration; every doubt removed as to His special interposition in human concerns; the free and gracious exercise of His Fatherly mercy together with the creative power of His renovating Spirit gloriously acting upon our fallen humanity. But this is not all that is here presented to our notice. For we behold, moreover, in the divine seal thus again set to the prophetic credentials of Elisha, a substantial Amen to all the promises of God, proclaiming to sinners His willingness and power to save and to grant to the "Gentiles also repentance unto life."

Every other instance of redeeming mercy is, like that of Naaman, a living monument thickly covered with the words of sacred writ. The stars in the heavens, the flowers of the field, the birds of the air are all epistles of God, sententious sentences. But every regenerated person is a "living epistle," often indeed despised of some, but "known and read of all men," and rich in meaning. For the renovation of a sinner as a new creation in Christ Jesus testifies more of God than all creation besides; it is an exhibition of the crowning work of God and a strong evidence of the truth of His written Word. Let those who wish to find health and peace in this world seek it here.

15

The Decision

"Make thee an ark of gopher wood; and come thou and all thy house into it, that thou mayest live!" Thus the Lord spoke unto Noah, His friend. And Noah conferred not with flesh and blood; but, submitting his reason to the word of the Lord and disregarding the sneers of an unbelieving world, he immediately began to build the marvelous vessel; and by this implicit subjection he glorified God.

A fearful judgment was approaching. A flood that should deride the strongest barriers and whose waves should overtop the highest mountains was appointed to destroy all flesh from off the face of the earth. What a prospect was this for the children of Adam! But do not be deceived; the same wrath that called forth these destructive waters still burns against all who are not born of God; and, by means of death, it daily sweeps its victims down to hell. Do you desire to provide yourselves a vessel against this time of need? O build it not of your virtues and good works! The justice of the Eternal is a sharp rock against which your bark will be dashed into a thousand pieces. To the Ark, then, my brethren! To the Ark, all who love their souls!

To the Ark? Yes, for there is one also provided for us. Look toward Bethlehem. There you behold it, as it were, lying still upon the land; but it will soon be afloat, and it is destined to enjoy but little pleasant weather. We shall see it contending with the winds and with the waves amid whirlpools and rocks. Storms will beat upon it, and the billows of ignominy and persecution will roll over it. Yes, we shall even see it sinking in a bloody sea of death, but it will soon rise again to display the flag of victory and to steer under full sail into the harbor of eternal rest. Do you ask, For what end is this per-

ilous voyage? Behold the ark of Noah! Neither does it remain on the
land, but it is launched forth upon the stormy billows. And for what
end but to preserve Noah and his family? For a similar purpose,
Christ, the living Ark, is exposed to the surges of divine wrath
against sin, and thus He becomes the Ark of salvation to all who
flee to Him for safety.

As Noah's ark lay upon the land, it was to all who beheld it a
prophetic intimation of danger. When the engines rattle through our
streets we know there is fire. When the people hasten to the
embankments with their barrows and their spades, no one doubts but
that an inundation is threatened. When a king raises an army, estab-
lishes military posts, and causes fortifications to be erected, we need
not be informed that the state is in danger. And when the
Almighty Himself sends for the preservation of the world not a
prophet or an angel but His only begotten Son, what are we to think?
How great must be the impending danger which requires such an
arrangement for its removal! Yes, the very appearance of Jesus in the
world is the most powerful sermon on the lost state of man that was
ever delivered. The cross, the wonderful sign of our redemption,
admonishes us more awfully than any other thing can possibly do of
the depth of that abyss of ruin into which we are sunk by nature.

When the ark was completed, the fountains of the great deep were
broken up, and the windows of heaven opened; and Noah entered
the ark, as the Lord his God had commanded him. The entrance into
the real ark takes place under similar circumstances. The waters must
first rise. Till the floods wash their feet, and the fountain of their tears
is opened, none will enter it. First feel the wrath; then escape the
curse. First experience the pain of sin; then seek refuge in the grace
of Christ. Such is the prescribed order.

Do you now inquire what it is to enter Christ the Ark? I reply first,
that we do so as often as with the eye of faith we realize the fullness
of those blessings which are treasured up in Him; we enter Him with
prayer when we solicit of Him any peculiar blessing, as did the leper
when he besought Him "to make him clean." But merely thus to
enter Him is not to eternal salvation. The entrance into Him, which,
like the entrance of Noah into the ark, is in consequence of our perceiving no escape in time or eternity from the coming wrath due to
sin except in His wounds; the entrance of our very souls into Him as
our Surety, depending on His atoning sacrifice, with all the hope and

earnest desire of a soul thirsting for mercy; this, this is the only right and saving entrance into the Ark.

When Noah had entered, "the Lord shut him in." This, in a spiritual sense, does not always take place immediately. With many who have thrown themselves into the arms of Jesus, the door remains long open, that with sorrow and anguish they may review the dreary waste of their past lives. But before they are aware, the Lord likewise shuts them in. The alarming prospect behind them is suddenly hidden from their view; the mountains of their iniquities are swept away by a mighty hand. They know themselves to be in a state of grace; that all is atoned for, pardoned, and forgotten.

When the Lord had shut in Noah, he was at once cut off from a wicked world. Yes, if Jesus frees us from the world, we are then free indeed. It may be possible personally to withdraw ourselves from the world, while the heart we cannot withdraw. But when Jesus has shut us in, then we are effectually shut in and are inwardly separated from the world. Were it possible for us then to desire a return to its practices, still we should find the return itself impossible, we should feel as if surrounded with closed gates and impassable barriers.

The Lord shut Noah in. Noah was then removed from the sight of those who remained outside. And thus it is with all who enter the true Ark. The world knows them no more. As to their spiritual life and experience, they travel *incognito*. Their "life is hid with Christ in God." But of how little importance is it to their own absolute safety and well being, whether the world be able to comprehend and rightly to estimate them or not! They are satisfied that "the Lord knoweth them that are his." They know that the Lord views them with complacency and love. What can they desire more!

"The Lord shut him in." Noah was then concealed. The waves did not come near him, and he was perfectly secure from falling into the floods. In the same manner are all shut in who are in Christ. "My sheep," saith the Lord, "shall never perish, neither shall any man pluck them out of my hand. My Father, who gave them me, is greater than all; and no man is able to pluck them out of my Father's hand."

When Noah was shut in, the ark went upon the face of the waters; and the waters increased, and bare up the ark, and it was lifted up above the earth. How frequently may it have been exposed to rocks and whirlpools! How often may the billows have rolled over it, threatening its destruction! But what then? Our voyager was in perfect safety. Amid the most tempestuous seas, he found himself secure in his floating castle.

Thus let us confidently steer through the ocean of life. Are we in Christ, the true Ark? Let the tempest roar, yet we are sheltered. Though the waves of temptation and sorrow roll over us, we need not fear. Should some violent concussion dislodge us from our seat or from our couch, we shall not sink into the flood, we are still secure in the Ark; we shall continue in it till the day of our landing, till we cast anchor on Mount Ararat and enjoy the rest of an eternal Sabbath. Happy voyager, continue your course in peace, and let the promises be to you as the olive leaf in the mouth of the dove! Behold Naaman, likewise, now appears to go into the Ark. Come, let us rejoice with him and congratulate him on such an entrance into peace.

2 Kings 5:15,16

> And he returned to the man of God, he and all his company, and came, and stood before him; and he said, Behold, now I know that there is no God in all the earth, but in Israel; now, therefore, I pray thee, take a blessing from thy servant. But he said, As the Lord liveth, before whom I stand, I will receive none. And he urged him to take it; but he refused.

The miracle of healing has been accomplished, and we have seen the happy man come forth from the waters of Jordan, renovated in bodily health and, we trust, renewed in the spirit of his mind. Let us, therefore, now attempt to gather a few flowers from the garden of this new creation. Its gate is thrown wide open, and every obstacle is removed. We shall first consider Naaman's frank confession of belief in the only true God, and then the grateful offer which he tendered to Elisha the prophet; and may the blessing of the Lord rest upon our present meditations, that they may prove a means of sacred refreshment and strength!

Naaman's Confession

I. Three remarkable transformations are presented to us in the kingdom of nature. The first, when a seed, which dies on being cast into the earth, reappears in all the splendor of foliage and of blossom. The second, when under the quickening warmth of a feathery covering, life is generated in an egg, and a bird breaks through the shell. The third, when a creeping caterpillar is transformed into a butterfly, gaily sporting on brilliant and delicately formed wings.

Three similar transformations, though far more sublime and wonderful, are observable in the kingdom of grace. The first is an invisible one, when in the process of justification, a sinner is instantaneously changed into a saint of God. The second, when, in regeneration, the Almighty a second time exercises His creative power and breathes new life into one who is spiritually dead. The third, when, in the moment of glorification, the weary pilgrim lays aside his cumbrous earthly mantle and, beautiful as an angel, is translated to the company of the just made perfect. The first two of these transformations Naaman, we may hope, had already undergone; and if so, what he is now before God, faith alone can estimate. But the personal change which he has experienced on earth is visible to all, as visible as a city set upon a hill or as a burning and elevated beacon.

Naaman, with his company, arrives again at Jericho. Interrupted by the press of the astonished multitude, the procession advances slowly through the streets, a triumphal procession and to the honor of Jehovah, who leads His healed captive in triumph and "makes a show openly" of the spoil which with a single stroke of His sword He has rescued from the hands of Satan. What is there then so remarkable in this man? Much that is beautiful and gratifying. With what a delightful train is he returned! He is conducted from Jordan by the living God. Angels attend him with their joy; peace, bearing the palm, is seated on his right hand; and hope, with blissful vision, on his left. How matchless the adorning in which he shines! His renovated body, cleansed by the hand of the Almighty Himself. His soul washed in the pardoning grace of God and attired in the righteousness of the Fairest of the souls of men! What light, joy, and love appear to have taken possession of his soul! Surely no seeker of goodly pearls ever rose from the deep laden with so rich a treasure; he appears to have found a pearl of inestimable worth; and if his soul has indeed found it, he shall know its value to all eternity. With thrilling emotion he commands, for the second time, a halt before Elisha's cottage; and a scene presents itself which must complete our admiration of the change which Naaman has undergone. He is no more the proud courtier whom Elisha's reserve had so much offended. The lion is changed into the lamb. As a man of really humble spirit, he now alights from his chariot to hasten into the cottage and to assure the prophet, in person, of his most devoted attachment.

That perverse heathenish temper with its exclamation, "Behold, I thought," he has left behind him, as if he had buried it in the stream of Jordan; and the temper of an enlightened man of God now appears in its place; the temper of one who knows how to approve things that are excellent and to value what is truly divine. The form of the turbulent warrior, swelling with rage and displeasure, is no more seen; but a being, peaceful and gentle as a dove, seems to have sprung from its ashes. The vain, deluded mortal, to whom the prescription of the prophet, "Go, wash in Jordan seven times," seemed but as mockery and absurdity, has disappeared from the scene, and we welcome in his place the appearance of a child of light, animated with living faith in the assurance that Jehovah is "glorious in all his works and holy in all his ways."

Naaman was about to enter the cottage when Elisha doubtless advanced to meet him with the most cordial and vivid congratulations. What overflowings of brotherly love and elevated joy must have met together from their united hearts! What fervent praise must have ascended like clouds of incense from these two living altars to the throne of Jehovah! Overpowered surely with deep emotion, Naaman now stood before Elisha, while we seem to see the holy prophet silently overjoyed and lifting up his heart in thankfulness to God. The happy stranger then breaks the silence and pours forth an ingenuous confession which we admire for its glorious import and for the energetic decision with which it was uttered. "Behold, now I know that there is no God in all the earth, but in Israel." And this is spoken by the man who only a few hours before was evincing the most deplorable blindness of heart. But the satanic delusion is dispelled, the charm is broken, the captive liberated. A new creation stands before us in unveiled beauty.

His confession is nothing less than an irrevocable renunciation of the service of idols; it is an eternal and joyous renunciation of the kingdom of darkness; the animating war-cry with which he joins the standard of Zion, and the first token of homage and devotion which he presents on the altar of Jehovah. By the declaration he has made, he virtually denounces as slaves of falsehood all who cleave to any other god than the God of Israel. Hereby he casts from him the religion of his nation as a tissue of errors. How his attendants may like it, Naaman is perfectly unconcerned. He persists in the declaration he has made, "There is no God in all the earth, but in Israel." And this confession is eternally true, if by Israel *we* understand the people who, confiding in "the sure word of prophecy," press through the strait gate of humiliation for sin into the blood-sprinkled sanctuary of the New Testament. Here only, and nowhere else, is God known, experienced, and felt. Here only does He come forth from His inaccessible light, and the heavenly hosts exultingly exclaim, "Behold the tabernacle of God is with men!" Here only do we perceive the sound of His footsteps, the light of His countenance, the words of His mouth. This is Jerusalem, this the temple, this the ark of the covenant!

The rationalist, the deist, the infidel have *their own* notions of God; but they have no God, no living God, known to *them*. In their retirement they are lonely indeed. Of a Friend in solitude they know nothing; nothing of a heart open to their griefs; and their spirit within them is as desolate as their closet. Alas! how gloomy is *their* world, uncheered by a single ray of divine consolation, destitute of all experience of heavenly superintendence, and only wildly and confusedly pervaded by the flitting fires of passion and fleshly imagination!

Destitute and forlorn is their whole existence. They discern no Jacob's ladder reaching up to heaven; strange to them are the scenes of Horeb and of Tabor. They are never conscious of the footsteps of an invisible Being at their side; and "guidance," "visitation," and "bowing down the ear" are to them words without sense or meaning. Yes, what John says is indeed true; "Whosoever abideth not in the doctrine of Christ hath not God." "There is no God in all the earth, but in Israel!" "Happy are you, O Israel; who is like unto you, O people saved by the Lord!"

The happiest persons on earth, indeed the only happy ones, are those who are in Christ Jesus, who "walk not after the flesh, but after the Spirit." They are also the most important and the most mysterious phenomena under heaven. Their exterior, it is true, indicates little or nothing of such importance. What chiefly distinguishes them from others is "that life of God" from which they are no longer "alienated" like the rest of the world. They are "born from above"; they are "begotten of God"; they are "a chosen generation, a royal priesthood, an holy nation, a peculiar people." They may be "poor in this world," but they are "rich in faith, and heirs of the kingdom" of the Lord of sabaoth. Their "conversation is in heaven," their treasure is there, and their heart is there. They "were by nature children of wrath even as others" but they "are washed, sanctified, justified, in the name of the Lord Jesus, and by the Spirit of our God." Who shall lay anything to their charge? It is God who justifies them; it is Christ who makes intercession for them. Who shall separate them from the love of Christ? "Neither death, nor life, nor things present, nor things to come, shall be able to separate them from the love of God, which is in Christ Jesus, our Lord."

Such is their character. "Ungodly and sinners" as they have been, "the righteousness of God" is not in the least offended by their justification and glorification. Where their "sin abounded, grace has much more abounded, that "as sin reigned unto death, even so might grace reign through righteousness unto eternal life by Jesus Christ our Lord." For the righteousness of their divine Mediator and Advocate is imputed to them, and by Him has their perfect "ransom" been "found." Hence God, the "just God and the Savior," "spares them, as a man spareth his own son that serveth him." He not only spares them, but "loves them with an everlasting love."

And what does the Scripture say respecting their outward condition while they remain in this world? They "have the promise of the life that now is, as well as of that which is to come." "The Lord provides" for them. "He is their Shepherd," and they "shall not want." "Bread shall be given them; their waters shall be sure." They "have all and abound"; they "learn in whatsoever state they are, therewith to be content." They are bidden and privileged to cast all their care on Him who cares for them, and who, to the promise that He will "never leave nor forsake them," adds, that "all things work together for their good" so that no one shall really "harm them, as being followers of that which is good." Temptations and tribulations may await them, but over these they are more than conquerors. They may not always meet with what they would naturally wish, but it shall be always what they shall sooner or later have to be thankful for; inasmuch as He, "with whom all things are possible," can overrule every such thing into a blessing; and "He is faithful, who also will do it." Whoever, therefore, is a real Christian, and yet doubts concerning such things, does not understand His own mercies. Therefore "let the righteous be glad and rejoice" before God; for it is written, "Such honor have all his saints."

But to return to Naaman. "Behold, now I know," he exultingly exclaims, "there is no God in all the earth, but in Israel." He is now fully confident that Jehovah lives; for he has the seal of this truth in his miraculous cleansing and in his conscience. Here is knowledge based on experience; and it is only in experience that faith grows and flourishes. Faith, indeed, "cometh by hearing"; but this is something more than that of the outward ear or even of the intellect. As long as it proceeds merely upon the report of men and books, it is but a sickly and unfruitful plant, unworthy of the name of faith. It is only by striking its root into the experience of God's power and presence and into the palpable demonstrations of grace, that it amounts to "the victory which overcometh the world."

Such is "the confidence and joy of faith" with which St. Peter declares, "We have not followed cunningly devised fables, when we made known unto you the power and coming of our Lord Jesus Christ, but were eyewitnesses of his majesty"; and with which St. John also declares, "WE HAVE SEEN HIS GLORY." It is only by virtue of experience analogous to this that our confession of the only true God and of Jesus Christ whom He has sent will endure unto the end, because thus only has our conviction any life, and our confidence any firmness and consistency. It is only thus that we can cheerfully endure afflictions and necessities for Christ's sake, and thus indeed we can do it effectually; for we then believe, though the whole world may deny, because "we have seen his glory"; and hence we only pity the unbelievers who mock and raise objections concerning the living God and concerning "his great love toward us." For then we bear about us the seal "that he is, and that he is the Rewarder of them that diligently seek him." The new heart which He has given us, and the new spirit which He has put within us, the peace of God which passes all understanding and which keeps our hearts and minds through Christ Jesus, will not suffer us to doubt that He hears prayer or to distrust His exceeding great and precious promises.

We have thus "seen his glory," we have thus "heard his voice," we have thus "handled with our hands the Word of life"; and such promises granted us are the focus and fire of our confession of Him before men, serving to establish our hearts in the truth, against the delusions of these antichristian times, and to nerve our arm unto holding up against every assault the impenetrable shield of faith.

It is only this demonstration of the Spirit and of power that can bear us safely along through every storm of the present mortal life. The mettle of mere accidental excitement and the outworks of cold calculating intellect are alike inadequate; and the adversary laughs at these as things from which he has nothing to fear. But that spiritual shout of triumph, "We have seen His glory," makes him tremble; for it is the signal of his becoming "bruised under our feet shortly."

His Offer to Elisha

II. Naaman, in having thus made his courageous and decided confession, is disposed to follow it up, as soon as possible, with some substantial proof of its sincerity. "Now, therefore, I pray thee," he exclaims, "accept a blessing of thy servant." He would at once make him a present of gold, or silver, or valuable raiment. He evidently did not intend it as pay or remuneration, but only wished to express his heartfelt gratitude by something more than words; to express his thankfulness to God by honoring a servant of God. That nothing more and nothing less than this was intended by him is evident from considering that a man of his high rank and importance in the world was humble enough to speak of himself as a "servant" to Elisha, and earnestly to beg, as a favor, his acceptance of what he calls "a blessing," by which he means a token of his very best feelings. It is as if he had said, "I am quite aware that no gifts or services of mine can really be wanted by yourself, but if you will accept anything I have to offer, it will gratify me not a little."

Here was no effusion of vain compliment; it was the language of open heartedness and simplicity. And who among us that has ever experienced any mercy from heaven by the instrumentality of God's servants does not enter into every feeling of Naaman upon this occasion? Who is there on whom the Sun of righteousness has once arisen "with healing in his wings," that can be a stranger to the fervency of spirit that will and must inspire to acts of homage and humiliation, to acts of dedication and self-denial, to acts of gratitude and love; that fervency which at such seasons is kindled in the soul and cannot but break forth into expression and gratification? In such blessed seasons, the love of Christ constraining us, we desire to pour out our all into the treasury of God; and that all, however little, is more valued by Him than the talents of gold which may be otherwise contributed out of men's abundance.

At every such time of love are those deeds performed of which it is written, "Their works do follow them"; though their left hand may not have known what their right hand does, yet as being done unto even one of the least of our poorer brethren, they will be regarded by the Supreme Brother as done unto Himself; and it is He who will recount and recompense every such deed, yes, before men and angels long after it has even been forgotten by the doers themselves. At such seasons as we have referred to, "the fig tree putteth forth her green figs, and the vines with the tender grape give a good smell," though unconscious of the many graces with which they are adorned; and then are the words of the royal psalmist again fulfilled, "I will run the way of thy commandments, when thou shalt enlarge my heart."

Christians resemble those flowers which droop at night and are closed and scentless, but which no sooner feel the first rays of the morning sun, than they again unfold and straighten upward, expanding their refreshed leaves to the light of day and appear again as beautiful altars, spreading around nothing but refreshment and perfume. You cannot, therefore, better provide for your sanctification than by studying to be more deeply immersed in the love of God and more constantly washed by the plentiful dew of His grace. Oh, if but a ray of that love penetrate the heart, how quickly does the desert blossom and the barren land become fruitful! For this reason it is that we so frequently preach to you of all the blessings that are treasured up for you in Christ Jesus. Yes, of a truth, it is with this that the earth must be watered and replenished or with nothing. "Joy in the Lord" is the fructifying fountain of all that is holy and beautiful. Oh, that such a fountain might flow more abundantly among us! If, alas! with reference to this congregation, we must take up the lamentation of one of old, "Help Lord," how is it, that while so much is spoken of spiritual life, there appears so little reality? We explain the afflictive appearance simply by the fact that so many of our brethren, while they know the goodness of the Lord, do not make it their business to taste and inwardly experience it. Were it otherwise, our congregation would be as a garden of lilies, and the smoke of our sacrifices would constantly ascend from our domestic altars.

Elisha, no doubt, felt exquisite gratification at beholding that spiritual gem which was presented to his view in the request, "Now, therefore, I pray thee take a blessing of thy servant." The sight, however, contented him. The proffered gift he declines to accept. "As the Lord liveth, before whom I stand," he replies with serious solemnity, "I will receive none." Naaman urged him to accept it. "Do not imagine," he may have replied, "that I propose to requite Jehovah for his benefits, or that I confound the instrument of my preservation with my Preserver himself. As little do I aspire to confer a benefit on you. On the contrary, you will be conferring one on me by not despising my gift; for my soul swells with the most ardent desire to praise the Lord with heart and hand. Accept then my offering." But Elisha, whose motto was the same as that of the great apostle, "I seek not yours, but you," persists in his refusal. "As the Lord liveth, before whom I stand, I will receive none."

His motive for rejecting the gift is easily perceptible. All things must conspire to uphold that important truth, that when Jehovah blesses, grace reigns, and grace alone. It was, therefore, the honor of Jehovah that, in this instance likewise, determined the conduct of the prophet. It was that it might not be said in Syria that the gifts of God can be purchased with money, or that He had respect of persons. This fully accounts for the solemnity of that decisive answer, "As the Lord liveth, before whom I stand, I will receive none." The honor of Jehovah was ever the first object of these servants of the Most High. This elevated principle gave to their whole deportment that wonderful dignity which inspires us with a veneration for them as for beings of a superior order and taught them, under all circumstances, that holy tact which they always exhibited as the agents and ministers of Jehovah.

Elisha was poor, the sons of the prophets no less so. Another person in Elisha's place might have thought Naaman's present most seasonable and might have imagined that God had designed it as a provision for him and for those about him. And his joy at this accession of temporal aid might so have clouded his judgment that no room would have been left for the higher consideration, whether the honor of Jehovah might not rather require its rejection than its acceptance. But Elisha was not so anxiously concerned for his external welfare as that the prospect of temporal comfort should make him indifferent to every other sentiment but that of extravagant joy at blessings of this sort. The conviction that He who feeds the sparrows and clothes the lilies would not suffer him to want was too habitual to his mind for the occurrence of such divine interpositions in times of need to excite in him even the smallest emotion of surprise. With a free and unembarrassed mind he could look beyond the temporal blessings that flowed to him; and, whenever he deemed it advisable, it was an easy thing to him to subordinate all temporal advantage to higher considerations; yes, he could joyfully sacrifice it when possessed, for he had certain assurance that some better provision would be made for him.

Oh, may the Lord raise us to so expansive, free, and cheerful an eminence! May He impart to us such large and comprehensive views! May He refine our sentiments to the same holy sensibility! May He more and more strip the budding blossom of spiritual life within us of its heavy fleshly covering! The new man unencumbered is the most beautiful object that can be seen beneath the sun. How can it be otherwise! It is created after God and of God and is the express image of Christ—the image of the sun in a dewdrop of the dawn; only it is a living image; an image which has become a being. Christ in us! God glorified in a worm!

16

A Flower of Sincerity

The words in the epistle to the Hebrews are familiar to us "Whose voice then shook the earth: but now he hath promised, saying, Yet once more I shake not the earth only, but also heaven. And this word, Yet once more, signifieth the removing of those things that are shaken, as of things that are made, that those things which cannot be shaken may remain. Wherefore we receiving a kingdom which cannot be moved, let us have grace, whereby we may serve God acceptably with reverence and godly fear" (Heb. 12:26-28). Words deep as the ocean; who shall fathom them? It is in vain to cast the lead. But let us attempt to dive near the shore, that we may obtain at least a handful of pearls.

The apostle in the above passage reminds the brethren that they have passed from the economy of Sinai and have entered upon that of the New Testament. He combines with this remembrance a solemn warning, that rejection of the gospel of grace is even more reprehensible than the transgression of Moses' law. He further reminds them that the voice of the Son of God shook the earth at the giving of the law, and that a thousand years afterward the Lord spoke by Haggai, "Yet once more, it is a little while, and I will shake not the earth only, but also heaven." These prophetic words had reference to the days of the new covenant and began to be accomplished at its establishment in Christ.

All history points out the nature of the agitation which since that time has pervaded mankind. The sound of the gospel goes out in all lands, and wherever it is heard, there revolution, agitation, and commotions arise. Sleeping lions are roused from their lairs and show their teeth; children of darkness become light and cry, Hosanna!

Ancient prejudices, rites, and customs suddenly or gradually disappear and are succeeded by a new order of things. Whole communities undergo an inward and outward transformation. Laws, constitutions, and civil ordinances are slowly but irresistibly buried in the vortex of change. Institutions of charity, till then unknown, spring vigorously from nothing. Entire new creations start into existence as by enchantment in spite of the opposition of raging enemies. Agitations of a thousand kinds are felt everywhere. Yes, wherever the gospel has penetrated, agitation has succeeded, and it continues the same to this hour. This agitation, which commenced in the world with the entrance of Christ's kingdom, is not restricted to the earth. "The heavens" are likewise "shaken."

What a movement was there when the Eternal Son prepared to assume the disguise of human flesh, and wondering angels flew down to soothe His infant slumbers! What agitation when He, who is the Life itself, endured a bloody death! What a commotion of joy upon His priestly entrance into the heavenly sanctuary with the pardoned malefactor at His side! What a movement at the introduction of so many children of God to eternal glory!—a movement that will continue till the heavens are possessed by Christ; as Peter says, "Until the times of restitution of all things, which God hath spoken by the mouth of all his holy prophets since the world began." But has Christ not yet possessed Himself of heaven? There is a sense in which He has not fully done it but is still engaged in possessing it. For He and His spiritual members are one; and, till they are all with Him above, His possession of heaven is not complete.

Let us hear the apostle still further. What he chiefly designs to unfold to us in these words we have not yet declared. He points out to us that the communication which the Lord makes by Haggai comprehends more than a simple annunciation of the shaking which should accompany *the entrance* of Christ's kingdom into the world. By these words, "Yet once more I shake not the earth only, but also heaven," the Lord designed to intimate great changes, alterations, and substitutions to be accomplished *in the course of time*. For this word, "Yet once more," says the apostle, "signifies the removing of those things that are shaken, as of things that are made, that those things which cannot be shaken may remain." There is therefore in all the visible world something that is movable, transitory, and subject to change. It comprehends whatever is evanescent in its design as having been called into existence for a certain period and then to pass away in order that only what is unchangeable may last and remain. To these belong, for example, the Levitical types and shadows of the Old Testament which were only intended to continue for a time and then to be annulled. But the Jews in the blindness of their hearts clung to these as though they were immovable; whence arose their unnecessary despair when the fire of dissolution was hurled among them. They had not the faintest conception that what was imperishable was to be sought in the tents of an Abraham, an Isaac, or in the unpretending dwellings of a Simeon, a Zacharias, or a Hannah. They mistook for it that which was splendid to the eye, such as the pomp of the typical priesthood; and when this disappeared together with the temple, their cry was "Ichabod! The glory is departed!" Instead of gladly embracing what was unshaken and immovable, they perished by thousands in vainly anticipating the re-establishment of what was shaken.

To *the perishable* belongs the entire system of this world, glittering and splendid and durable as it may appear. If we open the history of mankind as it lies before us, whither are we conducted? Our footsteps wander over the sites of endless ruined states, extinct princely families, moldered thrones, subverted religious systems, departed glory both spiritual and material. The dust of oblivion covers them, and their place knows them no more.

The chill blasts of desolation play fiercely about us; and at every point in the traces of history the reminiscence meets us, saying, "The things which can be shaken are mutable, and they change; the things which can be moved pass away." This truth, indeed, is legible almost everywhere we look. It is imprinted on the very foundations of the place where we dwell; that itself shall but accomplish the time appointed by God and then cease forever. It is inscribed on the political and civil relations under which we live, for they too belong to this mutable kingdom. It is visible in the pleasant family circle where our happiness centers; here likewise is the flower of the grass. We discern it in our official appointments and in the rank we occupy. Yes, it is written in our own foreheads; for we also belong in part to that which is transient and changeable. Thus everything around us is but as a fleeting shadow. Splendid as any sublunary thing may be, it fulfills but its appointed time; then the whirlwind of desolation sweeps over it and hurries it away.

Nor is the earth itself, nor the heaven with its sun and stars, exempt from this change; the former will be burnt up and renewed, and the latter rolled together as a scroll. How great a folly then is it to allow the affections to rest upon what is perishable! O let us fix our eyes on that which does not perish! Do you ask if there is such a thing? Yes, it exists in the midst of all this change and movement.

If we follow universal history once more over the ruins of past events, we shall perceive in the midst of the general overthrow an appearance that is lasting, which survives all things, which rises uninjured above the tide of every change that threatens its subversion and seems indestructible and eternal. If we look to the beginning of the world, we shall behold it there. If we survey century after century, where does it not meet us? At first we perceive it isolated and confined to one spot of earth. Within the last eighteen hundred years it has pervaded countries, islands, nations. Do you inquire what it is? A temple, a living temple; but one which no Nebuchadnezzar can plunder, into which no soldier of a Titus can throw the torch of destruction. It is a little company of people—a number of quiet, peaceful brethren. We find them with cheerful countenances assembled round a table which first exhibits to us a paschal lamb, then a significant loaf and a cup of blessing. They sing, and hosanna is the burden of their song. One like unto the Son of man stands benignly in the midst of them. He is their delight, their only and entire hope. They bear His cross. Everywhere despised for His sake, they "esteem his reproach greater riches than the treasures of the world." They are indeed in the world but only as quiet pilgrims who are careering through it. They have already cast the anchor of their affections on the opposite shore.

Such a phenomenon upon this earth is, and always has been, the kingdom of grace, invisibly but effectually upheld by the counsels of Eternal Mercy and by the atoning merit of a holy and immaculate Sacrifice. It is that peaceful kingdom of sanctified souls, arrayed in the most costly garments and purified by the Spirit of life, who reckon themselves "dead indeed unto sin, and alive unto God through Jesus Christ our Lord." Verily, this peaceful kingdom with its immunities, possessions, prospects, and customs is the only immovable thing in the present world of change and transformation. It will remain when heaven and earth shall have passed away; neither shall the gates of hell prevail against it. It will remain unchanged in its King, in its institutions, in its individual members; and when it can no longer tarry upon earth, heaven will be open to receive it. It will exist beyond the duration of the universe itself; it will survive all that is visible. Many of the forms, relations, and decorations in which it appears here below are indeed mutable, but the kingdom itself is immutable.

The outward construction of the church is transient as are many of its institutions and regulations; the kingdom itself blooms for eternity, and in eternity it will exist without symbols, catechisms, or any temporal organization. Yes, it will survive the fires of persecution and the general conflagration; it will survive every horror and devastation of death. "Wherefore we receiving a kingdom which cannot be moved, let us have grace," is the exhortation of the apostle. As is the kingdom, so is this order, "Salvation by grace," eternally and unchangeably. Let us not therefore follow the example of some who, after receiving grace, suddenly turn back again upon works; that is, make their peace depend upon the degrees of personal holiness to which they have attained. They misapprehend what is unchangeable, and range it again among the things that are changeable. They misrepresent the kingdom of grace and act as if they would transform it again into a kingdom in which the spirit of bondage, only in a more insidious manner, prevails. In this they act absurdly inasmuch as the kingdom of grace remains the kingdom of grace forever and ever. In eternity, grace alone reigns, has reigned, and will reign. Let us then be careful for one thing only, that the light of grace may shine in us, and let this one thing suffice us.

After the lapse of ages we this day extend the hand of fellowship to a man who appears again a living witness of the unchangeableness of our kingdom—his heart like our heart, his hope like our hope, his state like our state, his faith like our faith. And in the same way in which he was saved, are we saved to the present hour. Naaman found that which is unchangeable in this world of change. Let us rejoice with him and congratulate him on his great attainment.

2 Kings 5:17

> And Naaman said, Shall there not then, I pray thee, be given to thy servant two mules burden of earth? for thy servant will henceforth offer neither burnt offering nor sacrifice unto other gods, but unto the Lord.

The inmost soul of the Syrian appears to display itself to us more and more. Even the lesser chambers of his heart seem open to us.

Generally those who are born again are as enclosed gardens: peering above the walls of which may be just seen here and there the tops of trees, kept in motion by the breezes of heaven. But in the present instance we will think ourselves permitted to *enter* one of such gardens of God and to take a near view of its flowers and pleasant fountains. How delightful to wander in a region so peaceful, as if smiling with the light of paradise; where the discord of human passion is overpowered by the harmony of divine sentiment and emotion; where ardent longing after God, like the thrilling note of the nightingale, bespeaks the arrival of a vernal season of which the world knows nothing; where the fragrant blossoms of pure love betray to us the hand of that Keeper of the garden whose most minute demands are satisfied, when with the "Rabboni" of a Magdalene we cast ourselves at His feet! Naaman's spiritual state of mind, his fixed resolve, and the request put to Elisha are the subjects that will now occupy our attention.

Naaman's State of Mind

I. Naaman's confession has already shown us the character of the man. He appears not to be the creature of fleeting impressions, one whom the arrows of grace have touched obliquely. He decides at once for the Holy One of Israel and acts like a man who is altogether what he professes himself to be. How great a gratification must it have been to Elisha to behold the Gentile so quickly, so thoroughly changed! We may well envy the prophet such a satisfaction, and the more so, considering how rare a sight among us is the fulfillment of the words of the prophet Micah, "They have broken up, and have passed through the gate" (Mic. 2:13). For what a dearth is there of thorough-going and full-grown Christians at present! The generality are too well contented to stop half way. Whether they are indeed children of the Jerusalem which is above or, after all, only children of this world is a doubtful question. Whether they are bondsmen under the law or freed men under the gospel remains all along undecided. If now and then awakenings take place, still it is but by a tedious and precarious process. Though the children seem to come to the birth, still oftentimes, alas too often, there is not strength to bring forth! If we witness an eager rushing toward the kingdom of God, presently there is a dead stop; and after that a listless turning back again to the world. If a new excitement ensues under which men resolve and say, "I will turn unto the Lord," and even put their foot forward to do so, still, still we see not a decided entering into the narrow way.

Profession after profession is made, but there is no decision. Continual signs are given of an intention to cleave to the Lord, but there is no courageous execution of this purpose. There are buds and blossoms occasionally and abundantly put forth, but every time we are about to welcome in the spring with songs of praise, a night-frost destroys all, and the vernal appearances vanish. Sometimes the hope-giving blossom glistens with tears of agitated confession and fervent vows; still it droops and dies, it yields no fruit. An effort is made to rise above the world, but it proves like that of the morning mist around our hills, which being too heavy to soar through the chill air, sinks down into water and mingles with the dust of the cliffs. There is often a fluttering like that of the swallow around the towers of Zion, but how little of that nestling of which the Psalmist speaks; "The sparrow hath found an house, and the swallow a nest for herself, even thy altars, O Lord of hosts."

The principle of Naaman's decision was that he had chosen the Lord, the Lord having first chosen *him*. There is, indeed, a way of choosing the Lord which proceeds only from carnal selfishness. As its impulse is not from God, so it elicits only *human* purposes. Perhaps some of our beloved relatives have been converted, and we do not like to differ from them; we are intimately connected with them, we highly esteem them, or we depend on them, and therefore we will be like them. Perhaps some near and dear friend has entered upon the way of salvation; how, therefore, can we remain behind! Or, we feel the urgency of the times, and therefore we desire to possess a God of help and consolation. We observe how peaceful and happy are the saints of the Lord, and we desire to share in such prosperity.

Now, persons may from such motives seek the kingdom of God; but, "I say unto you many will seek to enter in, and shall not be able." Though they even use prayers, and are constant at their devotions, and have put on a form of godliness like a garment made ready to their hand, still, if there be nothing more, it is all mere mummery. It may be a Christian drama, but it is not Christianity. To seek to apprehend Christ without "giving all diligence" to prove that we are also apprehended by Him, and without giving "all diligence to make our calling and our election sure," is a vain effort that will end in a spirit of bondage as its only reward. As a plant never seeks the light till it has felt its secret influence, so man never vitally seeks Christ till his *whole* soul is attracted by the Spirit of God the Father and of Christ.

The first approach to union with the Lord is made by Himself and not by us. The relation of the needle to the magnet exemplifies the mystery of true conversion. His word, "Arise," must awaken us; His attraction must stir and set us in motion. When once He has apprehended us, as He did Saul going to Damascus, as He did the Samaritan woman when He set before her the mirror of truth, as He did Matthew the publican when the words "Follow me!" penetrating his soul, glowed like fire, and winged him with the speed of a tempest; then a valid connection is established between us and Him, then our approaches are no longer laborious and reluctant; but they prove our entire surrender as if from irresistible necessity, and we seem induced and led on by a holy violence. We feel a new spirit put within us, sweetly constraining, overcoming, and possessing us.

This seems to have been Naaman's condition. The change brought about in his mind was no preconcerted device of his own, but it evidently proceeded altogether from the Lord. He became the Lord's willing captive, and yet, precisely as such, the Lord's free man; a free and royal personage by whom the command to love God is no longer dragged about as a chain, but worn as an ornament and crown. His conduct seems to bespeak that though the Lord should slay him, yet would he trust in Him. His inclination toward Him has become a second nature, like that possessed by an old tree with a new graft. As a mountain stream hurrying down to the ocean allows no impediment to hinder it on its way, so all that is within him seems to fly as on new wings toward Jehovah; and he appears to count it an honor and a happiness, not a constraint, to present whatever he possesses or that the world can yield him as a sacrifice and whole burnt offering to the Lord.

Naaman's Fixed Resolve

II. Naaman's spiritual decision displays itself in a noble confession: "thy servant will henceforth offer neither burnt offering nor sacrifice unto other gods, but unto the Lord." This is his oath of allegiance, his subscription to the covenant now divinely established with him. He styles himself Elisha's "servant." He sees in him the interpreter, the representative and favorite of the Almighty, and this glory now surpasses in his estimation the splendor of royalty and the dignity of princes. He has learned to measure human greatness by a different standard from that by which he had been accustomed to estimate it. He no longer measures by the eye; he has learned to judge spiritually. "Thy servant!" This is spoken in perfect sincerity. Reverence, love, and inward abasement prompted the expression. Whether his attendants would approve this condescension of their master is doubtful; but Naaman is perfectly indifferent about that. Liberated from the insincerity of worldly compliment, he finds within him the elevated disposition of a David before the ark of the covenant. A sneering Michal would receive from his lips likewise the reply, "I will yet be more base in my own eyes, and with the despised in the land shall I be had in honor." "Thy servant," says the Syrian, "will henceforth offer neither burnt offering nor sacrifice unto other gods, but unto the Lord." He will not sacrifice to strange gods. His resolution is made.

This decision of the will is a decision indeed; as that ever must be which is wrought of God. It does not change but is as the Spirit who created it, and this is what constitutes *the man*. Naaman will henceforth not sacrifice to other gods; this is now the will of his soul, of his whole self. His personal self will not participate in the act. The operation of the *divine will* in Christians is what constitutes the Christian *character*, and thus a Christian ceases *from sin*; "he cannot sin because he is born of God" whereas he who is not in Christ can only sin at every step and movement of his life. Nevertheless, even in the regenerate, there is, as we may say, both Christ and antichrist. A regenerated person is the most mysterious phenomenon under heaven, a complex existence indeed. He is continually sensible of "a law in his members, that warreth against the law of his mind." With the law in His members He is, however, at perpetual war; and it often costs Him many a conflict and wound. But His constant aim and endeavor is to "crucify the flesh with its affections and lusts"; and to "put off" even more and more, "as concerning the former conversation, the old man, which is corrupt."

Naaman *wills*. It reminds us of that divine necessity in the Christian which, nevertheless, is personal and perfect freedom, for there is such in every Christian. The *converted* are not machines; they yield, but it is voluntarily to what they feel as a divine necessity laid upon them. They feel it to be their greatest liberty to be acted upon by the Holy Spirit. And now, what is the *natural* man? Is he free? He thinks himself so, but he is blind from his birth. In what delusive liberty is he not tied and bound! He sins, indeed, from no compulsion and yet from the necessity of his nature, just as the Christian is holy from the necessity of his *new* nature, most gladly and willingly. Real liberty in the unconverted man's acceptation of the word has no meaning or else is another name for slavery, however little he may be aware of it. But if in every case subjection to one power or the other is unavoidable, who would not prefer being under the influence of heavenly guidance to being sold under the power of darkness? A *third* spiritual power does not exist.

"Thy servant will." To such a resolve is everyone brought who is effectually called by grace. It is the signal cry of true conversion. Where there has been no ear for it, the great turning point has never been attained. There are, indeed, many among us from whom we may hear expressions like these, "I *desire* to give myself up to the Lord!" "I *hope* some day to do so!" "I *would* do it willingly!" But such mere assertions avail nothing; such impotent resolves will not save from hell. Yet thousands remain satisfied with these alone and spend all their days under the dominion of the power of darkness. "I *desire*," must be changed into "I will"—into a determined, cheerful, ready, comprehensive, energetic, unchangeable, "I will!" "I will!" My family shake their heads; but "I will" be the Lord's. My friends dissuade me; but "I will."

What can my friends do for me in the hour of death and in the day of judgment? The world would daunt me with its ridicule and contempt; but the world passes away and the lust thereof, I care not for such a world: "I will." Many accusations will be made if I suddenly forsake the worldling's haunts and vanities so as to join with heart and hand the people of God; but it matters not; "I will" be the Lord's. "I will," though all the powers of darkness should arm themselves in array against me, or though I should be trampled under foot as the mire of the streets; "I will."

Away, you idols, which I have hitherto served. You vain circles which have hitherto been my delight, adieu! Be accursed, you follies with which I have hitherto squandered my time. I swear unto the Lord my God that I will perform all the statutes of His covenant, and that irrevocably. Yes, my brethren, a resolve no less than this must be begotten in the soul; a purpose, which like a rock against the billows shall withstand every opposition and pretension—an "I will," which like a scythed chariot shall cut right and left and break through everything incompatible with Christ; an "I will," that shall morally re-echo far and near throughout the place where we reside and shall stamp our every action with the impress of its decision.

Yes, until such decision as this has begun to possess *the whole man*, our faith is vain, and our Christianity is but an empty show. O remember this; take notice of it; do not forget it, for any mistake here may be fatal.

Naaman will no longer sacrifice to other gods but to the Lord. We congratulate him on this holy and sacred resolution. O for the formation of the same in all our hearts! For surely no period ever deserved to be styled more idolatrous than the one in which we live. There are three attractive idols which the world principally makes use of whereby to keep its votaries ignorant of the power of real religion. The first is *Temporal Enjoyment*. Robed in the gaudy attire of the pleasures of sense, this idol exercises a magical sway over young and old of every rank. Thousands quench entirely for its sake the last departing gleam of soberness of mind and give up the very wish of immortality. An hourly succession of either sensual or sensible enjoyments is all that their refined materialism desires or pretends to desire.

The second of these idols is the phantom of *Political Liberty*. The imagined coming of its reign is a kind of *millennium* looked for by this present world. This idol absorbs in the minds of thousands every essential interest and, by its deceptive and dazzling influence, amuses the multitude farther and farther away from the one thing needful, beckoning the whole world to seek its *regeneration* and *salvation* in institutions which past experience has long since condemned as delusive swamp or at best as wells without water.

The third idol before which this infatuated age is seen to bow is the false illumination of unsanctified *Human Intellect*, yes, of genius, of exuberant wit, or of the creative power of thought however much these talents are devoted to the worst of purposes. Admiration of this or that splendidly gifted poet or philosopher has risen almost to *religious* devotion. To be captivated by the writings of some master-spirit, a Goëthe, for instance, or a Hegel, is now avowed to be the meridian and highest pitch of cultivation.

Men consciously or unconsciously worship in the pantheon of literary heroes, and many scruple not to acknowledge that they do so. Corrupt as we know the natural mind of fallen man to be, they are absurd enough to speak of it as if it were (to use their own words) "*a portion* of the Divinity"; yes, as if it deserved a kind of devotional regard, it only sparkles with those earthly radiances which they idolize. One step further, and the abomination of the antichristian period will have attained its complete development. May the Lord look down in mercy and dissolve the fascination, wherever it has gained ground among us, and thus preserve our feet from the snare of the devil! May Naaman's watchword become our *received* and *popular* warning against "destruction and misery": "No other gods; the LORD alone!"

Naaman's Request of Elisha

III. To the frank *confession* he has made, Naaman unites a peculiar *request*. When Elisha had declined his gift, the Syrian solicits from him a present for himself: "Shall there not then, I pray thee, be given to thy servant two mules' burden of earth? for thy servant will henceforth offer neither burnt-offering nor sacrifice unto other gods, but unto THE LORD!" This request may appear surprising and cast a doubt upon the *evangelical* nature of his sentiments. But let us not exercise an unchristian judgment, nor form from appearances a shallow opinion. Naaman desires to have a few sacks full of Israelite earth, material earth, but to which he attaches a kind of spiritual importance. This extraordinary freight he desires to transport to Damascus. But for what purpose? This, he has himself intimated. He designs that immediately upon his return home, every vestige of his former delusion shall be abolished and effaced. No idolatrous image, no heathenish symbol shall be tolerated in his house, but an altar to the living God shall be erected there that to everyone it may testify of the great blessing which had been conferred upon him. He is determined to make no secret of the change of mind he has undergone, but that all shall know and see whose banner he has sworn to follow.

Whatever may be the temporal consequences to himself, this altar shall proclaim to the world and to his latest posterity that Naaman is become a servant of the God of Israel, that Jehovah is his rock and his fortress, his defense and his salvation. But the altar was not designed to be a mere memorial; Naaman intends to sacrifice upon it to the Lord and by this expressive symbol daily to renew the confession of his sin and his ardent and longing hope in the only Savior. By Elisha he is not forbidden thus to take upon himself the priestly office. As an isolated man of God in a distant heathen land, Naaman was at liberty to give to the Levitical law a wider interpretation. If he thereby anticipated the gospel period, his doing so would be the more acceptable to the Lord, the more his exalted faith entitled and qualified him to exercise it.

Besides, in the person of this sacrificing heathen proselyte, a period of richer grace surely dawned upon the heathen world. His appearance, like an early morning star, seemed to skirt the dark clouds of an idolatrous region with a most cheering light. It pointed prophetically to a priesthood which should rapidly pass the boundaries of Canaan and the fences of the ceremonial law, and which, ramifying like a vein of living gold, should spread in due time through every people and nation. And this prophetic prefigurement, as Elisha might well have anticipated, was certainly intended of God.

That Naaman designed to erect his altar on *Israelite* earth must not, with narrow-minded illiberality, be interpreted to the prejudice of this happy man. Should we suppose that he associated with it any *superstitious* notion, such a surmise would only show our inability to estimate and comprehend some of the more refined and nobler natural feelings of the human soul. What is there in a mere leaf gathered from a tree now growing on the Mount of Olives? And yet we were much affected lately at beholding one. What would be a few wild flowers brought to us from the very spot which was once the Garden of Gethsemane? And yet did we possess one of these, it would vividly touch our feelings. So the Syrian Naaman, though perfectly aware that his few bushels of earth imported from the neighborhood of Jordan could not, in physical properties, be at all superior to that of Damascus, yet *with him* it was earth from the land which the Lord had distinguished above all other lands; it was earth upon which His footsteps had been heard as they had been heard nowhere else; it was earth on which the divine glory had shone repeatedly with refulgent splendor; and, lastly, it was earth from the memorable place where this delighted stranger had experienced inestimable benefit, where he had found the living God and in Him eternal life; consequently, if any earth can deserve the name, it was to him *sacred* earth.

Suppose that he found pleasure in the thought of possessing some of this earth in his own distant heathen country and sweet recollections in praying and sacrificing upon it; what if he imagined that stepping upon this earth would subserve, by mental association, to promote and animate his own feelings of brotherhood toward the servants of Jehovah in distant Canaan; shall we shrink back in pity at his weakness, or shall we ridicule it as childish folly? Far from it. Let innocent natural feelings have *their* privilege, no less than everything else. We have our treasure in *earthen* vessels; we cannot seize, all at once, the spirituality of angels, neither is it necessary; we may remain mortals and feel as mortals. Christianity requires not the destruction of human nature, but only the crucifixion of the old man. The endeavor to cast away *every* thing that is pleasing to the senses arises from mistaken and narrow notions of holiness and has never produced any better sanctity than that which is distorted, self-flattering, proud, and pharisaic.

While I contemplate Naaman and his company preparing with his singular treasure to set out on their journey into Syria, various reflections occur to my mind, and I can imagine much that is figurative in the procession of this unpretending cavalcade. Earth of Canaan borne away into the distant heathen world; what a significant symbol! "Salvation is of the Jews"; and from the "land of Judah springs the salvation of the people!" Naaman, even in Syria, will worship on Israelitish *earth*. And *our* altars are well placed, if erected on the soil of Israel; that is, on the ground of the promises and of experience. Naaman's altar is to be erected in a house which was lately the scene of unutterable misery. The providential guidance of all the elect terminates before an altar of praise and thanksgiving.

Naaman's altar will be a solitary structure in Damascus in the midst of heathenism and darkness. An altar dedicated to the Lord, and often similarly surrounded, is found in every regenerate heart. Gloomy as all may be about them, dreary, barren, and often stormy, the altar in their heart exists; and sighs and secret aspirations, like clouds of incense, are constantly ascending from it to God. O that in all our houses there could be found an altar like that erected by Naaman! An altar with the inscription, "Salvation is come unto this house!" and inscribed also with the names of all its inhabitants;

an altar from which the incense of life never ceases to ascend and on which everyone is resolved joyfully to offer whatever the honor of Immanuel may require. O that the Lord would erect for Himself such spiritual altars in our habitations and soon bring about the blessed moment when the declaration of the Syrian shall be unanimously repeated among us, "I will henceforth offer neither burnt offerings nor sacrifice unto other gods, but unto the Lord!"

17

A Scruple of Conscience

"If we walk in the light, as He is in the light, we have fellowship one with another, and *the blood of Jesus Christ His Son, cleanseth us from all sin!*" (1 John 1:7). Observe, these are the words of John with whom so many among us, forgetting that all the writings of the New Testament are equally inspired, think they can better agree than with the writer of the epistles to the Romans, Galatians, and Hebrews. But will they not, now, secretly protest against John himself? Of the blood of Christ, the world, as such, is determined to know nothing. The bare mention of it is sufficient to produce in many a distortion of countenance, as though their ears had been wounded by some most offensive sound. That odious appellation, "the blood theology" (for by this our evangelical doctrine is designated), abundantly indicates men's cordial aversion to "the blood of the Lamb." Sermons and hymns which treat of "redemption through His blood" are cast aside with the most indignant displeasure as "the productions of darker ages." Thus "Christ crucified" is still the offscouring of the people and will be so till the last contemner of His blood has taken the downward road to perdition. For of a truth, all who despise His blood are "accursed." "The preaching of the cross," says the apostle, "is *to them that perish* foolishness" (1 Cor. 1:18).

Thousands in the present day profess a certain kind of Christianity, but the precious blood-shedding of the Son of God is excluded from it. This omission is proof enough that their Christianity is false; yes, properly considered, it is enmity against Christ. "We believe," they say, "in the divine character of Christ; we believe in his divine mission; we believe in the reality of his miracles."

185

But all this will not constitute a Christian. An earnest "receiving" of and attachment to His *"atonement"* is one of the most essential and striking features of a disciple of Jesus; and where this feature is wanting, it matters little what others may be found. They may, indeed, constitute a man decked in Christian *ornaments*, but not a Christian. The blood of the Lamb is the very life-blood of Christianity. The temple of the New Testament is grounded upon the merits of that precious blood. Remove this foundation, and the temple itself ceases to exist. Deny the efficacy of the blood of Jesus Christ, and you deny all the salvation which is in Him.

What color shines most conspicuously through the whole Bible? In what color was the first promise arrayed with which God cheered the transgressors in Paradise? In what color did Abel appear before the Lord when he brought his acceptable offering? What is the prevailing color of the significant types, the sublime institutions, which God devised and arranged? What color was it that preserved the children of Israel in Egypt from the exterminating sword of the destroying angel? In what color did the Lord decorate the forms and ceremonies of the tabernacle? In what color shone the ark of the covenant and the altars at the holy festivals? In what color did the people, when bowed in the dust, receive the absolution of the high priest? Of what color were nearly all the predictions of the holy prophets concerning Him that was to come? Of what color is the gospel of the Old Testament—the fifty-third chapter of Isaiah? And say, of what color is the whole New Testament itself? What did the apostles choose as their established, their favorite color? What color glittered in the standard which they bore among the heathen? And even those who stood before the throne of the Lamb with palms in their hands, in what color had they washed their robes? Do you not know? Oh, how can you be ignorant of it? It is the color which is still most grateful to the sight of the humble and repenting sinner, the most consoling and dearest to his heart. It is the color of BLOOD!

Oh, what songs of praise echo through the world for "the blood of the Lamb"! What songs of praise have echoed from the beginning to the present hour! During our thousand years its strains were those of *desire*. For nearly two thousand years it has assumed the accents of *joy*. Now it is the song of jubilee proceeding from the redeemed, who, on beholding the blood, have been relieved of all their sorrows. And now it is the song of *hope*, ascending from hard-pressed wrestlers, who, looking upward through their night of gloom and beholding the blood, no longer doubt of a happy issue out of all their troubles. Sometimes it is the song of *peace* from those who are severely tempted; who, amid the assaults of Satan, suddenly find the most soothing consolation on recognizing the blood. Then, it is the song of *triumph* proceeding from the righteous at their death, on perceiving death, sin, hell, and Satan, vanquished at their feet; for they know that as the lintel and side-posts of the Israelites' houses were sprinkled with the blood of the paschal lamb, so the door of their own heart has been sprinkled with the blood of Christ. And again, it is a *festal* hymn from the once distracted and sorely perplexed, but who in this blood have discovered the first solution of their doubts and long embarrassments. Yes, many things in the world may be more loudly and pompously celebrated and applauded than His blood; but there is nothing more ardently, cordially, and inwardly extolled.

What the Scriptures understand by the blood of Christ, it is not necessary that I should now explain. It comprehends the shedding of His blood, His sufferings and death, in so far as they represented His having endured punishment in our stead; His bloody sacrifice by which He satisfied for us the immutable justice of God. Therefore, undoubtedly it includes the *salvation* and *life* of the wretched sinner.

What then is the efficacy of this blood? Our connection with it decides our eternal state. To participate in it or not is to be eternally saved or eternally lost. What says the apostle John? "The blood of Jesus Christ, his Son, cleanseth us from all sin." "*Helpeth* to cleanse us?" No; but "cleanseth us." "Encourages us to cleanse ourselves?" No; the blood itself cleanseth us. "Cleanseth us from the lust of sin?" No; it cleanseth us from sin itself. "Yes, from the sin of spiritual drowsiness and indolence!" No; read the words again, "from *all* sin." "His *blood*?" Yes, yes, His *blood*. You think, perhaps, Christ's *example* makes us clean. Behold, the apostle John is of a different opinion. You proclaim Christ's *doctrine* does it. No; John says His *blood*. You assert that it is done *by walking in Christ's footsteps*. No; it is His blood, His blood! You say that it is the desire of amendment, of conformity to the precepts and example of Christ. Oh, how little does this sentiment exhibit of the savor and peculiar character of true Christianity.

"But John himself says, 'The Spirit cleanseth from sin.'" Yes; but that is quite another thing. It is not the subject here treated of. Here blood is spoken of, the words are "and the blood." All must admit—believers and unbelievers, those who reject blood and those who are sprinkled with it—that the power of cleansing, of cleansing from all sin, is here unequivocally ascribed to blood.

Cleanseth FROM ALL SIN! It is impossible to describe how grateful such an enunciation is to one who beholds sin in its true light and is aware that he is himself a sinner. How avidly he seizes upon it—like the hart panting for the water-brooks, like the hungry sheep in a sandy desert on discovering a verdant spot. None can imagine but he who, like the thirsty hart, has himself found a spring of water or, like the hungry sheep, has discovered a spot of rich verdure! Many of us have read the words, "The blood of Christ cleanseth from all sin," but they have been to such of us as so many unprofitable words. Yes, such declarations shine first in *darkness*; *then*, they appear as stars or as lights upon a peaceful shore.

But how is this declaration that the blood of Christ cleanses from all sin to be understood? Simply according to its obvious meaning, as a child would understand it. Those to whom the blood of Christ is by faith applied are in the sight of God freed from sin. Their "trespasses," having been fully atoned for by Christ, will not be "imputed" unto them. Lo, my brethren! here is the point on which we have not the happiness to possess the concurrence of all our hearers. They wish that the efficacy of Christ's blood should be less frequently dwelt upon; that on this subject we should be *piano*, that is, fritter away the gospel; that we should employ less energetic language than is our custom; in other words, that we should darken the splendor of Christianity where it shines most gloriously. They require us on this head to encumber the consolations of grace with all sorts of *ifs* and *buts*; that is, diminish and circumscribe the merit of the Surety.

But we admit only one *if* and it is that which precedes the inspired words we are considering, namely, "IF we walk in the light, as God is light, and in the light (we have fellowship one with another, and) the blood of Jesus Christ, his Son, cleanseth us from all sin." Therefore we shall continue to proclaim aloud the power of Christ's blood, and having done so with our utmost energy, we shall retain the feeling that our testimony has still been but too feeble and inadequate. To this we adhere, that for him who by faith applies the blood of Christ to his heart and conscience, there is *now* no more condemnation, as Paul declares. He is now, as the Lord Himself testifies, "clean every whit." Is such then the power of Christ's blood? Yes, such is its power.

Witness, the crucified malefactor, the woman who was a sinner, the persecuting Saul.

But may it not be said that the blood of Christ has reconciled all? Certainly not. "He gave himself a ransom for *all*"; but, that all are *actually ransomed* cannot be said; for it cannot be said of anyone who lives in sin; and however he may assert his having been ransomed, he only shows himself to be under satanic delusion. No; he who is not submissive to "the law of the Spirit of life" which is graciously vouchsafed to make him "free from the law of sin and death," and who does not resist, if required, even unto blood, in his strife against the "law of sin in his members," to him the consolation does not belong; and though he presumptuously assume it, he but renders himself worthy of the greater condemnation. Those to whose conscience the blood of Christ has been applied have both received and yielded to the Spirit of Christ, whereby they have solemnly repudiated all the sin of their nature and have begun to delight in God and in all that pleases Him; yes, they cordially renounce everything that belongs to the kingdom of darkness. In them sin has ceased to reign, and notwithstanding it may frequently reappear, though more to themselves than to others, still it is as a crucified enemy; it is, by the power of grace, mortified and subdued, so that it is not allowed to reign in their mortal body, that they should obey it in the lusts thereof. No; their Prince is Christ, and Him they obey. Sin is an intruder, a foreign oppressor, against whom they zealously guard and fortify themselves. Such is the organization of the people to whom the consolation of the blood of Christ appertains. They are, in themselves, sinners; but they are cordial lovers of holiness "in all manner of conversation."

These people console themselves with the belief that they are cleansed before God, and they are justified in this confidence. But must not carnal security spring from such a conviction? Not if, as is really the case, this blood purifies the heart and quickens the conscience. Should what is sinful reappear in their hearts and lives, you imagine they have only to recollect that the blood of Christ has atoned for this also. But that is not the case. By a mere thought or emotion, sin is not purged from the conscience. The Spirit of Truth that is in them will not permit such superficiality. The cleansing of the conscience can be effected only by the blood of Christ, which is not to be applied by an operation of the memory but by a living faith.

And the restoration of their peace of mind being not always at the command even of the converted, who, after a renewal of unfaithfulness, have frequently to endure conflicts of which the world has no suspicion, their faith, still alive, causes them continually to wait upon and thirst after a reconciled God in Christ till their peace is restored. He to whom great faith is given has likewise great peace. He who, as "walking in the light," is always able immediately to apprehend the full atonement of Christ may quietly pursue his way, for the blood of Christ cleanses him from all sin. May we not hope this of Naaman, as we now proceed to consider the sequel of his history?

2 Kings 5:18,19

> In this thing the Lord pardon thy servant, that when my master goeth into the house of Rimmon to worship there, and he leaneth on my hand, and I bow myself in the house of Rimmon; when I bow down myself in the house of Rimmon, the Lord pardon thy servant in this thing. And he said unto him, Go in peace.

The text here presents to us a feature in the history of Naaman which seems incompatible with his inward state as it has appeared to us, and which threatens to darken the gratifying impressions we had begun to entertain concerning him; a feature which from misapplication has been snare to many, and which, therefore, requires serious elucidation. We propose, I. To defend; II. To illustrate; III. To apply it. May the Lord send His light and truth to guide us.

To Defend

I. It is unquestionably a remarkable circumstance that now demands our consideration, a circumstance which seems to place the sentiments not only of Naaman but of the prophet in a dubious light. From the lips of a man who with most joyous and decided alacrity had just enrolled himself under the standard of the living God, to hear a moment afterward the request that the Lord might pardon him if on his return to Damascus he continued, as formerly, to attend his master to the house of Rimmon, with him to bow the knee before the altar of this idol, seems alarming. And how does Elisha receive this offensive proposition? We should have expected him decidedly to protest against it as halfhearted and despicable. Yet he not only acquiesces in it but appears to sanction it. What are we to say to this?

Can it be any wonder that scarcely any passage of Scripture has so perplexed expositors? Can it surprise us that, down to the present moment, thousands should have imagined they have found in this incident a plaster for certain injuries and wounds of their violated consciences, infinitely more acceptable than the thoroughly healing and radical one presented in the blood of Christ?

They make Naaman the patron of their spiritual indecision, lukewarmness, cowardice, insincerity, and halting; and the prophet Elisha the sealer, defender, and voucher of this lamentable state of feeling. In the conduct of Naaman and Elisha they find the fig-leaves behind which they seek to hide from themselves and from God the shame of their own spiritual nakedness. Tampering with the world under certain circumstances is thus thought justifiable, as if Naaman had practiced it, and the prophet, in the name of God, had approved it.

Against such a view of the fact before us we most solemnly protest as false, and erroneous, and as outrageously unjust to both these personages. It not only discovers a superficial, unenlightened estimate of their conduct, but it even amounts to a wicked calumny against them. Therefore we gladly come forward in their defense and to discharge the first part of the obligation to which we have pledged ourselves.

What are we to think of the sentiments of those who, in order to justify themselves in their own disingenuous doings, will interpret a passage like the one before us in the manner above mentioned? This is the first question to which we have to address ourselves. The spiritual condition of such persons will be discovered with tolerable accuracy by the following statement. "We desire," say they, "to be Christians, for we wish to die happy; and we have heard again and again, and we believe, that none but true Christians can die happy. But the kingdom of God consists not in outward forms. God requires that we should serve Him 'in spirit and in truth.' Consequently, what is denominated a public rallying round the standard of the Lord is not so indispensably requisite. It is not necessary that we should molest the neighborhood with noisy declamations about our surrender to Christ and make a parade of our spiritual decision by temporal differences. Why do you require of us an external separation from the world and its customs, so far as they are not avowedly sinful? We worship the Lord in the temple of our hearts. Why do you require of us an open and exclusive recognition of merely *serious* persons and *their* practices? We erect in secret an altar to the Eternal. Why do you enjoin it upon us as a duty to renounce connections, occupations, amusements, and social pleasures which do not prevent us from approving ourselves as Christians and worshiping God in secret?"

Such are the thoughts of these people; and they act up to their principles. They desire to be Christians, but they will not quit the world to which they assimilate in innumerable particulars; yea, with which they continue to live upon a secret good understanding. They bow their knee to God where it costs them no sacrifice; the next moment they do homage to their idols. Their dominant inclination attracts them to what is carnal, and only a momentary dictate of their mind to that which is God's. And with this divided and hypocritical devotion they flatter themselves that they are standing on *scriptural* ground. They say, "We do at most only as Naaman did; and we have Elisha's sanction for our conduct."

Is it possible to hear such language without holy indignation? In what a light do they thus view these two men of God? They make Naaman only a pretended brother whose profession of faith was insincerely made, who had merely in appearance abandoned the service of Satan, who by his conversion was far from intending the renunciation of sin, but who only wished to find a method of going on as usual in peace and quietness. And thus also they make Elisha a false prophet, as one who had approved of the most scandalous temporizing, as one who had even pronounced a blessing upon deliberate idolatry, who, most palpably contradicting his great predecessor, the Tishbite, had sanctioned men's "halting between two opinions," and had made concessions worthy only of an emissary from the father of lies.

But I would ask these persons, if in their conscience, they really believe that the example to which they appeal does indeed sanction their own religious duplicity? In my opinion they are not so much mistaken as hypocritical and dishonest. I believe they willingly proceed against their own better judgment when they attach to the proposition of Naaman and to the reply of the prophet so unworthy a meaning; and I doubt not that would they openly avow the secret motives of their hearts, my suspicion would be too well confirmed. How can they honestly imagine that this ingenuous confessor could ever intend to addict himself again to the idolatry of his country? Again: Do not their consciences unequivocally testify that a holy man like Elisha could never have been seduced to a decision like the one charged upon him, so directly opposite to the entire spirit and most explicit declarations of the word of God? For in what manner the living God requires to be worshiped, the Bible leaves no one in doubt. He will possess His people *entirely*. The lukewarm He "speweth out of his mouth." It is said, "Thou shalt worship the Lord thy God, and Him only shalt thou serve" (Matt. 4:10). "How long halt ye between two opinions? If the Lord be God, follow Him: but if Baal, then follow him!" (1 Kings 8:21). "He that is not with me is against me; and he that gathereth not with me scattereth" what is mine (Matt. 12:30). "Who saith unto his father and to his mother, I have not seen him; neither did he acknowledge his brethren, nor knew his own children; for they have observed thy word, and kept thy covenant. They shall teach Jacob thy judgments, and Israel thy law; they shall put incense before thee, and whole burnt sacrifice upon thine altar" (Deut. 33:9,10).

The Lord "seeketh" such to worship Him who not only worship Him in their hearts, but cannot refuse to enlist publicly under His banner and openly to confess Him in word and deed. "If thou shalt confess with thy mouth the Lord Jesus, and shalt believe in thine heart that God hath raised Him from the dead, thou shalt be saved" (Rom. 10:9). "Whosoever shall confess me before men, him will I also confess before my Father which is in heaven. But whosoever shall deny me before men, him will I also deny" (Matt. 10:32,33).

The Lord requires that our whole deportment should testify that we are no longer of the world, but that we are essentially different. "Be not conformed to this world" (Rom. 12:2) is an exhortation which He also causes to be addressed to us. Again: "Be ye not unequally yoked together with unbelievers; for what fellowship hath righteousness with unrighteousness? and what communion hath light with darkness? and what concord hath Christ with Belial? or what part hath he that believeth with an infidel? And what agreement hath the temple of God with idols? for ye are the temple of the living God. Wherefore come out from among them, and be ye separate, saith the Lord, and touch not the unclean thing; and I will receive you" (2 Cor. 6:14-17).

The Lord requires that we should abandon everything rather than practically deny the faith and truth of His gospel. "Whosoever shall be ashamed of me and of my words in this adulterous and sinful generation, of him also shall the Son of man be ashamed, when He cometh in the glory of His Father with the holy angels" (Mark 8:38). "He that loveth father or mother more than me, is not worthy of me; and he that loveth son or daughter more than me, is not worthy of me. And whosoever he be that forsaketh not all that he hath, he cannot be my disciple. But whosoever forsaketh all for my sake, shall receive a hundred fold" (Matt. 10:37; Luke 14:33; Matt. 19:29).

The Lord is so little satisfied with a so-called *hidden* worship, that He has pronounced a woe upon those of whom all men speak well. He expects from His followers such an open and decided taking up of the cross as shall render it impossible for them to escape the ignominy and ridicule of the world. Hence the apostle exclaims to all Christians, "Let us go forth therefore unto Him without the camp, bearing His reproach" (Heb. 13:13).

What sort of worshipers are acceptable to the Lord is, and ever has been, abundantly evident. He desires to be followed by sincere and faithful disciples, who, in consequence of inward dissimilarity to the great mass of the world, are even externally distinguished from it; cheerful confessors of His name, refusing the honors of Egypt for His sake; meekly, charitably, and temperately protesting by word and deed against the follies and vanities of their fellow men, and absenting themselves from the scenes of their sinful or questionable practices.

And yet Elisha is to be supposed to have intimated to Naaman that it was not necessary for him to be one of that number, but that he was at liberty to divide his conduct between the service of God and the service of Belial! Can such an opinion be seriously entertained? I must be permitted to doubt it. Everyone is sufficiently susceptible of truth to be aware of the falsehood and injustice of such an interpretation. Should I, however, be mistaken, and should there really be any who persuade themselves that in this incident they have an excuse for their double dealing, let them weigh well the following considerations.

You wish to believe that Naaman's heart was still half devoted to the idolatry, or at least to the good opinion, of his countrymen and of his sovereign and that Elisha did not account this any sin. But hear to your confusion Naaman's own solemn protestation. "Behold, now I know that there is no God in all the earth, but in Israel. Thy servant will henceforth offer neither burnt offering nor sacrifice unto other gods, but unto the Lord." You persuade yourselves that

Naaman would conceal his newly adopted sentiments, or rather, his faith, from the world; but have you not heard him make his confession in the presence of his whole retinue, who would doubtless publish it abroad. You console yourselves with the supposition that Naaman is desirous to avoid, on his return to Damascus, outwardly separating himself from idolatry, and that the prophet approved this temporizing; but reflect that he distinctly declares his intention openly to appear what he really is: that he proposes for this purpose to erect in Damascus an altar to Jehovah and to expose it to the view of all as a sign of his change of mind. You quiet your consciences with the thought that Naaman, in order not to offend the world, will studiously abstain from the intercourse and practices of other servants of God; but what does that significant burden of Israelite earth which he carries with him to Syria mean? Is he not here striving, I might almost say by coarse and violent means, to make this external communion as close as possible? You would have it that Naaman was minded not to abandon in some points at least his former idolatrous course; but can you suppose that in such a case he would with so little reserve have opened his mind to Elisha? From him he could then have expected nothing but the most decided disapprobation and rebuke. You would maintain that Naaman persuaded himself that under the shadow of God's pardoning grace, he might quietly continue in the pursuit of many things which his conscience condemned; but how utterly false, unfounded, and injurious is such a supposition proved to be by the ingenuous manner in which he submitted his case to the decision of the prophet, a manner which even evinced an anxious scrupulousness of conscience!

How entirely vain then is it to seek in the conduct of Naaman a sanction for men's disingenuousness and to regard Elisha's approbation of that conduct as a cover to their own halfhearted and underhand regard for religion! Surely the example of these two eminent persons ought to overwhelm our modern temporizers with shame and confusion. Naaman's integrity condemns their falsehood; Elisha's frank and disinterested behavior was anything but their hypocrisy and perverse self-deceivings.

To Illustrate

II. What then was the object of Naaman's proposition? What was his intention? What his desire? Let us endeavor to solve these inquiries. With the most exulting joy he has just dedicated himself to the service of the living God when his thoughts naturally turn upon his future life, and a scruple presents itself to his mind, the disturbing force of which is somewhat softened by the fact that the man of God is at hand to direct and counsel him.

"I am now about to return," he thought, "to Damascus. My sovereign will not dismiss me from my office on account of my altered faith; but my duty among other things requires that on festal occasions I should attend the king to the temple of Rimmon, and when he prostrates himself before the idol, and when he rises again, that I should offer him my hand. I have forever renounced idolatry and its gloomy services. What part am I in future to take? If I refuse to attend the king, nothing is more certain than that I shall lose my office and with it my influence over Benhadad and the people. Should I continue to perform that service of my office, how will such conduct comport with the character of a servant of Jehovah? Would it not be sinning against Him and against His word? Shall I not incur the guilt of denying His holy name?"

Such were, probably, the thoughts that crossed the mind of Naaman and discomposed it not a little. He was determined to be entirely the Lord's. This resolution was unshaken. He meant to serve Him exclusively and in every respect to maintain Jehovah's rights. But he was uncertain whether he ought still to extend his hand to his prince on these occasions or not. Were this sinful, he would a thousand times rather sacrifice favor, office, influence, and even life itself, than lend himself any longer to this ceremony. Whether it were sin or not, he was as yet in doubt. That question he wished to have solved.

He therefore disclosed his mind to the prophet and frankly submitted his conscientious scruple to the decision of infallible authority. He betrayed his anxiety in the broken accents of doubt and embarrassment—"In this thing the Lord pardon thy servant, that when my master goeth into the house of Rimmon to worship there, and he leaneth upon my hand, and I bow myself in the house of Rimmon: when I bow down myself in the house of Rimmon, the Lord pardon thy servant in this thing." It seems as if the Spirit testified within him that a worshiper of Jehovah in such an observance was not in his place, even though he were only an outward participator in it; and beyond a doubt such was Naaman's feeling; but he desired to know if this were not one of those few cases which though,

when strictly viewed, cannot be approved, yet under the divine forbearance might be permitted. This he wished to ascertain, and he left
the decision to Elisha.

What was Elisha's reply? The prophet did not misunderstand the
words of this open-hearted inquirer. Had there been the smallest reason to suspect the purity and singleness of his sentiments, he would
certainly not have been indulgent on this occasion but would have
answered with reproving severity, "You must on no account again
enter the temple of the idol!" But he is aware that it is the serious
intention of this man to live in all things to the glory of the Lord. He
will not worship the God of Israel in secret, but he will confess Him
before men in his own country. The question at issue, therefore, was
not whether he should participate in idolatrous worship, but simply
whether he should continue in the performance of a civil, official act
which could not possibly be misapprehended by the people.
Naaman would offer neither sacrifice nor worship to the idol, but in
all his other acts would approve himself the more unequivocally a
servant of Jehovah, the more such an act of civil attendance exposed
his character to misapprehension. This Elisha knew, and allowing the
upright and conscientious man to retain his influential office, he
replied, "Go in peace!" and thus dissipated at once the uneasiness
that oppressed his heart.

"But what!" it may be asked. "Does Elisha consent to his entering
an idolatrous temple?" Elisha opposed no objection to this *mere* act.
"But did he not by so doing sanction Naaman's committing an evident sin?" Certainly not. The mere act of entering an idolatrous
temple was not *in itself* sinful. I can imagine, for instance, a sick heathen thus addressing a Christian missionary, "Go with me to the
house of my god, that I may pray before his image. If he will not hear
me, I will believe your God to be the true one, and an idol nothing."
The missionary attends him, and while this pagan leans on his shoul-
der, he with a view to assist him in rising seems in bodily attitude
merely to bow with him before the image. Has he sinned in so doing?
Who will venture to assert it? In such a case the outward action is
indifferent; it only becomes sinful if associated with sinister designs
or by the spiritual stumbling which it occasions.

But would it not have had a better appearance had Naaman at all
hazards abstained even from the *semblance* of communion with idolatrous worship? That it would have had a better appearance I will not

deny. But whether it would have deserved the credit of great wisdom and self-denial is another question. What is most striking to the eye does not at all times prove itself the most important when weighed in the balance of the sanctuary. The mummery of excitement, mistaken for inspiration, will not infrequently command more *eclat* than what proceeds from the quiet fire of true faith. But does it not seem as if Naaman himself felt that this courtly service was inconsistent with his new character? It undoubtedly appears so for he expresses the hope "that God would pardon him" if the act were sinful. "Does he not then propose to sin, that grace may abound?" By no means. That would only be the case if his conscience testified to him, that his attendance would be absolutely sinful; but his conscience testifies no such thing.

"Still it gives him the feeling that it would be better entirely to keep away from the scene of idolatrous abomination?" This might have been the case. "Did Elisha then intend to lull such feeling asleep?" Why should we think so? Weigh well Elisha's words. He does not say, "Your scruple is unfounded." Neither does he say positively, "You will be doing what is lawful in bowing down yourself in the house of Rimmon." But as little does he express the contrary sentiment. He does not feel himself called upon to place a yoke upon the neck of the willing man or to burden him with a variety of legal or self-imposed injunctions. He could have made of his proselyte what he pleased. Naaman surely was ready to acquiesce in everything advised by Elisha, even to have given up the thought of returning to his native country and to have relinquished all his civil dignities and prerogatives.

But the more sensibly the prophet feels this, the more circumspect is he in the exercise of his influence. He does not assail the new convert with direct demands nor constitute himself the holder of dominion over his faith. He does not ignorantly confine himself to the letter or act like a narrow-minded formalist, as a strict observer of technicalities. He takes a comprehensive and considerate view of the circumstances of the man, and instead of violently cutting the knot as many of us would have done either with the sword of some moral sentiment or with some humanly based ascetic aphorism, he solves it in the free exercise of his judgment with a truly holy liberality. Entering fully into the worthy man's circumstances, situation, and state of mind, he dismisses him with the friendly salutation, "Go in peace!" Whether he laid any particular *stress* on the words "in peace," and thus have intimated, "If you can *in peace* pursue this course, and without any upbraidings of conscience, then do so," we cannot determine.

This much, however, is evident, that the prophet, far from indulging any timid and distrustful anxiety for the *perseverance* of his proselyte, joyfully consigned him to the Lord and to His Spirit under whose guidance he knew him to be and was fully confident that He would inform and teach Naaman in the way wherein he should go so that his farewell salutation seems only to mean, "Go your way! I am under no apprehensions about you, you are in good keeping. He who has received you to His grace will guide you into all truth!"

Application

III. What has been already said appears sufficient to remove from Naaman and the prophet all suspicion of sinful temporizing and indecision and to explain the seemingly mysterious occurrence recorded in the text. The application of the subject to ourselves will not be difficult. A few short hints will serve to bring it home to us. In the first place I shall address a word to those who are censorious among us. Take a warning from our history never hastily to pronounce judgment on any man. It does not necessarily follow that a person cannot be a Christian of whom you have heard that like Naaman he has been seen in the temple of idols or in some noisy assembly of the world. He may have been there most unwillingly and simply because his vocation had made it necessary or because his lawful superior had required his attendance. Say not that in the latter case he should rather have risked the favor of his superior and his own influence over him, yes, all his official appointments and usefulness rather than have seemed to participate in such vanity and folly. Such a decision, easily as it may be mistaken for heroism, might be only superficial, unenlightened, and crude, or, to say the least of it, hasty and inconsiderate. Besides, tempted by the devil or by his own carnal nature, he may have been there *for the first time* and suffering such anguish and remorse of conscience as to render it little probable that he will ever feel inclined to venture into such an uncongenial climate again. Thus, by a most unjust judgment, you may condemn one of God's sincere "people," one of the "sheep of his pasture" because upon a single occasion while wandering from the fold, the forgetful one had been unhappily torn by the wolf. O abstain above all things from judging or at least begin with your-selves.

In the quiet circles of the more retired but self-satisfied, it is often, alas! not much better than with those who face the public theater of open worldliness, for to such also the words of our Lord, which He addressed to the scribes and Pharisees, are but too frequently applicable; "Ye pay tithe of mint and anise and cummin, and have omitted the weightier matters of the law, judgment, mercy, and faith. Ye strain at a gnat, and swallow a camel" (Matt. 23:23,24). For let me state how things often proceed in your social circles. At first you have some religious conversation in order to constitute yourselves a *Christian* company. As soon as you imagine your *Christianity* is suf-ficiently established and placed beyond suspicion, the limits of conversation are *extended*, and the truth of James 3:5,6, 10 becomes at once apparent, "The tongue is a little member, and boasteth great things. Behold, how great a matter a little fire kindleth! . . . And the tongue is a fire, a world of iniquity. My brethren, these things ought not so to be." Did everyone first endeavor to pull out the beam out of his own eye, he would leave the mote in his neighbor's eye untouched from very weariness. Remember, "he who judgeth, shall himself be judged; but he who judgeth himself, shall not be judged" (1 Cor. 11:31).

Let me next address myself to those who are oppressed, whose family connections or whose occupation places them in such society as abounds with unbelief and blasphemy, scorn and derision, where only sin, impiety, and darkness reign. For you, isolated children of God, who in the family circle or in your worldly business are com-pelled to see and hear what perhaps is worse than anything that ever happened in the temple of Rimmon, and who know not how to escape from this disagreeable attendance; for you I express my heart-felt and brotherly commiseration. But you know the words of your Lord, "In the world ye shall have tribulation." In Christ you have peace. Your dwelling among these "tents of Kedar" does not alter your true and genuine character. Protest, then, meekly yet firmly by your words and above all by your example against the reckless sentiments that prevail around you, and so "in patience possess your souls."

Continue in the furnace till God shall open to you a way of escape. As often as you have opportunity, heap coals of the fire of love and charity upon the heads of your adversaries. In the midst of their opposing darkness, be thankful if God has made you to differ. Console yourselves with the remembrance of righteous Lot. How was "his soul vexed!" Remember Joseph in Egypt and Daniel in Babylon; and while you call to mind the prayer of your everlasting High Priest, "I pray not that thou shouldest take them out of the world, but that thou shouldest keep them from the evil" (John 17:15); forget not the words of promise, "The Lord preserveth the souls of his saints; he delivereth them out of the hand of the wicked" (Ps. 97:10).

My next exhortation is to the halting, the insincere, the undecided among us who, though numbered with the children of God, have not utterly renounced the world and its vanities. You labor to no purpose when you seek to convince us that your constant participation in the vain and idolatrous practices of a benighted world is only the same as Naaman's supposed participation in the service of Rimmon. Tell me, I entreat you, what have you to do with Naaman? What have you in common with his spirit? Even your outward circumstances are not to be compared with his. Were you solemnly to renounce the maxims of the world, you would not by so doing lose any salutary influence in your neighborhood; it would only be increased by it. Were you to declare with decision to your friends and acquaintances that your attachment to Jesus and His words forbid you any longer to join in certain practices, would *you* be exposed to royal indignation or to dismissal from any important official employment? I doubt that. The worst you would have to encounter would be a little ridicule, a little reproach from an insipid and deluded multitude.

But *reproach* for the name of Christ *belongs* to the condition of the redeemed. He who bears not *this* mark of the Lamb has reason to distrust the genuineness of his own Christianity. But it is not in *outward* circumstances alone that you differ from Naaman; you are in no respect of Naaman's *spirit*.

How great is the contrast between you and this convert! To Naaman the worship of the god Rimmon was an abomination; your hearts, on the contrary, are still attached to and set upon the vain trifles of the world. Naaman entertained great scruples of conscience about the further continuance of even a ceremonious participation in the feasts of Rimmon; you continue your carnal pursuits without hesitation or scruple and are only anxious to defend and justify them.

Naaman studiously and with all seriousness sought to obviate the supposition of his being a contemner of Jehovah and an associate in heathenism; you, on the contrary, are only careful to remove all suspicion of your belonging to the despised number of Christ's faithful followers and desire to be respected by the children of this world as one of themselves.

Naaman was deeply solicitous in all things to live to the glory of Jehovah, and therefore it was that he communicated his doubts to the man of God that *he* might decide how he ought in future to act. You, on the contrary, are indulging the deceitful imaginations of *your own heart.* You refuse to listen to the condemnation pronounced *by the word of God* on your ways and actions and are only solicitous to exculpate yourselves by perverting the testimony of Scripture and converting it with disingenuous ingenuity into a palliation of your own double-minded or halfhearted conduct. Naaman would instantly have resolved at whatever cost never again to enter the idol temple had Elisha condemned it as sinful or as incompatible with the character of a servant of Jehovah. We may warn *you,* on the contrary, a hundred times by the testimony of the written Word of God that certain things are inconsistent with the Christian character; that this must be sacrificed, and that must be avoided; while you in the insincerity of your hearts close your ears and will listen to none of these things.

Or, do you imagine us illiberal in our opinion of you? Then let us proceed to the proof. Place yourselves for a moment under the scrutiny of the words of truth. Take *one* instance of your conduct. You frequent circles in which time is killed at card-playing, and you ask, Is it wrong to do so? We answer distinctly, Yes. If you desire to pass for Christians, you must not take part in such things. To what *extent* this miserable amusement is sinful, it is not on this occasion necessary to inquire. It is enough that it is offensive and mortifying to the brethren. On this ground alone we are authorized to enforce it upon you as a duty to withdraw from such company.

Take *another* instance. You go to balls, masquerades, etc. You ask again, Is this also inconsistent with the character of a Christian? We reply in the name of God, It is not consistent. In these scenes of vanity, of sensual pleasure, and often of the wildest dissipation, no one ought to appear on whom it is enjoined to "crucify the flesh with its affections and lusts." Such an one *cannot* continue there; and yet you *can!* Tell me then, what must be thought of *you?*

You, likewise, frequent the theaters. What! you exclaim, is this also forbidden to a Christian? Certainly it is altogether forbidden to a Christian. For what are the theaters as they are at present conducted, but the rallying points of every kind of worldly delusion and falsehood where sin itself is glorified? What are they but the *propaganda* of self-deception, pride, and vanity; temples dedicated to sensuality; decoys of Satan, beset with snares; places from which everything really holy is proscribed, where it is either derided or at best desecrated and depreciated! Can a Christian be in his place at such resorts?—a Christian whose very name imports that he is sensibly alive to the great end of his existence, that he has dedicated himself entirely to the service of Him who calls to all those that are His, "Come out from among them, and touch not the unclean thing!"

You take part in clubs and what are called *cheerful* societies in which, if the reigning spirit be not that of frivolity, yet the spirit of inanity, materialism, unbelief prevails. What! you say, may we not even frequent social circles such as these? No; these are not proper places for a faithful servant of Christ. Are we then, you ask, so restricted by Christianity as this? And I answer, Do you consider it a *restriction*, a *restraint*? If you do, truly it is a melancholy sign. But you may say, If we should happen to err in one thing or another, the Lord, we hope, will be merciful to us. No; to you He will not be merciful, for your joining the circles and participating in the pleasures of an unenlightened world proceeds from inclination not from unavoidable necessity. It arises from a secret attachment to "the pleasures of sin" and from a disregard of those who are offended by it. Then depart from unrighteousness. Cease from the maxims of the world. Yes; we call upon you in the name of God; but you ignore us. What need we further witness? No; you are not of the spirit of Naaman.

But enough of this. May God make us of a pure heart and to become decided and devoted; even as Moses, who "esteemed the reproach of Christ greater riches than the treasures of Egypt"; or as Paul, "who counted all things but loss, that he might win Christ, and be found in Him." Away with that insipid Christianity of modern times which is made compatible with all things; that takes all things under its patronage and conceals them with its capacious mantle under the name of things indifferent; that covertly returns to a world which has been apparently renounced, and herewith to the enjoyment of every fleshly gratification. Away, also, with that narrow-minded, pharisaical piety which passing lightly over the weightier matters of the law becomes itself the fabricator of innumerable minor laws and insignificant regulations; and with "Touch not, taste not, handle not," would put a yoke upon the necks of those who are called unto liberty, only not to use their liberty as a cloak of sin which in place of that liberty wherewith Christ has made us free, would impose a yoke which Christ has not laid upon His people. A LIBERTY ACCORDANT WITH THE SPIRIT OF HOLINESS is the liberty which is inscribed on the banner of the God of Israel. May love then ever constrain us and love *only*, even the love of Christ and of the brethren. Love always guides aright. May it be the moving principle of our whole life. Amen.

18

Gehazi

It is a very mysterious event that is recorded in Matthew 21:19; it appears suspended like a thunder-cloud in the midst of the serene sky of the gospel. The Savior, being on the way from Bethany to Jerusalem, is assailed by hunger, not apparently only, but in reality. He was "touched" and can be so still, "with the feeling of our infirmities," having been "in all points tried like as we are, yet without sin," that no trouble might ever afflict us, in which He had not already participated. Trees of various kinds grew here and there by the roadside, but they were leafless at the season referred to, for it was as yet early in the year. Their naked branches extending toward heaven presented significant emblems of genuineness and sincerity, as seeming to say, "Did but the reviving warmth of a vernal sun call up our juices and empower us to bear fruit, how gladly would we offer you refreshment!"

These trees were not cursed by our Savior. No; the humble, the unpretending, the faithful, He bids to prosper. Many plants and shrubs likewise grew by the wayside which had, as yet, no fruit to offer, but they exhibited tender promising buds. These He blesses. He perceives the fruit already in the germ. The young and hope-inspiring stem is spared by Him. But as He silently pursues His way, He descries at a distance a tree which promises abundantly to satisfy His hunger. It is a fig tree, and one that greatly out rivals all the others that surround it: while they are naked and bare, it exhibits a luxuriant crown of foliage and glitters in all the freshness of living green.

Now, you may be aware that it is the nature of fig trees first to produce their fruit and then their leaves. The verdant appearance, therefore, of this tree gave promise of fruit nearly ripe. Our Lord approaches it: the tree flaunts in all the pride and promise of a summer attire, but though there are among the branches leaves, indeed, in abundance; yet, notwithstanding its sunny situation by the open road, notwithstanding the advantage of its native oil and every other requisite advantage, there is no fruit, none at all.

In what light, therefore, are we to view this tree? It resembled a hypocrite, a deceiver. And what are you who are assembled here for the worship of God? Are you anything better? The ornament of leaves with which you are adorned is visible enough. I see you bow before Almighty God; I observe the seriousness and devoutness of your outward demeanor and hear the accents of faith and of contrition which issue from your lips. But what fruit is there beneath? Are you in truth so contrite, so averse and inimical to sin, so hungering after God and His mercy? Alas! not many of us are really so. Falsehood of one kind or another has gained fearful prevalence among us. It would command my respect did I hear one and another declaring, "I know I produce no fruit as yet; and as for the leaves, I will not wear them upon me till I do. I will not join in singing this and that hymn, or in uttering this or that devout expression, or in making a strong and loud profession!" But many of you act the *part* of saints and yet are as whited sepulchers. Your whole deportment, carriage, and appearance are but the leafy covering of the fig tree. It seems to offer fruit for the Lord to gather; but woe unto you if He approach and find your worship nothing more than dissimulation and self-delusion!

The Lord having thoroughly searched this fig tree by the wayside and having found it to produce nothing but leaves, He pronounced upon it not a blessing but a curse; and said unto it in the hearing of the disciples (that they might remark and not forget it), "Let no fruit grow on thee henceforward forever!" And, behold, the words were no sooner spoken than they fell like a blight upon the luxuriant tree, and it began to wither and die! The disciples passed by it the following day, and behold the tree was withered away and fit only for fuel.

The history further relates that at this sight the disciples were amazed and said with deep feeling, "How soon is the fig tree withered away!" The trees which appeared as they were, making no pretensions to what they did not possess, but patiently awaiting the fructifying influence of the sun, were left teeming with their swelling buds and smiling under the genial influence of the season. "Every plant," the Lord once declared, "which my heavenly Father hath not planted, shall be rooted up" (Matt. 15:13). Consolatory as this declaration must be to those who know themselves to be planted by the Father, yet horrific must it sound in the ears of those to whom it is the announcement of an alarming and melancholy fate. The plants here intended are doctrines professed to be scriptural and practical, yet producing no fruit; or they may further denote unfruitful members of the Christian church; *professedly religious* people: not dissolute persons, not enemies to the truth; no, men of biblical knowledge and exterior sanctity. But their religiousness is not the work of God, it is the work of man. It is *their own* or wrought into them *by others*: a Levitical mantle upon the shoulders of a Canaanite; the colors of the sanctuary covering the Ethiopian skin, the old Adam. They have worked themselves into the ranks of the pious without divine preparation and guidance; and they cannot abide in their place but are swept away with the ungodly.

The corn-flower, though beautiful in appearance, is but a weed. The husbandman says, "Thee I have not planted. Why cumberest thou the ground? Let it be cast into the fire!"

From many among you I hear the sigh, "Ah! what sort of a plant may I then be?" Such a declaration proceeding from the Lord may disquiet even the real children of God, those of them, especially, who have been piously and so well instructed from their youth that they have submitted themselves to the Lord almost imperceptibly, so to speak, and can hardly remember any time of their conversion. But let none of such too hastily yield themselves up to needless doubts and fears. In the garden of nature, you know that plants may be distinguished in reference to their mode of propagation into two classes, layers and seedlings. The former are green scions put into the ground which gradually take root and thus have life and existence independently of the parent tree. The latter spring gradually from seeds. Thus, with reference to the soul's life in God, there are two classes of real Christians; the one, resembling plants which spring from seeds, are in a remarkable and wonderful manner without any special preparation suddenly arrested in their sinful course and begotten again to a new life. Such were the three thousand on the day of Pentecost; such was Saul; and such the jailer at Philippi. Their confidence of having been planted by their heavenly Father would not be easily darkened. Others, which resemble slips and layers, are shoots from godly parents, pious friends, or tutors; by these they have been imbued with Christian knowledge and trained to godliness. Their Christianity may, indeed, for a considerable time be but lifeless formality; yet, by degrees and imperceptibly under the silent influence of God's grace, they strike root and become, equally with the former, not merely separate *branches*, but distinct *plants* in the garden of the true church, thriving with life to the glory of the Lord. Thus all depends on the root, on the vital and living root; and by the root of the matter in Christianity we mean a believing view of Christ as the one and only ground of salvation and of all hope revealed to a heart oppressed and broken by sin.

In the following portion of sacred history we shall see this symbolical account of the fig tree, together with the rooting out a plant not planted by our heavenly Father, lamentably realized in a man whose spiritual exterior justified the expectation of something better than what it was found to cover. "The Lord preserveth the simple." "The meek will He guide in judgment." Hypocrites shall not dwell in His presence. Liars cannot prosper in His sight.

2 Kings 5:19-27

> And he said unto him, Go in peace. So he departed from him a little way. But Gehazi, the servant of Elisha the man of God, said, Behold, my master hath spared Naaman this Syrian, in not receiving at his hands that which he brought: but, as the Lord liveth, I will run after him, and take somewhat of him. So Gehazi followed after Naaman. And when Naaman saw him running after him, he lighted down from the chariot to meet him, and said, Is all well? And he said, All is well. My master hath sent me, saying, Behold, even now there be come to me from Mount Ephraim two young men of the sons of the prophets; give them, I pray thee, a talent of silver, and two changes of garments. And Naaman said, Be content, take two talents. And he urged him, and bound two talents of silver in two bags, with two changes of garments, and laid them upon two of his servants; and they bare them before him. And when he came to the tower, he took them from their hand, and bestowed them in the house; and he let the men go, and they departed. But he went in, and stood before his master. And Elisha said unto him, Whence comest thou, Gehazi? And he said, Thy servant went no whither. And he said unto him, Went not mine heart with

thee, when the man turned again from his chariot to meet thee? Is it a time to receive money, and to receive garments, and oliveyards, and vineyards, and sheep, and oxen, and menservants, and maidservants? The leprosy therefore of Naaman shall cleave unto thee, and unto thy seed forever. And he went out from his presence a leper as white as snow.

Who does not feel it painful to hear of such an account in a narrative which has hitherto filled our hearts with high and holy delight? But nothing here below, not even what is most attractive and beautiful, is without some alloy of sin, and what is most holy is commonly set off by some gloomy contrast. Nevertheless, from the event here recorded, distressing as it is, we may derive spiritual benefit. The dismal termination of Gehazi's career serves to exhibit the uprightness of Elisha, together with the purity and simplicity of Naaman, in a still more striking and amiable light. This occurrence, therefore, so far from casting a gloom over the whole account, serves to make its splendor more intense. Let us devote a few serious reflections to the melancholy event that it may serve as a warning to ourselves and as a test for the examination of our own hearts. We shall first consider Gehazi's character; then his crime; and, lastly, the punishment it received; and may the Lord dispose us all to attend and learn with ingenuousness and simplicity!

His Character

I. The young man whose character now engages our attention was not a neglected, uncultivated being, picked up from the dregs of the people. He must have received instruction from Elisha; he was his servant and companion in travel: and why may we not fairly suppose he was taken by him from the schools of the prophets? There is every probability of the kind, considering the previous employment by which Elisha himself is designated, namely, as having "poured water upon the hands of Elijah" (2 Kings 3:11), considering, I say, the similar nature of Gehazi's employment in general to that which had formerly belonged to the prophet Elisha. Nor can we suppose that Elisha would have taken him about with him as his constant attendant and companion had not this young man already appeared the subject of a change which resembled some awakening to a new life.

What that change may actually have been cannot now be precisely determined. It was undoubtedly a more gratifying impression, a better feeling, a hope-inspiring emotion. This apparent regeneration, if seen in its origin, would probably have exhibited little more than the false fire of natural feeling and youthful sensibility.

How often do we notice in the present day persons offering themselves for missionary service whose flaming, proselyting zeal forbids, at first sight, any suspicion that the beautiful flower from the root upward is but of earthly origin! How much more frequently still do we see persons with unquestionable ardor uniting themselves to the people of God and adopting their habits, who yet have never discovered their own sinfulness nor experienced what it is to hunger and thirst after righteousness!

But then is it possible that Christianity itself should contain anything alluring to the unconverted mind? Certainly it is possible and is found to be the case. The natural *fancy*, for instance, can ruminate with much entertainment and delight in the field of sacred narrative; the natural *feelings* can find much gratification in the solemn excitement which religious meetings, religious fellowship, or various forms of religious worship produce; the natural *understanding* can enjoy an intellectual feast in deciphering the sacred mysteries; the natural *conscience* can obtain a pharisaical satisfaction by its complacency in religious observances.

Moreover, the Christianity of modern times often brings temporal *honor* and worldly *gain* to its professors. A return from the insipidity of the common ideas of *rationalism* to Scripture truth is often reckoned as the sign of a better understanding, or it is attended with some temporal advantage. What wonder then is it that the flesh should occasionally desire to wear the cloak of piety! I do not know what it was of this kind that Gehazi sought from the children of God: whether it was the imposing tranquillity of their order that first attracted him; whether he was tempted by the dignity and distinction of the prophetic calling; or whether it was the hope of one day shining among the foremost in Israel by receiving the power of working miracles. Too plain is it that he had not entered through the door into the sheepfold but had climbed up some other way; and that what appeared in the excited proselyte to be the work of God was nothing more than natural emotion.

But how happened it that of all others Elisha should have chosen Gehazi to attend him and to enjoy such constant and familiar relationship with him, especially also if his selection was made from among the children of the prophets? This is a question too difficult satisfactorily to answer. Yet it can hardly be doubted that Elisha entertained high hopes respecting this spirited and evidently gifted young man; possibly, too, he had already perceived diseased spots in his character, and thus, being aware how easily he might be seduced, he thought it necessary to take him more immediately under his own special superintendence. But never surely could he have dreamt of being so grievously deceived in him as he was; and we may well suppose this to have been one of the most afflictive occurrences of his life.

Gehazi's conduct in the present instance looks dark indeed. Surely at his very first entrance into the visible kingdom of God, he must have neglected to sit down and count the cost. He must have taken but little notice of the nature of that kingdom. He could never have well laid to heart the requisitions of its service which have ever been the same in all ages and are briefly comprised in the meaning of those forcible words of our blessed Lord, "Whosoever he be among you that forsaketh not all that he hath, he cannot be my disciple." Mere carnal illusion appears to have first attracted him into the exterior communion of God's saints; and such illusion, perhaps, having by and by become fainter and fainter till at length it disappeared entirely, the dull realities of everyday life were found not to yield him what his vain and selfish imagination had depicted.

He appears to have calculated upon a career of glory and pleasure; but he realized in the sedate and abstemious lives of such retired, unassuming brethren, what seemed to him the discomfort of a desert. He felt himself *trammeled* in the outward forms of the religious life he had adopted; he seemed as in a *snare* or in a *dungeon*, as a man painfully self-deceived and disappointed and yet not honest enough to acknowledge it; inconvenienced and oppressed, like a creature in all uncongenial element, but too pusillanimous to force his way out of it; as a hypocrite, burning inwardly like a furnace with the love of the world, but outwardly wearing the guise of singular abstraction from it; with the bodily eye directed to the heavenly Canaan, but with the mental eye lusting after the fleshpots of Egypt.

Had he only possessed courage enough to throw off the mask and openly to avow that he regretted his union with the brethren, that he lamented his having exchanged the world and its delights for the insipidity and privations of his present condition, possibly he might even have done better than thus to play the hypocrite. But he continued to dissemble; he remained in spite of his inward disgust among the children of the prophets, as the attendant and companion of Elisha; he joined as usual in all the devout exercises of those who were "quiet in the land" and yet suffered his inward corruption to "eat like a canker."

Alas! it is to be feared that at present also there are too many of such characters as Gehazi; indeed, one might everywhere almost venture to single out some as persons of this description; persons who once enlisted, apparently with enthusiasm, under Christ's banner, and with a kind of false courage entered, as it were, the ranks, and assumed the semblance of a warfare with the spirit of the world and of the flesh. And to this hour they may still be seen familiarly mixing with the people of God, though pitiably too much like persons who have overreached themselves, and who would gladly withdraw, could they do it with any credit; who, having precipitately put their hand to the plow, feel obliged to retain their hold, because, though they are continually looking back, they are afraid lest by relinquishing it altogether they should be either ashamed of *themselves* or that others would be ashamed of *them*. But, oh, cease from hypocrisy, you false brethren! Take back your pledge, for you are exposed. It is known without your giving yourselves the trouble to acknowledge it that in your hearts you are devoted to the world, and that you drag the form of Christianity about with you as an oppressive chain. We willingly exonerate you from the use of religious *phraseology*. We readily release you from the obligation of remaining in our communion. You but excite an evil report of the city of God and of Christ. You pollute and betray by your works that sanctuary to which, by your language and gestures, you pay a feigned homage. Be satisfied. Contaminate no further the courts of the Lord. Lay aside the crumbling mask of dissimulation. Be outwardly the children of the world as you are inwardly. Frequent your balls, theaters, and such places, and keep out of religious society altogether. Instead of holding that wearisome fellowship with God's saints to which you think yourselves by decency obliged, walk with "them that are without." Say to the babblers and scorners, "We are your associates." Your hypocritical fellowship brings needless scandal upon the cause and name of religion.

But to return. Naaman, rejoicing with childlike simplicity at the great blessing conferred upon him, had just given his farewell hand to the prophet. Elisha must have been not a little affected; his heart must have been raised with gratitude to God for the mercy and grace shown to this stranger. Even the attendants of Naaman must surely have shed tears of sacred feeling. And did not also angels before the throne then take their harps and attune them to notes of praise? But, behold, yes, in Gehazi's soul emotions also are excited! When the vernal sun shines in the heavens, not only do the feathered tribes arise and pour forth their cheerful melodies, but even the basilisk and the viper revive. It was now that the serpent moved in the heart of Gehazi. He does not rejoice: no; his soul is out of tune. His look is gloomy. Oh, it is a portentous sign! For he who participates not in the joy of heaven over a repenting sinner is certainly no member of the heavenly community; he is not born of God. Satan does not rejoice in such a case. He is chagrined and enraged. What then has so discomposed Gehazi? He is dissatisfied that his master had so disinterestedly declined the splendid present offered to him by the Syrian. He cannot digest his disappointment at seeing the hope of *gain*, with which he had been inspired on the first arrival of the noble stranger, dwindle to nothing. Dreadful! dreadful! How vigorously have the seeds of corruption already sprung up in this young man! How widely have the noxious germs of lust already expanded! A lust which, when it has conceived, brings forth sin; a sin which, when it is finished, issues in death! We shall now have to review the development of this lamentable process in Gehazi; and it may be seen to have taken place in the most melancholy manner.

Naaman was joyfully on his way homeward, and Elisha was returned into his dwelling with his soul devoutly raised to God. Gehazi paused behind for a few moments in abstraction and musing while he speaks with himself to the following effect: "Behold, my master hath spared Naaman this Syrian, in not receiving at his hands that which he brought." "Naaman this Syrian!" Does it not appear as if, by the latter contemptuous expression, he wished to palliate the villainy he meditated and to lull asleep his own upbraiding conscience? "Naaman," he thinks, "will praise highly indeed my master's remarkable generosity! but what shall I be the better for it, if he leave none of all that gold and silver behind! What a substantial man might I be with such wealth as the prophet has despised, because he does not know the value of money! Why, I could even purchase an estate with it; I could then plant oliveyards and vineyards! I could have sheep and oxen, and plenty of menservants and maidservants! Yes, and the Syrian is still within reach. I will seize the favorable moment. I will go after him. Yes; as the Lord lives I certainly will run after him and get somewhat of him." Thus the vain, deluded man reasoned with himself and resolved upon his mad project. Now, observe his baseness as well as artfulness in coming to such a resolution. He could not have entirely concealed from himself the magnanimity of the prophet in declining the present; and yet he shamelessly trampled the noble example underfoot and could venture to perpetrate an act of the most opposite character. Yes, though the thought could not have escaped him that he would thereby lower his holy, venerable, and revered master in the estimation of the stranger, yet even this in no way deterred him from lending a willing ear to the suggestions of his own vain and covetous heart! He was sufficiently aware that his nefarious act was likely to bring upon the people of God the suspicion of being hypocrites and lovers of worldly gain; but what was that to him! He cared only for himself and for his own advantage; and he was even depraved and impious enough in awful levity to seal his design with a profane oath, and thus virtually to call on God to witness and favor his design, even that God "who is of purer eyes than to behold iniquity," who abhors the covetous, and whets his sword against the liars. "*As the Lord liveth!*" he exclaimed, as if he were sneeringly alluding to Elisha who had employed the same asseveration in rejecting the Syrian's proffered gift, "As the Lord liveth, I will run after him, and take somewhat of him!"

His Crime

II. All this was scarcely sooner said than done. Gehazi sets off in pursuit of the Syrian procession which has already advanced to some little distance from the town. But Naaman, accidentally looking around him, observed and recognized the pursuer. He immediately ordered all to halt; he alighted from his chariot and hastened to meet Gehazi. Here was only another proof of the humility of his spirit and of his gratitude and veneration for Elisha. "Is anything the matter? Is all well?" inquired he, with some concern. "All is well," replied Gehazi, as if with the utmost artlessness. And then out comes his insidious falsehood: he was sent, he said, by his master; but foreseeing that Naaman might hesitate to believe that Elisha himself could desire a gift he had so recently, so persistingly, and so solemnly refused, he had got ready and now uttered with unprecedented effrontery an artful and well-digested lie. He stated that two of the sons of the prophets were just now most unexpectedly come from Mount Ephraim to the man of God, and he further implied that they were persons in great poverty and distress; that Elisha wished much to relieve them, but not having the means in hand, he knew that he could with the most perfect confidence apply to Naaman, and therefore solicited to that effect a talent of silver and two changes of garments. Who can forbear feeling an honest indignation at such imposture as this, such a cheat upon the grateful Naaman, such scandalous treachery to the holy prophet and to all Israel! So then, a few pieces of silver proved temptation enough to this man to compromise the honor of Jehovah and of His children, and to shake the world's belief in the existence of any religious sincerity or holy feeling under the sun!

Happily no such effect was produced upon Naaman. His childlike simplicity saved him from stumbling at Gehazi's offense. Naaman had conceived too high an opinion of the people of Israel, and of the sons of the prophets in particular, even to suspect that Gehazi's statement could contain anything but pure truth, and nothing could have made him distrust the integrity of the man of God.

"The Lord preserveth the simple." Frank and unsuspecting as a child, the noble Syrian not only believes all that Gehazi tells him, but heartily rejoices to have an opportunity of showing some substantial proof of his gratitude to the prophet by rendering a service to the children of God. He is not contented to give him a single talent of silver with the two changes of raiment as requested; but he obliges the man to accept two talents which, with pretended modesty and hypocritical reluctance, Gehazi affects to decline. Naaman does more. He sends two of his servants with him to carry the silver and the changes of raiment. One might have expected that Gehazi, on witnessing such artlessness and simplicity, would have sunk to the earth with shame. But no; his forehead is brass, and his heart harder than a rock. Too happy at the success of his villainy, he hastens away with the speed of a plunderer, only anxious how best to secure his treasure and escape detection. Miserable wretch! How much more enviable is the deceived than the deceiver, the defrauded than the defrauder, notwithstanding his triumph! O sincerity, simplicity, truth, you choicest pearls that decorate the Christian character! Oh, that we were more richly adorned with these ornaments! But the more intimately we become acquainted with Naaman, the more rare do we find persons of his noble simplicity.

His Punishment

III. And now what is the issue of all this wickedness and the fruit of all this plunder? Hear it, my brethren, and tremble! Gehazi accepts the escort of the two servants till he reaches a fortified mount at no great distance from the city, beyond which he is afraid to venture so publicly with his booty. He, therefore, invents doubtless some lying pretext to take the bags of money and the garments from his companions, and, after dismissing them with many hypocritical professions of thanks, deposits his booty in a convenient house, there to be preserved till he can further dispose of it. Thus fear and anxiety, those inseparable accompaniments of guilt, already begin to be felt; and he dreads detection. Before God he is not afraid, but the thought of being unmasked before man is dreadful. New apprehensions continually arise—"What if one of the sons of the prophets should meet me; or the two servants should relate to Naaman where I have deposited the treasure and so excite his suspicions that he should write an account of the matter to my master!" Thus the ominous cry of the storm-bird seems already heard by him, and he feels oppressed as by the gloomy sultriness that precedes a tempest. But he rallies himself to allay his rising terrors and to check his forebodings with such seemly sophistry as he can further invent.

In all apparent collectedness he hastens to Elisha; he appears before him with even more composure than usual, as if he would say, "I need not be afraid to look you in the face." But such a mask is now of no service. Elisha beholds him with a penetrating glance and pointedly inquires, "Whence comest thou, Gehazi?" A question, which, it has been well observed, ought to have been felt by him as that coming on of a hurricane, which warns the traveler to seek shelter in any neighboring rock where nothing can hurt him. But, as if his inmost soul could escape from the prophetic spirit even as his guilty eye now avoids that of the prophet, he boldly answers with a lie, "Thy servant went no whither." Nevertheless, as lightning flashes through darkness and discovers impending ruin though it is too transient to show a way of escape, so that Spirit of prophecy to which secret things are revealed confronts and overwhelms him; "Went not my heart with thee, when the man turned again from his chariot to meet thee?" Was I not in spirit present, when, unaffected by so much kindness, you falsely declared to the man that I had sent you, that I requested silver and raiment?

Elisha's words must have come as burning radiance upon the darkness of Gehazi's sinful heart; and you may imagine the shame, the biting chagrin, the astonishment and confusion which must have seized this victim of lust and vanity at finding himself so suddenly stripped of his dissimulation and exposed as it were to the blaze of noon. Behold him now, the wretched man uncovered to the very nakedness of his infamy and horrified by the conviction that Elisha knows all. Elisha's glance had even penetrated to the inmost thoughts of his soul and had discovered the use he designed to make of his ill-gotten wealth. For hear the rest of the prophet's remonstrance. "Is it a time to receive money, and to receive garments, and vineyards, and sheep, and oxen, and menservants, and maidservants?" What must have been Gehazi's confusion upon finding these most secret imaginations of his heart thus unexpectedly exposed! Thy sin, Elisha would say, is awfully aggravated. The time, the occasion, the circumstances wherein such an offense has been committed give double provocation to your guilt. That deceit and dishonesty like this could be deliberately devised and practiced by a highly privileged man bearing so important a character and office at a time of general apostasy and degeneracy in Israel, when it was especially incumbent upon all who professed to adhere to the standard of Jehovah to maintain his cause with the most undeviating rectitude and consistency; that he should be capable of perpetrating it on an occasion which might have been expected to impress even a base heart with noble sentiments and feelings; that he could venture upon such a deed in the face of the clearest conviction and thereby cloud and desecrate a sacred work, cause the name of the Lord to be blasphemed by the heathen, risk the honor of Jehovah and His prophet, compromise the divine laws and the Spirit of prophecy, and expose to ridicule Israel's light and privileges, its priestly and prophetic office—all this rendered his sin extremely aggravated and atrocious.

Elisha had already received from the divine oracle his commission how to act. After seriously remonstrating with Gehazi upon his crime, he announced to him in the name of God, "The leprosy therefore of Naaman shall cleave unto thee, and unto thy seed forever." The sentence was immediately put in execution, and Gehazi "went out from his presence a leper as white as snow." The honor of Jehovah required that this tainted sheep should be thus marked and separated; and it was necessary to hold him up to the world as a living testimony against the abomination of hypocrisy. Moreover, the same leprosy which as a stigma inflicted by the divine judgment, was thenceforth to rebuke the hypocrite, would remain a lasting monument of the grace and favor of Jehovah to all who were seeking salvation in Israel; for it was "the leprosy of Naaman"; of him who had been so wonderfully and gloriously healed. That this calamity was not merely inflicted upon Gehazi but was likewise suspended over his posterity, let those dispute with God who will. Doubtless the Judge of all the earth well knows how to justify His own proceedings. And if this affliction was productive of the same results to the posterity of Gehazi as it accomplished in Naaman, surely *they* never regretted in this earthly pilgrimage, their having been thus made living remembrancers of one of the most splendid exhibitions of divine power and grace.

We have now done with this melancholy part of the narrative but not with the instruction which may be derived from it. Therefore, my heart impels me for my own and your benefit to make some further use of it.

Some Lessons to Learn

In the first place, my friends, I adjure you, by the welfare of your souls, to beware of the leaven of the Pharisees which is hypocrisy. Be upright, be sincere: adhere to truth before God and man. Learn to abhor dissimulation; and if you know yourselves to be as whited sepulchers, place no confidence whatever in your disguise. For like as to Gehazi so also to yourselves, the hour of your detection will surely come; it will not tarry; it even may come while you are still in this world; however, it will certainly come in that great day which shall bring to light the hidden things of darkness and make manifest the counsels of the hearts. And remember that the hour of detection will to many be the hour in which they are ripe for destruction, the hour of completed and final impenitence. In the moment in which

Judas perceived that his Master saw through him, the enmity of his dark soul was perfected, and Satan entered fully into him. Believe it, the same is the case with many an hypocrite. Before they are aware, the wickedness of their hearts is made manifest, and the fruit of this discovery is not humility and contrition but that satanic hatred to Christ and to His people which places them entirely in the hands of the powers of darkness. May He who knows the way of the righteous and destroys the ungodly and profane, yea, all liars and hypocrites, preserve you by His grace from such a dreadful doom. May He purify you throughout; may He sanctify you wholly; may He guide you into all the truth. May He remove from you every false notion which conceals from yourselves your true character, and then all inclination to deceive others will be far from you.

When conscience is oppressed by sin, of what avail is it to be esteemed by man? The favor of God is everything. Therefore, brethren, I further entreat you, as long as it is not your serious and fixed determination to surrender yourselves entirely to the Lord; so long do I entreat and beseech you to abstain from using the language and garb of Christians, that you, at least, may not give cause for the repetition of that common remark, that the church of God has always received more injury from false brethren than from open enemies. Let some consideration for God's people, or rather for His own holy cause, keep you back till you can declare with the intimate conviction of Paul, "What things were gain to me those I counted loss for Christ. Yea, doubtless, and I count all things but loss for excellency of the knowledge of Christ Jesus my Lord" (Phil. 3:7,8). Why will you put a constraint upon yourselves and involve us in embarrassment and grief by entering our ranks; your motives will soon be recognized in their impurity and furnish the scorners with another occasion to insult the God of Israel with their blasphemies. Abide with the multitude to whom in your hearts you belong. Wear the insignia of the master whom you serve. Put not on the Christian uniform till the love of Christ Himself has constrained you to join His standard. But remember your danger every moment in the meantime, whether you profess Christianity insincerely or not at all. Real Christianity is a plant of our heavenly Father's own planting. So that whatever you profess instead of it can bear only the fruit of perdition.

Lastly: Put no confidence in the promises of Mammon. Whatever prospects he may open to your view, believe not such a powerless god. His abundance of treasure is a vain dream; his enjoyments are a delusive phantom. The only good thing upon earth that can impart real happiness is the peace of God. Seek it with all your might. It is worthy of your most strenuous efforts. To sacrifice it to a carnal project, as did Gehazi, is the worst of madness and satanic delusion. Could I gain the whole world, still what should I be but a miserable being if I lacked those consolations which spring from the love of God! Without them I am poor indeed; but with them I need not inquire after earth or heaven— I AM RICH!

Other Resources for Your Study of Bible Characters

Mark These Men   J. Sidlow Baxter
A treasure house of Bible biographies including Elisha, Elijah, King Saul, Daniel, Gideon, Balaam, and Nehemiah. Also included are New Testament characters such as the Apostle Paul, Lazarus, the rich young ruler, Ananias, and Simon of Cyrene, and many others.
ISBN 0-8254-2197-7   192 pp.   paperback

The Training of the Twelve   A. B. Bruce
(Forewords by Olan Hendrix and D. Stuart Briscoe.) The monumental classic on discipleship and leadership training. A complete exposition of how Christ prepared His twelve disciples.
ISBN 0-8254-2236-1   566 pp.   paperback

Great Cloud of Witnesses in Hebrews Eleven   E. W. Bullinger
A classic exposition including an examination of the great heroes of the faith. Full of rich, practical applications.
ISBN 0-8254-2247-7   462 pp.   paperback

Meet Jeremiah: A Devotional Commentary Burton L. Goddard
The "Weeping Prophet"— Jeremiah— comes to life in this devotional commentary. With many years of study, teaching and preaching on Jeremiah, Goddard breathes life into this important Old Testament Book.
ISBN 0-8254-2728-2   160 pp.   paperback

The Apostles of Jesus   J. D. Jones
Dr. Jones' knowledge of human nature, principles of leadership, and
how to draw the best out of people, all find expression in his timely
study of the Apostles. This treatment deserves to be read carefully,
for we have much to learn from "The Twelve."
ISBN 0-8254-2971-4   192 pp.   paperback

Joshua: Mighty Warrior and Man of Faith   W. Phillip Keller
The author of *A Shepherd Looks at Psalm 23* provides an interesting
look at the successor to Moses and conqueror of Canaan. Keller
examines the man and mission and gives tranferable and practical
insights for those in the "Christian battle."
ISBN 0-8254-2999-4   184 pp.   paperback

Elijah the Tishbite   F. W. Krummacher
A thorough, analytical work on the character of Elijah. Here is a
moving Bible biography that will give the reader new insight into the
man, his message, and his ministry.
ISBN 0-8254-3059-3   208 pp.   paperback

Designed for Conquest   Roy L. Laurin
This unique book offers practical help for life's problems. Through
the experience of these biblical models, you will discover the secrets
which will enable you to be an overcomer.
ISBN 0-8254-3139-5   192 pp.   paperback

Great Women of the Bible   Clarence E. Macartney
A collection of sermons from a master pulpiteer of yesterday.
Macartney's unique descriptive style brings these women of the Bible
to life and provides inspirational reading for all Christians.
ISBN 0-8254-3268-5   208 pp.   paperback

He Chose Twelve   Clarence E. Macartney
This careful study of the New Testament illuminates the personality and individuality of each of the Twelve Disciples. A carefully crafted series of Bible character sketches including chapters on all the apostles as well as Paul and John the Baptist.
ISBN 0-8254-3270-7   176 pp.   paperback

Paul the Man   Clarence E. Macartney
Macartney delves deeply into Paul's background and heritage, helping twentieth-century Christians understand what made him the pivotal figure of New Testament history. Paul, the missionary and theologian, are carefully traced in this insightful work.
ISBN 0-8254-3269-3   208 pp.   paperback

Portraits of Bible Women   George Matheson
(Foreword by Warren W. Wiersbe.) Readers looking for fresh insights into Bible characters will find a rich treasure in Matheson's work. Warren Wiersbe says of this blind author, "No evangelical writer . . . surpasses George Matheson in this whole area of Bible biography. . . . God has closed [his] eyes— only to open other eyes, which have made [him] one of the guides of men."
ISBN 0-8254-3250-2   144 pp.   paperback

The Apostle John: His Life
    and Writings   W. H. Griffith Thomas
(Foreword by Arthur L. Farstad and Introduction by Warren W. Wiersbe.) Written especially to help those "who are called to preach and teach," Griffith Thomas's material is presented in systematic, organized fashion. Rich with homiletical outlines.
ISBN 0-8254-3822-5   376 pp.   paperback

The Apostle Peter: His Life
and Writings   **W. H. Griffith Thomas**
(Foreword by John F. Walvoord and Introduction by Warren W. Wiersbe.) The author's main purpose was "to offer Christians help and guidance in their personal meditation on the Scriptures. . . ." Anyone who will trace these outlines through Scripture will develop deep insights and new applications for preaching or teaching.
ISBN 0-8254-3823-3   **304 pp.**   paperback

Bible Characters from the
Old and New Testaments   **Alexander Whyte**
The most famous writing from this Scottish clergyman, complete in one volume, covers the personalities of both Old and New Testaments. The author was uniquely skilled, and through his sanctified imagination, brings to life the times and circumstances of these Bible characters.
ISBN 0-8254-3980-9   **928 pp.**   paperback
ISBN 0-8254-3981-7   **928 pp.**   deluxe hardback

Women of the Bible   **Frances Vander Velde**
Character studies of more than 30 women with lively discussion questions included. Excellent for women's Bible study groups.
ISBN 0-8254-3951-5   **260 pp.**   paperback